Closer to Quiet

"Think I'm going for a walk now
I feel a little unsteady
I don't want no one to follow me
Except maybe you."

-Ani DiFranco

4

In remembrance of Holly and Inge

To The Gang

Egypt

D-Day - 1
The one with solar panels

Fault: karma's strongest currency would suggest that I had taken a horribly wrong turn. Peering out the rear window of Mohammed's black taxi cab, I suddenly realized that my current predicament was entirely my fault. The fact that I was an expat, existing somewhere in the fog between foreigner and local, afforded me rare insights into the true meaning and subtleties of the local Egyptian dialect. Mohammed had given me fair warning by using the most alarmingly pervasive yet seemingly innocuous Egyptian mantra..."Insha'allah". Translated, Insha'allah sounds quite innocently beautiful: "God willing". Here are the practical uses that frequently strip expatriates of their proverbial marbles.

"Can you please pick me up at seven in the morning to drive me to the airport?"

"God willing."

"Can you please feed my dog while I am away for the week?"

"Insha'allah."

"Can you please trim a little off the bottom? I am letting my hair grow out."

"God willing.."

Soon you are bald, and stuck in traffic for four hours having missed your flight, but feeling lucky that your dog will be spared starvation. You count your blessings in Cairo. So I decided to take stock. Blessing number one: I was in a moving car. Although it was not going in the right direction, it was moving and that was a blessing. There was hope when vehicles moved in Cairo. As they ground to a stop so did their passengers' sanguinity... knowing full well that they could spend their remaining days in that vehicle without moving an inch. Blessing number two: Although I could see the road racing by under my feet through a head-sized hole in the floor, the seats felt secure and quite able to support my weight. I bounced up and down a few times to check. Relief swept over me. I would not fall out of the bottom of a moving vehicle on the highway. If I could only make it until the next day, I would not need a vehicle for the upcoming four months. I said a short prayer — prayers requiring immediate consideration were how I knew that I was living in the moment. Blessing number three: The ten crates of soda, four boxes of chips and two medium sized disco balls had not fallen out of the trunk yet. We waved excitedly at the family of four running across the highway, taking refuge in front of our stopped vehicle. Certain things you could never get used to no matter how long you spent in a foreign culture. For me, it was watching young children dragged across highways in a high-stakes game of frogger. Noticing that we were ready to move, the family takes off, weaving in and out of traffic lanes to make it safely to the other side. Phew! Why do the chickens cross the road? They don't in Cairo. Soon enough, we were clunking our way down the highway, blessings in hand.

The fact is that this cab was never supposed to be MY cab..., it actually belonged to a Nigerian man named Suen. I was not even supposed to BE in a cab. I had a bicycle waiting for me at the Cataract hotel, gearing up for a twelve thousand kilometer bicycle journey from Cairo in Egypt to Cape Town in South Africa. I was supposed to be lounging by the pool or nervously chatting with any of the other cyclists on our last day of rest before the journey began. There was one small problem: I was terrified. I was more terrified of poolside banter than death-defying cab rides. How could this be? As cyclists poured into the Cataract Hotel from all over the world, I came to an overwhelming conclusion...I was in over my head. From a comfortable distance in the hotel lounge, I inspected each cyclist's calf muscles with the precise eye of a coroner, and then reflected on my own feeble display...diagnosing my limited musculature as a probably cause of impending death. From a safe distance I poured over cycling jerseys like resumes, learning of the various Ironmen and Ironwomen I was up against. I scoffed at my own resume: a wool baby-blue jersey lacking pride and accomplishment. I watched faces light up as cyclists from all over the world spoke in "technical bicycle" language, the secret code of a club to which I could never belong.

Chastising myself for training my drinking arm more than my calf muscles over the past year, I decided to focus on what I could control...grit. If I was to survive in this superhuman gene pool, it would be through grit alone. Grit, my subconscious influencer who prefered to die fighting than surrender.

In moments of extremity, grit would blast barriers and storm my conscious yelling like a drill sergeant.

"IF YOU AREN'T PUKING YOU AREN'T TRYING HARD ENOUGH!"

Grit got this militaristic voice in two thousand and one when I went to Gagetown, New Brunswick on Basic Training, as a newly appointed artillery officer who could barely tie her boots. I was pushed beyond limits by some of the Canadian Forces best infanteers. As they hurled insults and yelled obscenities, I found all doubt drowned from my conscious. With their voices, I pushed past perceived boundaries. Since their voices were not along for this ride, I would need a good substitute; something to fill my head, leaving no room for pain to slither and bite. I would need tunes. Tunes became my secret weapon against the onslaught of prepared cyclists. Tunes required solar power and, though lacking in infrastructure, Africa had no shortage of sunlight. I decided to embark on a mission to find solar chargers in Egypt rather than show my woefully lacking cards poolside at the Cataract Hotel. This mission began with ten steps out of the hotel: right into a warzone!

Having been in Egypt during the Arab Spring, I prided myself on attentively watching for warning signs of societal unrest: cellular coverage cutting out, large gatherings of men protecting their buildings with batons, empty shelves at the local grocery. However, I did not see Suen coming. Literally. An innocuous looking cab was parked outside the hotel. I raced towards the cab and stuck my head in to greet Mohammed for the first time.

"Esallah elaicoum. Ana eisa barouh City Stars."

Using my meager Arabic reinstated some of my recently lost self-esteem as I enjoyed the surprised look on Mohammed's face that I was making an effort. City Stars, the most popular mall in Cairo, was bound to have solar chargers and here was a cab, ready to aid my escape.

"Iowa, tayeb."

I opened the rear door to hop inside. Suddenly, I realized that I was not alone. It would seem that I was sharing this cab with chip boxes and soda flats. Mohammed, solving the first of many problems, took a few flats out and plopped them unceremoniously on my lap. At least they were not livestock! You count your blessings in Cairo. As I came to terms with my lap being a deluxe cushion for three flats of soda and two boxes of chips, the first barrage let loose.

"Racist! How dare you! White privilege!"

Laden down with America's favourite food vices, it took me a few moments to realize that this barrage was directed at me. Two thoughts crossed my mind: Was this what "white privilege" was supposed to feel like? Could I begin a four month bicycle trip through Africa being branded 'racist' on day one? I did not have time to explore these thoughts as the rear door was opened and Suen relieved me rather angrily of my burden, throwing the chips and soda flats off my lap and onto the ground. Although I did not see Suen coming, he was a difficult man to miss. At five foot ten and carrying two large disco balls, Suen had the personality of a giant. He charged and changed the energy of any room at will, deciding quite effortlessly who gets to breathe easily and who will struggle. There is no escaping his nature and he is calling me a racist. This was not a good beginning.

"Get out of my cab! Entitled!"

One- word descriptors flew out of his mouth like stray bullets on a self-determined path of destruction. He took fire over and over, until I had finally regained enough feeling in my legs to exit his cab. Mohammed looked sheepish in the driver's seat. Apparently, he had neglected to tell me his cab was spoken for. Suen had booked a ride in Mohammed's cab long ago. Mohammed had no right to drive ME anywhere. When I realized this misunderstanding, I behaved as any moral woman would. I got out and commenced my walk of shame in no particular direction; just away. I could hear Suen rearranging his wares while chastising Mohammed. The engine sputtered and they were off. As I watched them pull ahead and wondered if I would ever find another cab, they pulled to the side of the road. I walked alongside the cab and came face to face with Dr. Jekyll, the smiling face of Suen, ordering me in. Mohammed jumped out of the front seat and piled the stock into the trunk. We were off.

"Where were you walking to? You would never find another cab out there. Where are you headed?"

"Thank you for picking me up, I'm headed to City Stars."

I learned that Suen was a Nigerian businessman who had moved to Cairo four years ago. He had two jobs. He was a party-hosting D.J. who brought talent from all over Africa to Egypt. He also supplied shops with groceries, and today we were embarking on his milk run together. He told me his story; his rise from poverty. He spoke with conviction and I was swept away. Mutually spellbound by the story, Suen forgot to mention that we were headed in the opposite direction to City Stars and, in fairness, I didn't ask. Unbeknownst to me, we were headed to a suburb which my Christian friend Samir referred to lovingly as "hell".

It is impossible to portray the absolute chaos that assaults the eyes and blinds the thoughts, in Dar El Salem. The expertise of city planners began and ended with a three-lane highway traversing the suburb. Like the fabled library that sank under the weight of its books, Dar El Salem was sinking under a mound of garbage. Three lanes of highway had become half a lane access for pedestrians carrying multiple garbage bags balanced expertly on their heads and it was traversed continuously as they dumped their waste. The garbage was piled so high that it threatened to fall, burying passing cars and contributing pedestrians. With no front lawns, sidewalks or gardens, children played on this pile of waste as nearby dogs ate from it. Nothing grew in Dar El Salem. The sense of resignation and boredom was palatable as spirits shrank and died. Donkeys were rubbed raw from chaffing carts. Horses were whipped repetitively as their hoofs struggled to gain a purchase on the road under their heavy loads. Cars belched smoke the colour of coal. Children sold goods enveloped and dirtied by smoke. I have never felt so hopelessly smothered by every type of pollution imaginable. People decayed from the inside in Dar El Salem and it manifested itself in apathy. Cars would park in the half remaining lane to buy cigarettes or have chai…without regard for the traffic jam they created. Feigning oblivion to the honking and the disrespect of their actions, they would re-enter their car half an hour later to carry on the slow procession through hell. Three-year-olds without helmets stood on mopeds weaving dangerously through traffic. Nobody cared in Dar El Salem. Hell was apathy. My spirit spent a full hour screaming "GET OUT!" and a sense of cold fear ran through my body. I could hardly believe that this place existed such a short drive from my own home of the past two years, in Maadi. Though also chaotic and polluted, Maadi maintained hope. It had green areas and baseball diamonds, clean shops and parks for the kids. Garbage was either burned or soaked in an effort to reduce growth and stench.

Suen, accustomed to such assaults on the senses, requested several stops along the way to drop off wares and to network. Finally, leaving me in the cab, he shook my hand and confidently strode homeward. I realized the strength in community that existed even in hell. It was clear from the smiles on people's faces, that Suen was welcome among them. He belonged in Dar El Salem and that feeling of belonging was not to be trifled with. If you trifle with belonging, your head gets sick faster than the stomach viruses of the kids I witnessed eating from garbage piles. If you trifle with belonging, your heart shrinks more than the overloaded horse's spirit. Suen was larger than life. He was happy. Hell may not be such a bad place in good company.

Suen's detour cost one hour and a half, thinking conservatively about Cairo traffic. As roadside optimism is a deadly sin, I anticipated arriving at City Stars with one hour to shop. I was wrong. I came to this realization as we hit our first roundabout. Driving in Cairo is intimate. Drivers know when to caress their gas pedals into inching forward millimeter by millimeter and when to pound on the gas. And when micromanagement is needed, the climate is rife with possible errors. Mohammed and I found ourselves in a circular traffic entanglement. Too many parts inserted to promote movement. The result was the world championship game of Rush Hour. After thirty minutes of violent horn-expletives, leadership was born. One man jumped out of his stationary vehicle and started manually moving vehicles backwards millimeter by millimeter until finally his car was freed. Yelling profanity as a new vehicle tried to fill the void, he managed to keep them at bay long enough to get the ball rolling. We were released from the embrace one hour later, which left me twenty minutes to shop Cairo's largest shopping center. Saying "Massalama" to Mohammed was bittersweet and I considered asking him to stay and drive me home. Sometimes we open ourselves to experiences regardless of the emotional toll.

Mission at hand but exhausted to the core, I came upon an electronics store a few minutes after entering City Stars. They assured me that solar panels were not for sale at City Stars. Oddly at peace, having adequately filled my day without dreaded bicycle conversation, I decided to change missions. Chinese food and decaf coffee before the trip would empower my legs to make it through. Edging my way to the food court I was not surprised to find every table occupied. In fact most Egyptians, knowing the system, had left an elderly representative to save multiple tables and dozens of chairs for hours while awaiting the family's return from shopping. Resigned to eating from my lap, I asked an elderly lady for a chair from her reservoir of six. She invited me to dine with her. Nadine and I had a lovely chat in Arabic and I basked in her generosity. Nadine's generosity stemmed from her hoarding six chairs around an empty table. It was typical Egyptian generosity flowing unabashed from the gross inconsideration that makes it possible. Today had been a lesson in Egypt's blurred lines between inconsideration and generosity.

Feeling sufficiently depleted but relieved that all the serious cyclists should have put themselves to bed long ago, I returned to the Cataract Hotel after dark. One cyclist was still awake, my roommate Holly. As I cautiously entered the room and introduced myself, prepared to bolt at the first mention of ironman accomplishments, Holly put me right at ease. She was not scared to be scared. She had not spent the entire day evading emotion; she was far braver than I was. I thus became acquainted with Holly's true gift of creating space around her for others to be the best or truest versions of themselves. She was madly unpacking, repacking, double-checking, and furiously trying to get the upper hand over her to-do list. We commiserated nervously about our lack of training and I began wondering if it was possible that behind every self-assured smile and technical bicycle conversation lay an emotionally fragile soul who felt in above their head. How could we not? We were about to embark on a twelve thousand kilometer journey across Africa. Anyone who truly felt confident surrendering to the Mother Continent was either mad or didn't understand the finer intricacies of motherhood. At times all mothers let their young cry it out. Would Africa put me through the paces? Although I didn't cry, I didn't sleep much that night wondering what the morning would bring. My mind twirled like a whirling dervish rotating through different frames and focusing on a few for stability; would my knee make it without pharmaceuticals? Would I die in Cairo traffic? Would I be the slowest? Would I be able to close the bag containing all my belongings? I didn't immediately realize that my greatest asset would be my newly gained understanding of Cairo's inconsiderate generosity and beautifully frustrating culture. Inshallah I would make it through the next day.

D-Day
The one in which the Egyptian Police disappoint again

Holly and I arose from our slumberless states riding on adrenaline's sharp edge. We moved swiftly and efficiently, focusing entirely on the tasks at hand in order to keep stress at bay. As our bags zipped shut without too much convincing, our fates became sealed...all our belongings would be accompanying us on this adventure. None would be left behind in the safety of the hotel, and so we must be equally brave...this was it...no more room for excuses; we were actually going. We hurried to the front lobby of the hotel to meet the other cyclists.

If energy is the universal language, we could sense the undercurrent of excited screams punctuating our polite conversation as we waited for the police to arrive. This was to be our first cultural lesson, a lesson I learned during the Arab Spring in two thousand and eleven...the Egyptian police are horribly corrupt, or at the very least, unreliable. Many reasons can be listed in justification of their corruption: being paid a low wage that creates a climate of bribe acceptance. Being a visible sign of authority, and therefore a target, in a country with such a polarization of wealth. In a society with large power imbalances it takes a special talent to carve out a niche as the most corrupt: the Egyptian Police force held that honour. At the heart of the issue lay a bunch of bored young men with guns. Most police officers under the age of thirty were assigned to crossroads in which to guard the peace. Boredom led to creativity or conflict and both were employed by the police at these crosswalks. It took me barely one month of living in Egypt to learn the universal question of why the Egyptian crossed the road... to get away from the police. The police officers would cat-call, sneer, hiss or verbally assault us as we walked past, and this was considered getting off lucky. Many citizens were fined without cause and subjected to lengthy unprovoked questioning. When a country's police force becomes its greatest liability you are sure to have an open revolt.

Caireans often claim that smoking increases your life expectancy. This is not education gone horribly awry but indeed logical when you factor in the thick, heavy air pollution that blankets the capital city. Cigarettes may bathe your lungs in a whole host of chemicals but at least they filter the polluted air. Net positive, if you ask a Cairean. In a country where pollution threatens all your senses, hope for change is felt viscerally. For this, the Egyptian revolution was predictable. The dead stale air suddenly felt energized in a manner only made possible by collective change.

The Arab Spring began on the twenty-fourth of January, two thousand and eleven, the day before a national holiday: Police Day. In Egypt, we never knew when a holiday would strike. You could repopulate a forest with the number of last minute announcements and changes to the calendar businesses sent home on a regular basis. This was not due to a lack of organization at the Canadian International School of Egypt. It was procedural. In order to declare a holiday, three local newspaper publishers were first consulted for their opinions. If the majority of newspaper publishers believed that a holiday was warranted, a holiday was announced. On the 24th of January, 2011, the Canadian International School of Egypt declared that "Police Day" would be a school holiday. This was a new holiday for our school. For a school that celebrated all Canadian, Egyptian, Christian and Islamic holidays, as well as those peppered into the curriculum by the Egyptian powers, we were quite used to not working. Though we were meant to stand in adoration of the Egyptian National Police on the twenty-fourth of January, 2011, we decided that celebrating a coworker's birthday was far more worthwhile.

We had heard whispers that the floorplan for the Arab Spring had been set in motion but, that day, we remained blissfully unaware as we celebrated at the beach playing ultimate frisbee and drinking games. As it turned out, Police Day was the perfect stage for protesting repression. Inspired by Tunisia, Egypt was feverish with potential for change and spent Police Day peacefully protesting outside the Ministry of Interior, demanding an end to corruption and the Minister's resignation. A political storm was brewing while, at the beach, we were enjoying the sunshine.

The next night we went to see Ahmed Harfoush. When you live abroad nostalgia takes on a new form. Not only does it transcend time but also space and that night it was bringing me back home and reminding me of those pieces left behind. Ahmed Harfoush is the master of nostalgia. Every Tuesday night Ahmed would take to the stage at club 55 in Ma'adi and croon to the likes of Frank Sinatra, Bing Crosby and Adele. Expats gathered at this oasis and danced until normalcy was restored. Albeit temporarily. We took refuge in the comfort of old lyrics that seemed to find common ground amidst vastly different cultures. There are few joys as temporal as live music.

Superficially, that night resembled every Tuesday night. Ahmed was a well-worn tradition who never disappointed his followers. We exited the club at our usual two a.m. and continued onward towards our ritual late night falafel at a nearby restaurant. Something was different. None of our cellular phones worked. Together, we conspired about what it all meant and strategically made a communication plan for the next twenty-four hours.

"What it meant" reared its aggressive head the next day when it became apparent that the proverbial fan had finally been sullied; cutting cell service was a last ditch effort on the part of the government to prevent scheduled organized protests. Ironically, for the Egyptian people, the government's manouver had the opposite effect. As it turns out, when citizens are clamouring for the increased protection of their human rights, stripping them of one of their rights isn't a smart idea. The twenty-eighth of January became the "Friday of Anger" as protesters filled the streets en masse and the revolution took form. Within twenty-four hours, our neighbourhood which usually caused enough noise pollution to rattle the grey matter was silenced as citizens took refuge indoors and we began processing our new reality. Firing tanks were squeezing into our recently quieted streets accompanied by a barrage of AK-47 gunfire. Prisons had been opened and burned, and men armed with batons were patrolling the streets protecting and securing their assets.

I processed what we were seeing a little differently from my fellow expats. For nine years I had been a soldier in the Canadian Artillery Reserve. Formerly serving with the Canadian Forces, I had released from the Forces and moved to Egypt, with the full intention of reenlisting once I returned to Canada. I had seen all this weaponry before, but it somehow struck me as grossly out of place. It was from a different life, one in which I understood the implications and took an active role. This I did not know or understand, and yet somehow it felt like my duty to do both. Thus my secret life came knocking. Early on in the international teaching hiring process I learned that showcasing military experience wrapped your CV with caution tape. Distrustful foreign businesses were unlikely to hire ex-servicemen and women. Having been rejected by a few international schools I learned my lesson and removed my military background from my resume. Now, with the military in the forefront, I felt as if I was being called to service in an evolving battle I could scarcely comprehend.

As per our late night plan, we gathered at Marcus' apartment - a fellow Canadian. He lived fifteen minutes away by cab and so we made the drive surrounded by gunshots. We arrived and there was comfort in company, yet I felt so alone watching the scene unfolding from Marcus' balcony. In rare moments, you can become vividly aware of storing experiences to be processed much later. Your senses heighten as if your brain compensates for its struggle to comprehend that particular moment. I stood frozen ingesting the scene deeply, keenly. An armoured vehicle passed through the street. Shots rang out. I waited to hear that telltale sign of military victory - cheering. None came so I assumed it must have been enemy fire. People were yelling in Arabic and I immediately recognized my single grossest expat flaw. I had not learned the language of my new home. I promised myself that I would learn Arabic, a promise I kept. Standing on Marcus' balcony, the air smelled ominous. My skin was trying to hide but my eyes were too curious for me to go back inside. I ducked around a corner and stayed extremely still, saturating my senses with this new environment. I stayed there paralysed until my senses released my brain back into thought.

Within twenty-four hours, my bearings were regained and gunshots became the backdrop of Maadi, our Cairean suburb. As a civilian, I will never forget how quickly people get used to the sound of gunfire. As a soldier, I felt I had gained some understanding of the roots of PTSD: sometimes things happen to your brain when you are living through your senses and unable to process thought. Soldiers cannot sit and wait for cerebral activity to recommence, they must make sense of it later in a completely different environment. How difficult that must be. The police were no longer visible on the streets. Nobody missed them but their absence left buildings and businesses vulnerable to opportunists. Boabs offered some measure of security. Boabs were loyal men hired year round to protect buildings. Each apartment complex had a boab. Expats considered boabs as filling the "overprotective big brother" role. The boab looked out for its occupants, protected them and made them tow the line. We paid our boab monthly for the ongoing service of keeping us safe, watching out for our apartments, unlocking our doors when we lost our keys and chasing away members of the opposite sex. We learned in turn when our boabs were most likely to be asleep at their posts and used those precious moments to sneak our love interests in. During the revolution, boabs bravely began patrolling with batons and homemade weapons. Boabs showed their true colours in the revolution and they were radiant. Egyptian and expat alike were made to feel protected, valued and cared for. Despite their best efforts, businesses and apartments were looted. Anyone living in first or second floor apartments became aware of increased risk as thieves would enter through windows. Allison, a close friend, entered her first floor apartment one afternoon to find a thief stealing her computer. She screamed in fright and yelled for him to stop. Unafraid, he took over twenty minutes looking through the rest of her apartment, knowing full well that he was safe. Her boab had stepped out and she had nowhere to turn.

Marcus had the one item that became a prized possession in the revolution, a landline. Cellular coverage and Internet was out off for days, but we were able to call home using his landline. We were also able to call the Canadian consulate. And call we did. Over and over and over. We simply wanted to see if we had been registered as expatriates with the Canadian consulate so that someone official knew we lived in Egypt. Being registered meant that we would be informed of any extraction procedures if the unrest became increasingly dangerous. The responsibility for employee consular registration was held by the school. Paperwork was not a forte of Egyptian International Schools. It turned out that back in Canada, my father was attempting to find out the same thing. At least he was able to leave a message on the consulate's answering machine. Having hightailed it out of there, employees at the Canadian consulate in Cairo had a full answering machine. This was a source of shame when our international friends were being contacted by their consulates. A shame that lasted until Marcus used his landline to broadcast the Canadian consulate's failings over Canadian Radio stations.

Marcus worked in radio and had many connections in Canada. As he called in favours, he was interviewed on Canadian radio. The war cry of the media demanded action and within twenty-four hours we were called on Marcus' landline by the Canadian Government. They took our information and informed us of a relief flight to Frankford leaving the next day. The fact remained that, of our coworkers at a Canadian International School, we were the only Canadians to be contacted by our consulate and/or government throughout the process. Only because we shamed them publicly. Their reaction was a disgrace.

Many factors played into an individual's decision to stay or leave Egypt during this very interesting time. Although my decision was simple, my inner critic kept questioning and judging my decision harshly. How could I leave my new home when it was taking such good care of me? In leaving, was I betraying those about whom I cared deeply? My boyfriend Salem pleaded with me to go; once I was safely away, he could focus on protecting his family. He even dropped me off at the airport. Resources were growing scarce, staples gone from the shelves. We pooled our remaining resources to support those left behind. We removed the burden of care and provided for those who had little. It made sense, so why did I feel so guilty? I had a personal reason for going. For the three months leading to the uprising I had partial blockage of my right ear. Local doctors told me that I had to have a hole drilled through the eardrum to release the pressure. This terrified me. I wanted desperately to be seen by a Canadian doctor before deciding on this course of action. So I went.

We almost didn't make it out. As we gathered at the airport I saw an Egyptian running through the baggage carousel trying to escape. Desperation had set in. We were shuttled to a smaller room and told to wait for our plane. Just as we were supposed to be released, the police locked the doors and demanded two thousand dollars to reopen them. With ATMS's frozen and insecure, we didn't have the money. Our pilot was nearing his final hours of being able to fly and we saw a long night stretched out in front of us. Finally, some tourists paid the corrupt policemen and we boarded the plane. The police were perpetrating exactly what had led to the uprising. While we were not used to being victimized in this way, the Egyptian people were. The revolution suddenly made much more sense. It would continue until Hosni Mubarak resigned on the 11th of February, 2011. Most expats had been glued to their television sets since leaving Egypt. Finally, we could return.

The fateful day on Marcus' balcony swept over me as we waited for the police to arrive in front of the Cataract Hotel. The feeling was eerily familiar: adrenaline. The problem with adrenaline is that it takes a sinister joy in creating need. If the initial threat is pacified, you feel dull, bored and somehow less. Adrenaline convinces you to create threat just to feel alive. After Hosni Mubarak resigned, pockets of citizens accustomed to adrenaline continued to create threat on a smaller scale. Stores were looted, stones were thrown. Once you boast a global audience it is hard to resume a less public life. Adrenaline was propelling the Egyptians to fight for change. And in the great fight vs flight standoff, I was reminded that I had fled. Thinking of the bike trip ahead, I was determined not to flee again. I would fight my way through this bike tour regardless of what I was up against.

The police didn't show up that morning and so we set out on what seemed like a suicide mission; we would convoy through the traffic without police support. Anyone who has visited the streets of Cairo knows that the lines on the roads are a waste of paint; laughable and without the power of suggestion. You would expect a veteran of Cairo traffic to stand immobilized at the thought of pedalling through such mayhem, but in actual fact things were not as they appeared (Egypt's mantra). In truth, the drivers around Cairo were extremely used to one important thing: reacting to the unexpected. They dodged misbehaving donkeys and erratic scooters as if life were a video game with serious repercussions. Most things were dodged successfully. Arguably, the drivers in Cairo were more welcoming of forty insane cyclists than their Canadian counterparts would have been. With endless highways, Canadians are lulled into dream-like states of apathy, resulting in disaster. No living Cairian driver has ever been accused of day dreaming at the wheel. Before that terrifyingly final tiny word "GO" I wriggled my way to the front of the pack. Starting at the front meant that I could slowly drop to the back of the pack as long as I made a show of socializing with everyone along the way. Thus, cyclists would consider me extremely social, not horribly out of shape. This plan did not work. I fell swiftly to the rear within the first few moments with no spectacle of socialization. I contemplated the many species of animals that kill their weakest link for survival while repeatedly thanking our homosapien overdeveloped prefrontal cortex.

The bike trip staff also showed their true colours. I was immediately impressed with their willingness to place themselves in sacrificial roles to protect their sheep. Perhaps the sheer spectacle of forty disoriented cyclists on these deadly roads was just enough to shock the locals into submission but our staff managed the impossible...they stopped road traffic at every intersection we crossed. No local egos were visibly bruised and we all made it to the pyramids intact and ready to begin our adventure. Grand success.

As any teacher will attest, there is something in a name. Names hold the power of persuasion. So I name my bikes carefully based on their salient characteristics and general energy. I rode Trinity, my graceful Devinci Destination across Canada in 2004. Trinity sat beneath me, followed my lead and deferred to my judgement, even at the worst of times. She was steadfast, dependable and quite content meandering for hours on end. General Kate, my Cannondale Ultegra toured me around Japan. She was decisively stylish with her zebra patterned handlebar tape and pink water bottles. She requested more frequent pampering and in return she kept me on schedule. For the African tour, I sat atop Buck, my Surly Long Haul Trucker. Whether I rode Buck or Buck rode me was dependent on the day and this surly bike's mood. When I first told my parents that I was looking for a "Surly Long Haul Trucker to ride across Africa" they quite understandably had a few questions. Buck lived up to his name. He would eventually get me there, although it was rarely pretty. Buck would push me to my limit and then handle the rest. Whereas I felt in control of Trinity, I felt controlled by Buck. He knew how he wanted to ride over every terrain and he tolerated my input solely because he needed my legs to pedal. I was actually a little afraid of angering him and under no illusions that we would be best of friends at tour's end. Buck tolerated me for what I brought to the relationship. We had an abusive relationship and I have rarely picked him up since the tour.

Buck frowned dimly at my squeals of glee upon seeing my friends at the pyramids. Trina, Chantel and Lindsay had come to see me off and it meant one last sense of normalcy before reality hit me like a brick wall. I felt proud. Suddenly Mama Tam, Hannah, Springs, Roberto, Monica, Kadija, and Omar rounded the corner sitting on bicycles. The first day of the tour was open to local cyclists who wish to join as a proper send-off. They were along for the inaugural ride. We couldn't help but laugh as Omar rounded the bend with his unattached helmet on backwards, holding onto the side of a police van, exhausted after a three minute cycle. I was relieved when he told me that he had already quit on the day's adventures. Being around other nervous riders who weren't sure they would survive the day was a source of great comfort.

The police, finally appearing after their lazy morning, escorted us out of Cairo. Amazingly, they orchestrated a professional and organized convoy; almost as if they cared. As they directed traffic and blocked intersections, I watched the reactions of the locals ranging from disgust to disbelief, from curiosity to joy. The majority looked at us with that special brand of pity reserved for those who are mentally imbalanced. I was beginning to question this very same logic as I sputtered and choked on the thick pollution. "Magnooneen" became a chorus we heard through the black fog assaulting our senses and declaring us "insane". With sight and breath obscured, what is the point of cycle tourism you might wonder? The answer lies in these letters: EFI.

The EFI club is reserved for an elite bunch of idiots willing to set aside all authentic purpose, reason and safety in order to gain the deepest of bragging rights. Telling yourself and others that you cycled down Africa is simply not enough. You MUST be able to say "I cycled EVERY F@*&$ INCH!" when others beg to know if you skipped any section. Not that anyone will ever ask. Ever. Nor care. But just in case they do, you are willing to cycle through cancerous fog, broken bones and extreme bum sores to be able to brag this deeply. On that first day, Holly had the wherewithal to climb onto a truck and take a deep breath. We would all eventually come to understand that this tour was so much bigger than the EFI club but on that day, Holly was the only enlightened one. I did, however, have revelation of my own; come what may, I was embarking on a profound goal. This was a goal which inhabited every cell of my being. A goal that had managed to find a crack in my marriage years earlier and wedge inside. The worst moments of my life were now being replaced with core moments of happiness. In these moments, you feel a stirring, your heart suddenly shouts "YES!" as you fist-pump the air in celebratory release. This moment seemed to exist uniquely between me and the universe and a chill ran over my body as I bared myself under the watchful eye of Mother Nature. That road felt like the perfect life path again, finally. I had made it. I bid goodbye to my friends. As they drove away seated tenderly on a bus I heard them yell: "Now we can literally call you a pain in the ass!" and I shivered. The last remnants of my familiar life just exited the stage. The grand adventure had commenced. The next day held the promise of 166 kilometers of cycling, our first "century" (100 miles on the bicycle in one day) and my longest day of cycling in over seven years.

Only maniacs sleep on the first night. Despite communal restlessness, nobody uttered a sound. Nobody wanted to showcase their discomfort. Separated by only a thin layer of nylon, cyclists lie immobile, entombed in their tents, hardly daring to roll over lest they sound like a rustling, dying animal. Against my better wishes I was betrayed by my bladder that first night. I rustled from my tent, dragged my body outside and ventured off to pee under the stars. The witching hour was upon us. The witching hour; seemingly calm but fully energized, seemingly dead and lonely but fully, vividly alive. The rest of the night has peaceful slumber, but the witching hour has lucid dreams. You cut through its essence with your wakened presence. You are meant to be asleep and not to witness the raw energy, usually so cautiously masked. Suddenly I was jolted to awareness by a distinct lack of sound clanging around in my brain. No snoring or heavy breathing resonated from the fifty odd tents scattered in the field. These little dark bumps scattered, silently basking in the moonlight, hiding their slumberless occupants from the watchful eyes of the stars. Absolute silence except the dancing of the wind. It was perfect. Finding relief I made my way back to the one unsightly large tent, which broke the perfectly blemished skin of the Earth. For no particular reason other than availability, I had brought a four man tent. Every day I leveraged my entire body to cram enough poles and nylon for four people into my tiny one person locker. I had no backup plan. The tent and I were "all in" together.

I did not regret my frugality. My cheap choice not to buy a new tent afforded many benefits. In Khayamiya, named in honour of Egyptian circus tents, I stood and stretched my aching achilles tendon, now blissfully lulled to submission by ibuprofen. I did some tent yoga. I tried to make Tasha proud. Tasha, my yoga instructor in Cairo, taught me how to breathe in one of the world's most polluted cities. I'm not sure any of us would have survived without her. In Tasha's presence everything became periphery as you graced your core with a much needed playdate. Honking horns dulled, barking dogs hummed, you saw your heartbeat. She was an oasis and I needed her that first night on the ground. My favourite yogic construction has always been pigeon pose; it never ceases to relax my brain. With a practiced exhale into the relaxing pose my achilles tendon inhaled sharply, coughed and spasmed in protest. "166 kilometers!" it screamed. "Are you mad?!?" I felt the cry pierce through my ibuprofen defence. Unwilling to admit defeat on the first night, I forced a stretch and absorbed my freedom. Little did I know the following night I would be staring down the barrel of an AK47.

D-Day + 1
The one with the AK-47

The next morning, I missed breakfast. How is it possible to miss breakfast after a slumberless night? Let me tell you a secret. There are few moments as relaxing as lying in a tent cozily nestled in your sleeping bag listening gently to the world coming to life. Emerging from dreams in my own personal monastic cell to noises that fueled the imagination was certainly the nicest way of waking up. It was fitting because today we would enter the town of Zaafarana, considered by many to be the birthplace of Christian monastic life. Around the year 270 BCE, St. Anthony wandered into the same desert mountains that we were about to travel with the desire to live in a small cell. The practice of isolation and self-denial was becoming an increasingly popular method of connecting with divinity. With time, others emulated St. Anthony and his Coptic monastery grew to house over one hundred and ten monks in small cells.

As Maximous Elantony mused after discovering these cells in Zafarana, "When you live in a quiet place, like a cell, and you are not busy with anything but God, you start to hear yourself and to see yourself."

That was the trouble. I suddenly saw myself. Trying to awake slowly was of no use. The soft "getting ready" sounds universally made by cyclists which I usually found soothing suddenly alarmed me. I could not face the pack as I did not feel like one of them. I hid. I needed a few more moments of blessed anonymity to fake belonging.

I was jolted from my sleeping bag by one sickening realization: Africa was devoid of Tim Hortons. Whereas in Canada I would pedal ten kilometers in ANY direction and be comforted by the promise of a Timmies breakfast and coffee, there were no obvious food stops here. I would have to cycle seventy-one kilometers before the next option of food. This realization propelled me into the pack, needing their support desperately. Anonymity destroyed, I loudly lamented missing breakfast until Andrew reached into his back pocket and pulled out a chocolate bar and crackers, handing them to me. Andrew was from Newfoundland, Canada, famed for creating the world's funniest and most generous people. Andrew was certainly funny. He hosted the popular television series Canada's Worst Driver. I stared at Andrew as if he were a world-class magician and I was witnessing his best trick. Where had that food come from? People carry food in their back pockets? Oh right! I thought suddenly. Everyone was better at this than me. They planned their life. They knew how to survive AND that I was the weakest link. I hung my head in shame and graciously accepted Andrew's offerings, trying not to think about what most animals eventually do to their weakest link. Andrew was not Newfoundland's most generous - I learned much later from Andrew himself that he did not reveal his entire trick, saving two more chocolate bars in his back pocket for himself. No matter how it may look superficially, it is a dog-eat-dog business cycling Africa.

I got on my bicycle and tried to hurry to lunch before my calories ran out. I felt strong, REALLY strong. I felt fast. This could only mean one thing. Whenever a cyclist's ego surpasses his or her ability it always means one thing...massive tailwind! Relief swept over me, I may just survive the morning.

I boogied down to the Red Sea. It greeted me beautifully with arms outstretched. The Red Sea was family. Since my arrival in Egypt, I had been drawn to the Red Sea. Advancing my diving qualifications and working briefly for a dive company brought me to her shores most months. Having explored the Red Sea inside and out you would think I would greet her with warmth and familiarity. I didn't. I had witnessed the Red Sea reveal both heads and tails. Its most magnificent splendor should never blind you to its deadly might. In one dive, we would see giant moray eels surrounded by lionfish as we passed corpse-filled remnants of shipwrecks. The Red Sea would give divers confidence and open up new worlds, only to periodically strip their egos. On one particularly horrific occasion, I witnessed as the Red Sea almost swallowed one diver eternally had it not been for the fast action of our Dive Tour leader who brought him back to safety under extreme duress. I knew not to trifle with the Red Sea. The Red Sea inspired awe in everyone, no matter the number of previous encounters.

Curving along the Porto Soukhna road I found myself gaining confidence in my legs and looking forward to each vista as the road twisted and turned. Perhaps I did belong in the pack. Just after being passed by a group of transport trucks full of palm trees and water bottles, I caught up with Jennifer. Jennifer was a twenty-five year old Canadian adventurer from Ontario. Although Jennifer had never lived in Egypt, we shared a friend from Cairo. Everyone has a story to tell and we shared ours freely. I learned that Jennifer went to an all girls' high school, she adored her brother and missed her late mother dearly. She was at once adventurous and driven, and was heading to New York City after the tour to complete an MBA. Jennifer had gotten whiplash during a pillow fight in eighth grade and had never fully recovered. These are the details that tell a person's unique story. From global perspectives to small anecdotes, we shared freely. Our stories wove tightly together to form ties. I remember thinking that exchanges like this one held the key to empathy. Understanding our connection despite our different threads was made possible through the literal and figurative sharing of common ground. We have a very real responsibility to support one another in this small world. Anyone who has trouble finding common ground should climb on a bike together.

Jennifer and I cycled well together. Together our tires sung soft lullabies rotating so slowly that even the Red Sea was lulled into meditative slumber. We also rested from our slow motion cycling a lot. Was our speed an effort to ease the mental load of one hundred and sixty one kilometers? Slow and steady wins the race? Perhaps. Where I never found out Jennifer's motivation for slowing down, mine was simple...I was mostly numb from the waist down. Before running into Jennifer, a pain cycle had swept through my lower half. It began with a sharp pain in both knees screaming for my undivided attention. I ignored its aggressive pleas. The sharp pain transformed into a wider, globalized pain across my legs. Given that ignoring had previously worked, I tried my hand again. Finally the cycle turned into numbness; my favourite stage. It would eventually cycle back to sharp localized pain, of that I was sure. When was anyone's guess.

"Whosh! Whosh! Whosh!" our lullaby had been interrupted by some aggressive cycling.

Suddenly we received a surprise visitor from the rear, Alaric. Alaric was a young attractive Namibian citizen who had been living in Cairo for over one year. The tour was a manner of transportation home for him, as he planned to stay in Namibia following the tour to set some roots. A few months before the tour began, I was put in contact with Alaric by a few common friends. We sized each other up over a meal at a small restaurant in Cairo. At the time, Alaric struck me as intense, his serious gaze never left mine. I remember wondering if he ever blinked or looked anywhere other than at my soul. In fact, he was dumbstruck. At the time, I struck Alaric as idiotic. He was incredulous that I had not joined the Cairo Cyclists Club to continue training for the tour. I did not tell him that my training hadn't even started. For the next few months I tried to 'balance Alaric's training' - his beer arm was sorely lacking - by inviting him to a few social gatherings. He always declined. Looking back, it was at that meeting that I first formed an opinion of what a REAL cyclist was and, by contrast, determined that I wasn't one. Unbeknownst to Alaric, he may have inadvertently begun "the Solar Panel Crisis". Alaric could have been called Anubis for his steady, judgemental yet honest eyes. Anubis, an ancient Egyptian God, the gatekeeper to the afterlife. Anubis would weigh the human heart to determine the soul's direction: heaven or hell. Alaric's penetrating gaze made me feel similarly judged. Deep down I knew that I deserved judgement; the audacity of attacking Africa without giving it the due respect of training. I realized how fear can be subconsciously paralytic. The moment Jennifer and I were passed by Alaric, my brain took a step back. Alaric WAS a cyclist. What in the world was he doing behind us fakers? With a flirtatious smile from both of us, he slowed his pace long enough to fill us in. He spoke quickly. Unluckily, he had experienced a flat tire at three kilometers from the starting block. After changing his tube and restarting his day, he subsequently got another flat. As I would find out many times over, there were days when the tire gods did not smile upon you. This was Alaric's day. He sped off quickly in true racer form leaving us quite literally in his dust. His day was far from over; he would fix three more flats before sundown, and he would still arrive at camp half an hour before the two of us. The rabbit did win the race that day.

Jennifer and I stopped to dip our toes in the Red Sea. I begged for the Red Sea's restorative powers to get us through a gruelling day. The water was crisp and cold, a sharp contrast to the fiery numbness enveloping our lower extremities. Three uniformed soldiers approached us wanting a photograph. I knew full well what this meant. In one snap, we would be forever entrenched and bragged about as their girlfriends to a wide ranging Egyptian audience. Girlfriends are effective left hooks in a fight for the macho. Fully aware of our fates, we accepted. We needed all the good karma we could get. As it turned out, I needed an abundance of good luck that very night when I encountered another pair of soldiers, this time under quite hostile circumstances (more on that later...).

Back on the water's edge, we saw an old fisherman in his ramshackle hut down on the beach. Life was challenging as he had with no safety net to fall back on. Exposed to the elements - Egypt is surprisingly cold at night in winter, my heart went out to him. He smiled at us and waved. Looking through my North American lense I felt pity as I returned the gesture. I was yet to learn how little my North American life set me up to understand happiness. I still considered wealth a top predictor. Ethiopia would rid this idea of its last vestiges. In retrospect, the elderly fisherman was looking at me with pity, and rightly so. Jennifer and I got back on our bikes slowly. We pushed forward as we carefully watched the sun descend into the horizon. We did not yet know the sun's schedule intimately. The sun set just as we crossed the finish line in Zafarana, precious moments before we would have been swept into a van reserved for those "who didn't make it that day". Sunset was a non-negotiable deadline on tour. Tour rules stated that for safety reasons, you must make it to camp before dusk. Every F&@*ing Inch (EFI) died inside active cyclists as the sun went down. Luckily for us on that one hundred and sixty-one kilometer day, the sun had our backs.

After downing a victory beer, Alaric helped me to set up my tent in the dark. This was to be the night where my opinion of Alaric started shifting towards the comfortable. He had seemed so intense in Cairo but laughing alongside him now, a few hundred kilometers from where we had both called home, the stars shifted. To get a better view of those stars, we decided to head to the beachside for a refreshing walk and a swim. Lost in the moment, it took a few long seconds before we recognized that we were suddenly looking down the barrels of two AK-47s. Loud people were shouting at us in hurried Arabic. Time froze.

"Should we run?" I whispered to Alaric.

A foolish suggestion as my legs were decidedly NOT running anywhere after such a long cycling day and certainly not outrunning a bullet. We could not hope to understand what they were yelling so we did what any great understudy of Hollywood would do; stuck up our hands. Much later, Alaric confided in me that he was strongly considering lifting my shirt and dazzling them long enough for his getaway...not sure which brand of Hollywood he was watching....

"We are cyclists!" were my first words to our captors spoken in English.

Luckily one spoke back. Alhamdulillah! Headlamps were illuminated and two young soldiers named Ahmed and Mahmoud approached. Quickly, my Hollywood brain classified Ahmed as the good cop and Mahmoud as the bad. Mahmoud stared at us scowling as Ahmed and I tried to make sense of one another in broken speech. This would be the first of many times that Arabic lessons saved my hide. I knew enough of the current state of Egypt to determine that being shot was a real possibility. I also knew the Egyptian male ego was our best approach at escaping unscathed. Cowing, belittling ourselves and flattering Ahmed's knowledge and power was the way to go. Appeased, Ahmed explained to us that the beach was extremely active and dangerous with drug traffickers at night. The exact information that had been passed on at the rider meeting before Alaric, Jennifer and I had arrived. Staff had forbidden cyclists from the beach with a grave warning. Soldiers had permission to shoot first and ask questions later. Ahmed relented and decided to walk us back to camp thankfully without a thorough search. Mahmoud, his fellow soldier, seemed much less impressed and kept his weapon readied throughout. I slept soundly despite the knowledge that armed soldiers and drug traffickers were waging war a few hundred meters away.

D-Day + 2
The one with the madman

The next morning I awoke to a wonderful surprise. If tailwinds ever reach divine status, today was the holy grail of weather. Perfect temperature, perfect wind and perfect distance; a measly one hundred and thirty six kilometers. Leaving camp I felt like I was floating. But African Gods aren't known for their unconditional gifts. In fact, today's many shades of brilliant were quickly marred with smudges of terrible. As perfect as the winds were, today could not be enjoyed. Rosalyn foreshadowed trouble that morning "I think I will get my first flat today." Rosalyn was a stunning and athletic thirty-two year old Canadian nurse who was cycling Africa with her partner Jay, an emergency room physician. I had the pleasure of knowing Rosalyn from Tour du Canada back in 2004 where she kept up with the quickest racers on tour without too much effort. I admired Rosalyn for her fearless and confident attitude. The fact remained, she was usually right. Sure enough, ten kilometers down the road, my throat closed. An ambulance had pulled to the side of the road. Ambulances on bike tours paralyse my breath while spiking my heart with adrenaline. It has been this way ever since the extremely tragic death of our fellow Tour du Canada cyclist Colin Krivy in Beiseker, Alberta in July 2004. Colin had just set his life on a new path and was listening to his heartsong when his life was tragically cut short by a dangerous driver. Not again. As we approached, my breath returned, relieved to see Rosalyn unharmed and sipping water while the paramedics fixed her first flat of tour. I suppose there are perks to being gorgeous, funny, athletic and confident.

Twenty kilometers down the same road, the ambulance had stopped again. My throat closed a second time as I came upon a horrendous scene; a rider was on the ground, unable to move. Shona, a middle-aged South African woman, was in obvious pain and distress.

Instead of showing concern for herself, she was yelling adamantly "Don't tell Mig!" "Don't tell Mig!"

I was slowly piecing together a picture of this incredible woman. My first recollection of Shona was at our first rider meeting at the Cataract Hotel where she was encouraging all women to partake in the race element on tour, regardless of riding style. At heart, Shona was a well-balanced, selfless advocate. She simply wanted everyone to be the best version of themselves. Shona was a fierce competitor but also a strong unifyer. In South Africa, Shona single-handedly raised her daughter to be a strong woman and opened Curves studios to help all women towards this same goal. Shona was the lifeblood of the tour. She was in distress and it made my heart sick.

What can only be described as a teenaged madman had come from the desert terrain and violently pushed Shona into oncoming traffic. Oncoming traffic was a transport truck. Shona was 'fortunate' in so far as she bounced off an immense transport truck tire and fell away from traffic and into the ditch. She was scraped, deeply bruised and in shock but alive and conscious. Rosalyn's flat tire had slowed Jay, who caught up to Shona just after the attack. He kept everyone calm until Shona was whisked off to the hospital in Hurghada.

"Don't tell Miguel!" was yelled out the window one last time. Miguel was Shona's partner. Through it all, Shona was most concerned about Miguel losing his EFI status and not being able to complete his goal. Shona was a force. Chained to another transport truck was the perpetrator, looking more than slightly "magnoon". One look suggested that his mental health was failing. Frightened and angry, I yelled "HARAM" as loudly as I could. Usually this two syllable word strikes fear in the heart of any good Muslim but he barely recognized my existence. I'm not entirely positive that he was lucid, but I am positive that he was released back into the desert once the coast was clear.

Patience has many of the same properties as time, it expands and contracts to suit the individual experiencing it. Although most drivers in Egypt seemingly check their patience at the door, the tour paramedics painstakingly followed me the rest of the way to camp. I suppose they deemed that anyone crazy enough to yell "SINFUL" at a madman would need extra protection. I was very thankful for their presence as, being lulled into a meditative state by the drone of the road, I missed the finish flag for camp. I also missed everyone yelling at me as they watched me ride uphill away from the camp. This introspective spell engulfed me until I heard the ambulance horn blasting me from behind. The horn jolted me back to awareness and I laughed my way to camp. I told Rosalyn that I simply wanted more from this beautifully temperate day.

D-Day + 3
The one with the Red Sea

We awoke to one hundred kilometers stretching between our desert camp and Safaga's sandy beaches of the Red Sea. It doesn't take long living in the desert to feel grateful for the restorative properties of the Red Sea. The Red Sea protects you from the harsher realities of the desert heat and provides a serene oasis from the abundant noise pollution engulfing even the quieter desert neighbourhoods. Newcomers to Cairo are told that in order for an expat to survive, one weekend per month must be spent rejuvenating in the Mother Sea. In a world where natural order has given way to overpopulation, submerging in aquatic beauty permits temporary amnesia regarding how far from the natural we are living. We would re-emerge a better version of ourselves. To me, Safaga holds the gold star. In my life, I have witnessed two completely awe-inspiring sights that stopped time and required every cell to come into focus. Coming face to face with a dinosaur-esque giant moray eel in Safaga was one such moment. The other moment would follow much later on tour. Needless to say, nothing was coming between me and my Red Sea today. Certainly not a measly one hundred kilometers. The immediate problem was, my legs had gone on strike.

I willed my legs to move and in return, they shot pain up to my skull. I sat them down and had a serious heart to heart with them yet their position didn't budge. I had no other option; I needed to cut them off. Popping two Egyptian painkillers, roughly equal in dosage to ten regular strength Canadian painkillers, I felt nothing from the waist down. Relying solely on muscle memory, I booked it downhill to the coast. My plan worked as my legs numbly drifted into the ancient port town of Safaga. This merchant port was founded between 282 BCE and 268 BCE. Today, it was touted as Egypt's capital of rejuvenation with it's pure air, black sand dunes and mineral springs. Tourists came internationally to treat their heart, liver and kidney disease in Safaga's sulphur baths, warm sands and mineral treatments. I hoped my legs would follow suit. I spent a blissful day on the warm beach and left the fly off my tent all night to bask my traumatized leg muscles in crisp seaside air.

D-Day + 4
The one with the jackass

We awoke with the reward of the Red Sea behind us and a camp called "Police Check" ahead of us. We had to dig deep for motivation. Headwinds decided to make their grand debut on our fifty-seven kilometer climb from seaside camp. When downhills feel like uphills you know the world is conspiring against you. I passed all the slower riders heading uphill. Feeling slightly otherworldly I kept pushing until the shocking and unexpected happened...I passed some of the faster cyclists. I had a secret weapon that day: fear. You see, when one of the most knowledgeable cyclists on tour tells you that the day you are currently facing has historically been the worst day on tour, you panic. You push hard, all day long. Convinced that I would not make it, I surrendered to a day of pain. What I did not anticipate was the sharp edge of beauty that can creep in while enduring pain. Was my breath being taken by overexertion or by the rigid mountains steeply bordering both sides of the road? Impossible to tell, both made me lightheaded in appreciation. Synapses fired wildly in my brain. I had done this before. Jackass Mountain, British Columbia, two-thousand and four.

In early July two-thousand and four, I had just embarked on my first bicycle tour. Not having any idea of what cycling meant, I was equally frightened to face the steepest mountain relatively early on tour. The name Jackass Mountain served a terrifying reminder that even the most risk-taking donkeys would turn on tail when facing this mountain route. "Jackass" would be the predominant refrain of self-talk while climbing. It was a well named mountain. In two-thousand and four Rosalyn and I arrived at the base of Jackass Mountain around the same time. We both had the same initial thought: "*@$#!" As the tar truck moved aside to let us pass we wondered what would give out first; our lungs from the tar fumes or our bodies from the additional ten degrees of heat tarring adds to any pavement. With steely resolve, I climbed slowly and steadily, the soft tar embracing my tires. Suddenly, the road flattened and Rosalyn was waiting. We had done it! We had conquered Jackass Mountain! Victorious pictures were taken showcasing our extreme musculature. Then we turned the corner and silently wept. Jackass Mountain had the last laugh that day as it continued uphill for many, many more kilometers. Mentally defeated, Jackass Mountain became the longest, most gruelling day on tour.

Today was Jackass Mountain stuck on replay. As often as the road flattened, I celebrated my victory, only to be defeated as I turned the next corner to greet more uphill. This continued until I turned that final corner and saw the telltale signs of a Police Check, our campsite for the night. No matter how grateful I was to see such a sight, no celebratory pictures would EVER be taken at an Egyptian Police Check. Too many times, while crossing the Sinai to go diving in Dahab or Sharm El Sheikh, would we encounter corrupt Police Checks. Police Officers would demand payment to pass, confiscate items unnecessarily or hold us up for hours without explanation. One time, while driving to Nuweiba with my boyfriend Nour and his best friend Omar, we were stopped at a police check. Four liquor bottles were confiscated, which was well within their right. However, having had enough of police oppression, Omar proceeded to smash all four bottles on the ground rather than hand them over for the police to drink themselves. The officers, reeking of alcohol already, hardly responded as they did not have a leg to stand on. I quietly entered the Police Check campsite and drank soup leisurely while licking my mental wounds. Little did I know that I would need this recovery time dearly before a hair-raising jaunt into Luxor the following day.

D-Day + 5
The one with sticks and stones

With the tantalizing smell of a day off, we awoke at the Police Check invigorated and excited. Although historically, today was not meant to be the hardest day on tour, it would end up making the day before look easy. We were entering tribal territory. As the streets became increasingly remote, so did the presence of police. We were entering areas where tribally based street vigilantism was the primary tenor of law and order and we were about to have a day unparalleled by any previous tour. It could hardly have been predicted unless you had witnessed the changes in post-revolution Egypt, which I had. As the police were stripped of power, tribal vigilantism filled the power void to disastrous extents. Expats living in Cairo were slapped in the face by this revelation in November, two thousand and eleven, a few months before the bike tour. By November two-thousand and eleven, expats had become accustomed to the new Egypt. Egypt was now under Army Command. Police weren't present to threaten or protect you. Street justice, speared on by boabs and neighbourhood watches, took form. This evolved predictably into tribalism in smaller towns. Yet, life carried on and, true to the adventurous form of expats, we traveled over the Eid holiday. Jean-Francois Pelland (JF), a French Canadian man in his thirties, was working as the vice principal at the British Columbia International School. JF was well known, well liked and a passionate educator. I used to see him at the baseball pitch where he would pepper me with questions about the upcoming bike tour. He was following his dream and very interested in this particular brand of travel. We joked that he could come along in my panier. Over Eid, JF traveled to rural Egypt with a friend. While going through empty police checks, JF's taxi found itself in the midst of a tribally-motivated gun fight. JF was caught in the crossfire and later died as a result of complications after surgery. The entire expat community mourned and grieved JF. He was a true adventurer and had passed on far too soon. At his memorial service, a card was handed out with the creed of St. Christopher, patron saint of travelers. As JF had mentioned to me that he wanted to see all of Africa and that he was very interested in the bicycle tour, I carried that card with me throughout the tour, and in all my travels for years after. Because of JF, I knew too well the current dangers of rural Egypt. So I approached the staff the night before our cycle into Luxor, told them about JF and warned them that any cyclist deviating off the prescribed route was placing themselves in potential harm. My warning did not go far enough.

The route was stunningly beautiful. A feeder stream to the Nile shimmed on our right and small towns tucked cozily to our left; we had entered tribal Egypt. The life-giving Nile welcomed many inhabitants over generations. Those living closely to the Nile were deeply rooted in their land. A group of young girls across the Nile saw us cycle by. They jumped and screamed while holding goats, in the hope that we would take a picture or two. Young ladies just out of school for the day stopped us to inquire about our journey and practice their English. For the second time, I realized what a blessing it was to speak Arabic. Keys unlocked safeguarded minds with the promise of creating connections and keeping us safe. Then the caning began. Sugar cane whipped between the spokes of our rims, rocks were launched at our heads. It was open season and we were prime targets, all because we did not belong in the newly re-tribalized Egypt. We were obvious outsiders. Egypt, having spent the better part of the year in turmoil and at times feeling abandoned by the international population, was not in the mood for us. We were visible signs of that unhelpful wealthy outside world. The locals, sensing that we were not in the giving mood - cyclists stop far less frequently heading into a rest day - rallied against us with sugar cane sticks and rocks. To be fair, most of the trouble came from curious, mischievous children, but certainly not all.

I was not in a rush. I was never in a rush. I lived by the mantra "There is no hurry in Africa." On this day forever referred to as the "day it rained rocks", the fastest cyclists had an advantage. Passing through the villages first, the fastest racers caught the locals by surprise, leaving them no time to plan their attack. By the time my group of leisurely riders passed through, the locals were coordinated, well armed and at the ready. Luckily, I also had the element of surprise. My secret weapon; Arabic. The repayment for hours upon hours of private Arabic lessons was to be the avoidance of being both caned and stoned by mischievous children and unruly adults. Every time I saw a group of young men with ill intent, I would preemptively strike; slowing right down and conversing with them in Arabic while maintaining firm eye contact. The rocks that they wielded would drop as quickly as their jaws. I could hear their internal debate.

"Who is this crazy white woman who speaks Arabic? Does she know my mother? Is she Egyptian? Will I get caned for stoning her?"

I became a curiosity rather than a target. We came across a group of six boys, with their arms cocked in unison, ready to hail rocks at us.

I slowed down to a halt and spoke extremely clearly, "Ana aerif umahatik - I know your mothers".

We had a great laugh as they ran away screaming. After that, a few curious riders asked for quick Arabic lessons and practiced alongside me. As we cycled into Luxor we saw that most of the cyclists did not finish the day unscathed. Most cyclists were battered and bruised this day. The worst case was Douglas, a powerfully-built South African veteran cyclist and bike mechanic who swerved into oncoming traffic to avoid a sugar caning. He was hit by an oncoming vehicle. Doug's bike was mangled and he was missing a piece of his lip, though he maintained his sense of humour making quips about them doing him a favour as he no longer needed to concern himself with sharing. Nothing ever got Doug down. One rider almost quit the tour after cycling through a hail of rocks all day long. I convinced her to ride with me on the remaining Egyptian roads. I was determined to use my Arabic to keep other riders safe. Eventually, my little trick made me popular and my cycling group ballooned for the remainder of Egypt. I became the safety net for the slow. At the end of a long dangerous day, seasoned staff gathered the broken group and told all riders that this was the first time in ten years that they had seen such dangerous riding conditions in this section of the tour. I felt completely unsurprised.

Every place on Earth has a touch of deep beauty. Getting intimate with a country exposes its raw personality. Although Egypt was a country in the midst of great change, its core was steeped in a history full beyond measure. I was determined to show the cyclists that Egypt was much more than sugar caning and rocks bouncing off their weary bodies. No better place than Luxor to do so. After a long emotional day on the bike, I guided three riders through a local market. Peter was a fifty-five year old man from New Zealand, a huge cycling enthusiast who was finally fulfilling a dream. Femke was a thirty-eight year old woman from the Netherlands, whose strength was matched only by her social graces and open-mindedness. Gennesse was a sixty-one year old woman from Australia, had completed an Ironman and embodied embracing life. Cycling tours bless you with many friendships from outside your demographic. All three of my new friends would go on to have extremely bad luck on the tour. But today was not that day. I guided Femke and Gennesse in bargaining for scarfs and revealed to them the secret of how to judge your bargaining skills. Upon purchase, if the owner gave you a little gift such as a scarab beetle or small figurine, the owner had made out like a bandit. This was a token of shame. If, however, the owner had such a scowl that you felt he/she may stab you in the back upon departure, you had done well. We ate kofta sandwiches in the souq and then set off on a two hour felucca boat ride on the Nile. We departed at sunset. After the reign of Mubarak feluccas gained the freedom to sail past sundown. We drank sugary tea and peacefully watched the sun setting behind the Nile. Our Captain, Ahmed, an entrepreneurial local man in his twenties, steered the boat with the help of his ten year old Second

Mate Abdel. They answered all of our questions about Egypt and even let us try our hand at steering the felucca. We experienced a sensation of tranquility only made possible after a sensory-rattling day. The magic of the felucca. We had stepped onto the vessel shell-shocked but now exited mentally rejuvenated...and hungry!

Of this I'm sure: there is no better fuel for extreme cycling than the traditional Egyptian kushari. Boasting over five hundred and forty calories per cup, this delicious concoction of carbs was perfect for long days in the saddle. Kushari consists of layers of rice, macaroni and lentils, topped off with a spicy tomato sauce, chickpeas and fried onions. For the best kushari, look for the most rundown small restaurant. We did. The paint was peeling off the walls, the floors were dirty and we were treated to a delectable feast. It is a traveller's misconception that somehow the cosmetics or plate price of a restaurant equates to "safer food". That night, a few cyclists fell ill after 'fine dining' in Luxor. Luckily, our koshari club felt better than ever. Foodborne illness was a real risk throughout the tour. As each country's population awaited our arrival, so did the microbes. Ethiopian microbes were particularly welcoming and enthusiastic. With our bellies full and minds rejuvenated, we settled in for our first night sleep without a looming agenda; tomorrow a rest day.

D-Day + 6
The one with Amun-Re

Our first rest day reset expectations for the remainder of the tour. Most cyclists began their day with a tourist's itinerary only to discover that it would be slashed viciously by necessary maintenance. This tour, it seemed, would not only be hard on our bodies, but our bicycles, tents and clothes as well. Half of the day was spent laundering clothes and cleaning greasy, sand-covered bicycles. Still determined to espouse the virtues of my new home, I set off with a group of riders to Karnak Temple; the daytime equivalent of staring at the stars. Karnak Temple merits introduction. Built for the god Amun-Re, Karnak Temple's construction spanned many periods of history beginning somewhere around 2000 - 1700 BCE. Almost every Pharaoh who reigned during construction added his own personal flavour to the site thus making

Karnak Temple a time travelers paradise. As such, it makes you feel small and insignificant but connected to the entirety of life. Everyone gets lost and found in the one hundred and thirty four towering columns of the Karnak Temple; lost behind columns measuring between ten and twenty one meters in height, with a diameter of over three meters, then found in the organization of the sixteen perfect rows. One expects Amun-Re, creator of the universe, to pop into view from behind a column at any moment in an elaborate game of hide and seek. Karnak Temple gets you in touch with the ancient wisdom of what matters. It immediately dwarfs you and obviates your insignificance in comparison to its magnificence. This feeling lasts until you exit the Temple towards the Sacred Lake and find the monumental scarab beetle. At this point, you feel tempted towards trivialities and begin to think a little too much of yourself. The scarab beetle was metaphorized as rebirth and regeneration in the heavenly cycle. Unwillingly, it has become a tourist attraction guaranteeing new love or the rejuvenation of old love, depending on how many times you circle the scarab. As you make the rounds of the scarab, you cannot help but feel downtrodden by how society has made such sacred ancient truths all about the self. Luckily, you cleanse yourself of this trivial feeling as you depart Karnak through the Avenue of Rams. Gazing at the stars one last time under the multitude of watchful ancient ram eyes, a feeling of oneness washes over your body, calming your core and you sit in the knowledge that we are all part of this great tapestry. The riders exited Karnak Temple and headed back a little more mindfully to mundane maintenance with the thought of another tough day in the saddle looming ahead. Shona had made it back to camp, which made us all thankful. But she needed time to recover, she would not be riding for a while yet.

D-Day + 7
The one with Youssef's tuk-tuk

Understandably, many cyclists decided to tag along at my snail's pace today. Not because they supported my lack of physical preparation for the tour, but because they felt no match for the hundreds of armed youngsters lining the roads. As before, speaking Arabic momentarily jolted the troublemakers out of their "us" vs "them" mentality. We became alike somehow, bridging the most important gap in humanity: communication. Nola and Bev, fellow Ontarians, learned Arabic greetings and enjoyed shocking the rocks from children. Youth and adults returned our greetings and welcomed us warmly. We even ended up with a police escort for a while, generously passing along orange slices when our stomachs began to audibly grumble at the unfair distance to the lunch truck.

Finally arriving at the lunch truck, our bodies were intact but our mouths were dry and parched from speaking to hundreds of Egyptians. I felt proud when Bev told me that she had seen a new side to Egyptian culture, a friendlier, more welcoming side. THIS was the side I saw every day as an expat living in Cairo. THIS was all that I wanted. However, it was not to be. The human brain is a remarkable instrument. Our long-term memories are often shined and polished towards the favourable. Nostalgia gets its name from this business. Our short-term memories edge and scratch towards the threatening. It only takes one threatening moment to refocus the brain, leaving little room for acknowledging the bigger picture. As we left the lunch truck, we found this one threat amidst hundreds of positive experiences. That one threat was thirteen year old Youssef and his tuk tuk.

We first noticed Youssef as he edged his tuk tuk closer and closer to our bicycles, mimicking our speeds. Unwilling to chance any collisions, we were forced off the road. He travelled ahead and stopped, waiting for our next move.Reluctant to play his brand of play cat and mouse, I went to speak to Youssef. I implored him to exercise caution but my reasoning fell on deaf ears. I stopped a few bystanders to ask for help but to no avail. They thought it was funny. It is human nature to side with those alike. In the end, we were forced to wait for the tour's ambulance escort to catch up to us. Sensing authority, Youssef immediately hightailed it home. My blood boiled because I knew that this day would not be defined by the thousands of friendly faces, but by Youssef and his power-hungry and dangerous game. I remembered Nour, my Egyptian boyfriend, remarking that it was a good thing that I was embarking on an organized tour. He said "In many parts of Africa, a person yielding minimal authority could hold you up for months". At the time, I thought he was exaggerating. Today, we were held up for over an hour by a thirteen year old tuk tuk driver.

We set camp in Edfu. Edfu was a town that superficially resembled most others in Egypt; tall buildings crumbling onto noisy streets. But in Edfu, the noise pollution kicked up enough dirt to hide a great secret. Edfu held the most preserved evidence of Egyptian history, more than any of the known tourist destinations. Experts flock to read the walls in Edfu as they contain detailed accounts dating back to 3100 BCE. Edfu was Egypt's diamond in the rough. At camp, I reflected on the day. I desperately hoped that my fellow travelers would be able to see the diamond that was Egypt. Today's story was rough and threatening. It would be difficult to see past the experiences of the day. I wondered how many of our experiences were being defined by the superficial. I prayed for safe passage on this long and unpredictable journey. Any hopelessness I felt that day would be eradicated later as I realized that most people we encountered would work to keep us safe, to better our passage. Humanity bears a common thread accessible through shared experiences. There was hope.

D-Day + 8
The one with a mounted defense

I awoke to our last full cycling day in Egypt and six eager cyclists wishing to survive it unscathed. Jennifer, Peter, Nola and Bev sat with John, a gentle and kind sixty-six year old Canadian man who was originally from the United States and L.S a young fit Torontonian who decidedly had a cycling habit. We set off together. After yesterday's ordeal I was hoarse and exhausted, but I took the lead all the way to lunch. Cognizant that I had a few quicker cyclists in tow, I tried to maintain a respectable pace, which nearly killed me. I was desperate to replace the memory of Youssef with a kinder goodbye from the country I loved so dearly. I decided to will the best from every Egyptian we met. To bring about friendliness on belief alone was improbable but I desperately wanted the locals to showcase what I knew was true; that they were hospitable. We came upon group after group of adolescents. Each time I slowed right down and greeted the group enthusiastically allowing all six cyclists to cycle by me to safety. I then struggled to catch the front of the line for the next group. Towards the end of the day, I placed my neck cover over my head to further confuse the youth. Confusing the teens into thinking I may be a covered Muslim was my last ditch effort to create a positive day. It worked. We all made it to camp at Aswan without a single stone launched in our direction. I felt relief but not happiness. I had spent the entire day on the defensive. The stress of maintaining this positive mindframe and feeling so connected to the outcome completely did me in. I collapsed into my tent.

Egypt was beautiful and I wondered how much of that beauty was lost on fearful riders. Hidden in the last few days of cycling were true Egyptian gems including Iman and Sayed, Egyptian staff hired to chauffeur our luggage. They welcomed us with open arms, sharing sugary tea, taking us for authentic kushari and buying us sweets. More importantly, they shared Egyptian customs and traditions with all those who would listen. I hoped the riders were listening as Egypt is so much more than rocks and sugar cane. Perhaps one day our brains would look back nostalgically but for the time being most riders were happy to leave Egypt behind.

That night, it turned out, I was also done with Egypt. It started when I went with Shona to purchase a bike helmet. The two men at the shop were so obviously trying to scam her out of money by inflating the price. Although usually good-humored about bartering, that day I had had enough.

Shona put it best "Jana lost her shit, yelled and stormed out of the shop."

I had simply spent too much energy that day willing the good from Egypt. I had no goodwill left for people who simply wanted to take advantage. I did not want to leave on such a note. Losing heart, I too felt thankful to move onto Sudan.

D-Day + 9
The one with a four-dimensional game of Tetris

I felt ready to leave Egypt. That is, until I arrived at the Aswan Ferry Boat. In two-thousand and twelve, there was no ground passage between the two neighbouring countries. We were to spend the night on a local ferry with Egyptian and Sudanese people, who tended to scoff at the laws of physics. Anyone who has driven Ring Road in Egypt will tell you that the laws of physics are mere suggestions in this part of the world. Your eyes deceive you as your taxi successfully wedges its way through a two foot space between fast moving vehicles. Space that doesn't exist materialises for your safe passage. You exhale in bewilderment and give your head a shake. Perhaps in the North American art of bubble-wrapping its citizens for safety, this is a lost skill. Our spatial awareness is founded on cultural safety precautions. Our definition of impossible is far too broad. We are wrong. Upon arrival, I was duly impressed with what resembled organization. We were told where to wait, when to load and where to stash our bikes and belongings with efficiency. Efficiency of which I dared not dream in my two years in Egypt. Nobody said Insha'allah. I noticed that both the doors and halls were narrow and tricky to navigate with luggage, there were low ceilings and heavy traffic blocked main arteries. Although our progress was slow, it was efficient. We soon discovered that our efficiency was orchestrated out of necessity. As soon as the tour was successfully stowed politely onboard, the regular boarding began. We were soon found to be amateurs, struggling with our individual luggage. We stood in awe watching hundreds of people competing for space to load what appeared to be all of their earthly possessions. Everyone was good natured and cutthroat, completely willing to crawl over their neighbour to secure a place on board. This is what happens when you have one ferry leaving weekly.

Imagine a four dimensional game of Tetris. The yellow square; countless refrigerators entering the boat - via narrow doors and hallways - on the backs of their owners. The magenta blocks; small chairs and tables of all shapes and sizes being carried by youth, negotiating every corner with far more yelling than movement. The inverse L; entire sofas being hoisted on the backs of men, hunched over while maneuvering through doorways. Then it got stranger. The snake block: Toilets being brought onboard which provided seating during the voyage, hopefully inoperational. Finally, the oddest piece of this Tetris puzzle: the line; hundreds upon hundreds of meters of shag carpet in bright pinks, reds and purples entering the ship to make the overnight voyage. I never got to the bottom of this one. The ferry boat became a magician's hat, and we stood with fascination as entire houses poured in. Then reality hit. This was not a magic show, physics exists and the boat may not bear the load. This thought made me a little nervous and my mind ventured to the many shipwrecks I had dived in Egypt. Swallowing my fear and refocusing, I thought that Jonas Neubauer, Classic Tetris World Champion, would have been proud of how neatly items were stacked away. We had breathing room and maneuverability and we were off. Once the boat hadn't sunk in the first hour I realized that we may just make it there alive.

There were not enough ferry cabins to go around. Many cyclists elected to sleep under the stars that night, which in theory, sounded very romantic and adventurous. While I was snug in my safe tiny cabin a dozen or so cyclists and staff got cozy in their sleeping bags on the ship's deck, settling in for a night's rest. Or so they thought. In romanticizing the Lake Nasser side upper deck, riders forgot to take one thing into account. In countries that celebrate Ramadan, nighttime is not always for resting. I learned this when working with students who fasted. In order to reduce the discomfort of fasting, families would often deliberately reverse their days and nights. They would begin their days at midnight, waking, enjoying meals, heading to school and then they would fall asleep upon returning home. This would maximize enjoyable waking hours and reduce the challenges of the hard fast. Day and night were not analogous to waking and sleeping. This was proven on our adventurous ferry boat ride. Opportunists often function best under the cloak of darkness. Cyclists on the upper deck awoke to find their food eaten and water drunk. Some locals, now pleasantly full and tired, were fast asleep spooning cyclists for warmth, which made for a very awkward morning. There would be no walk of shame, we simply became another story for them. Stories and experiences are true sources of pride when your prized possessions include dozens of meters of red shag carpeting. We had entered their world. It was our expectations that were out of place.

Sudan

D-Day + 10
The one with dirty laundry

The next morning the offload went as smoothly for us as the onload, with bags slightly lighter from the midnight snack fiesta. If first impressions are the business card of a country, Sudan was hired! The stress of the ferry ride was shed in the quick cycle to customs. Local eyes communicated less friction, the Sudanese were welcoming and gentle. We were immediately placated. Sudan felt like needed therapy after the jostle of Egypt. While the Sudanese officials rummaged through every bag diligently, we were treated to some local dance and music. Four women dressed in airy attire stood across from four men and partook in the universal language of dance. Bringing a few audience members into the mix brought our full attention to the joyous occasion playing out rather than to the dozen or so officials sifting through our dirty laundry, literally. Luckily our dirty shammy cycling shorts and personal pharmacies didn't look overly suspicious and we were released from their care, dignity intact. What struck me was the lightheartedness of the dancers. No obvious weight rested on their shoulders and just to bear witness released a weight we hadn't realized that we had been carrying. It would continue to amaze me throughout the journey that arbitrary lines drawn in the sand sever humanity so severely. Although only two feet wide, the border separates citizens based on their differences rather than serving as a common and uniting space. Survival in Egypt meant persisting through your body's protests. Survival in Sudan would mean listening to your body's every cue. The body's cues can be deafening if attuned to.

We cycled three kilometers to camp surrounded by tranquility and we collectively exhaled. At camp, we were greeted by the iconic Tour d'Afrique truck. Usually riders would be introduced to the great tour truck in Egypt, but due to political unrest, tour organizers had decided to bypass Egypt and park it in Sudan to await our arrival. In Egypt, we threw all our belongings into the cab of a large truck. Today we would meet our individual lockers aboard the official truck that would accompany us for the remainder of our journey. Our individual lockers, measuring roughly two feet in width and three in length, would house ALL of our belongings. More than one anxious face peered into our new lockers. Would this small Sudanese village be the lucky recipient of all our extraneous kit? At this point on tour, material possessions still mattered psychologically. We had not yet determined what we could live without, which turned out to be a great deal. Africa would be a glorious reframing of our consumeristic mentalities. But for now, we had to make it fit. When it simply didn't, various tactics were employed. I'll never forget Andrew, heading out on his first one hundred and forty-nine kilometer day in Sudan with his thermarest, plate and bowl stowed on his back rack. For months to come the van drivers kept finding kit stowed sneakily in various hiding spots.

D-Day + 11
The one with a wadi

Sudan has a way of creeping into your soul and comforting you before asking the impossible. I awoke to a body reset. No pain greeted me as I crawled out of my tent and onto my bike. Thirty-two degree heat warmed my breath but Egypt had accustomed my lungs to this. This was to be my first day pain-free! I was excited as we had entered a whole new world; Wadi Halfa. Wadi, the Arabic term for dry valley or riverbed. I looked forward to exploring the upcoming Wadi. Wadi Halfa was one of Sudan's most important trading ports, but it was not for the faint at heart. It boasted one of the world's highest amounts of bright sunshine and lowest amounts of rainfall. With an annual average temperature of twenty-seven degrees celsius, it often dabbled in the forty degrees or above range with no reprieve in sight. Only a Wadi sits as comfortably at such extremes. In the harshest terrain we find the most exotic beauty. A Wadi will kill you quickly but allow your soul to exit slowly; decomposition takes decades in the dry Wadi desert. Wadis will lure you in without expecting you to get out. It is nature at its most seductive and deadly. Even an amateur biker like myself can feel like Les Stroud in a Wadi. Lawrence of Arabia chose the Jordanian Wadi Rum as his backdrop. Arguably, the harsh beauty of a Wadi exists nowhere else in the world. Wadi Halfa was intense in every sense of the word. The people were vivid in character and dress, the environment harsh yet stunning, the animals ripe with personality. The shades of grey are small in a Wadi. Each day stretched to infinity slowing for the worst and best parts of your day. You became aware of how easily life is thrown off balance, the roots of humanity felt deeper here. There is a wisdom in Wadi Halfa and the time to ingest it. Cycling Wadi Halfa was akin to cycling on the moon. Wadi Halfa takes Wadi Rum's rugged beauty and frosts it with Egypt's Black Desert rock. Sun kissed sand flowed and veined between the earth's cracked blanket of scorched rock. With every step or track, black rock gave way to the tan desert blood contrasting sunlight off all angles, a dance between light and dark. Tiny wisping clouds trying desperately to keep their water add definition to the uniformly blue sky. Despite the shifting winds I felt strong. Sudan lulls you into a sense of security before showcasing its tremendous might.

Perhaps living in the harsh and unforgiving Wadi held the key to the contrasts we witnessed at the border crossing. One needed to be strong and resourced to survive in a Wadi. I found myself wondering if the Sudanese had learned from the Wadi about multifaceted survival techniques. Wadi's quickly instructed how to leverage a resource to one's advantage, how to gain quick and intimate knowledge of both friend and foe, how to be a wolf in sheep's clothing. Whereas the Sudanese welcomed us and inquired about our nature and business, the Egyptians had driven us away, disinterested. While the Sudanese valued gentle prodding, the Egyptians preferred aggressive questioning. Had the Sudanese concluded that information on outsiders was tantamount to survival and that this soft approach would yield the best results? Was this why the Sudanese soft-hearted nature contrasted so strongly to that of the hard-nosed Egyptians? Curious, and a little telling was the fact that we found our best wifi to date in the middle of Wadi Halfa. Every local we met seemed to ask the following three questions: "Where are you from? Where are you going? What are you doing in Sudan?" The thirst for information was evident.

At camp that night, a rider started playing frisbee. To some, prioritizing a frisbee in such a small locker space may sound insane, but it was a real icebreaker. The frisbee attracted the attention of ALL the local children and there were many. Having a median age of under twenty years, Sudan had no shortage of youth. Noticing that the young girls were firmly stationed on the sidelines, I encouraged them to join in. They quickly engaged alongside the young boys. When I encouraged them in Arabic, any remaining barriers seemed to break down and the girls participated as aggressively as the boys. We had fun together. Finally, their parents came to talk to us. One of them, a woman in a full burqa, asked me "the questions three". She was welcoming in tone and mannerism. In Egypt, I had encountered many burqa-clad women but they had never talked to me. To me, religious exclusivity was a firm tenant of those who subscribed fundamentally. Anyone belonging to an opposing camp, even an adjacent camp, was threatening and therefore looked down upon. Sudan was proving me wrong. These burqa-clad women were as unrestricted as they were warmly inquisitive. They wanted "the questions three" answered and their beliefs stood confidently in our presence. We had something to learn from one another. The young athletes jumped with joy when we gave them pencils from Canada, a small token of our appreciation for this brief moment of sharing country and culture so freely.

D-Day + 12
The one with L.S's lost Ten Pounds

What kind of lunatic tops off a one hundred and forty nine kilometer biking day with a rigorous game of frisbee? This was foremost on my mind the next morning when my legs were firmly on strike. Today was to be very challenging, physically and mentally. Every so often life makes you feel differently, though nothing discernible has happened. You put on your regular clothes and feel flawed. You brush your hair the same way and feel haggard. In these moments, it feels as if every fleeting negative thought accumulated over weeks, months, years, is finally being released in a tirade of self-loathing or self-disgust. You have to ride the wave in order to wipe the slate clean for the next time you put on your clothes or brush your hair. If the feelings recur long enough, or if you repress the release of such emotion, that's when your brain finds itself in deep trouble. Today I felt dirty to the core. My cycling clothes were in the usual state of filth... I had taken my usual wet napkin shower during my morning ablutions. There simply was no explanation. It was to be such a day.

Nothing was left but to take the helm and drag a few fellow riders uphill and headlong into a headwind. Perfect. The best part of our day was the Sudanese. As if knowing that we needed a complete overhaul, they gave us a boost. Sudanese men and women stopped their vehicles and asked us if we needed anything (after "the questions three" of course). Throughout Africa it would stand that those who had fewer worldly possessions were the most generous with what little they did have. Mohammed, the local village chief, stopped and welcomed us to Sudan. He thanked us profusely for being with the local people. Good leadership is good leadership everywhere. We made it to camp physically unscathed. Giving waterfront a new license in Sudan, Alaric and I decided to purify our mental state with a dip in the Nile. This time there were no AK-47s. The refreshing water soothed and removed the mind's dirt.

Exiting the Nile clearer-headed but still fragile, we met Mohammed. He was riding along the water's edge atop his donkey. He greeted Alaric and I with a strong belly laugh and offered to take us across the Nile for tea and for "the best" view of the sunset. Mohammed was as gentle as he was entrepreneurial. Both Alaric and I wanted to support him making positive connections being the ultimate goal of any traveler. This was one bridge too far for today's battered brains. We declined heavy-hearted and settled for taking pictures beside Mohammed's well-nourished donkey. He was a kind man. We headed back to camp. As the Sudanese sky enveloped us beautifully, I settled down for the night hoping to wake up refreshed. But tents are tricky shelters. They create the illusion of personal space, the illusion of walls and privacy. Tents will give you away every time and tonight, all riders had to contend with L.S's ten pound SIM card.

On our first night in Sudan, L.S went to town and purchased a ten pound SIM card to contact her loved ones at home. Ten Sudanese pounds equated approximately to thirty Canadian cents, enabling a call home that would last one nanosecond. In trying to activate the SIM card, L.S quickly realized that she had been scammed and threw the useless SIM card into the campfire. When people are had, and for the equivalent of a few cents, they can either laugh it off or go crazy. She laughed it off, then she went crazy. We all lay in our tents listening unabashedly to L.S on her cellular phone, trying to get her ten pounds back. She called the help line listed on the card's package and remarkably someone picked up. This must have given her false hope towards the legitimacy of her purchase. L.S demanded her ten pounds back, yelling at the operator to "check their system". The audacity in assuming any of our host countries placed value in an organized system. Perspective lost? That phone call lasted well over the time limits purchased by ten pounds. The question remained: would tenacity be a virtue in Africa? We had yet to discover. L.S finally surrendered and we all got a good night's sleep, bellies sore from the comedy we had just overheard.

D-Day + 13
The one with the Ten Pound SIM Cards

We awoke to our first time trial. Time trials are stand-alone team cycling competitions generally used to classify riders. Tour du Canada classified me as "the rider with the most time in the saddle". I wore this designation like a badge of honour as it meant that I was out adventuring. Today, there would be no such exploring and the fault rested squarely on my shoulders. Jokingly, I had invited Bryce to join our 'racing' team alongside Nola, Bev, and Carlos who was a non-racing young man from Spain. Beyond all reason, Bryce accepted. Bryce was an American-sponsored ultra cyclist who currently had the World Record for quickest thousand kilometers, completing the course in just over thirty three hours. He was forecasted to win a medal on tour. At the Cataract Motel, Bryce made heads turn for his accomplishments. In today's time trial, Bryce undertook the momentous task of creating racers out of our small team of tourists. This was a momentous feat but Bryce was skilled at challenging himself past his breaking point.

We called ourselves the "Ten Pound Sim Cards". Bryce took the helm and taught us to ride in a peloton formation. In peloton formation, the focus needed to remain steadily on the rear wheel of the rider ahead. I was amazed at how much wind resistance was cut and how fast we could be, however, lapses in concentration can result quickly in crashes. It felt exhilarating to be a synchronized team. Under Bryce's tutelage, we became racers for the day and finished respectfully. For some, this synchronized rhythm relaxes the mind, but my mind kept racing - how many locals, camels, goats was I missing along the way? Though I admired passionate racers, I was unwilling to stop soaking my senses in Africa. Perhaps, for the second time, I would win the classification of "slowest cyclist". The thought planted a wide grin.

After the time trial was completed we ended up cruising with Team

Eight Lumps for the rest of the day. Team Eight Lumps consisted of Esther, Marita, Jenny and Femke. Esther, a twenty-two year old from Australia, was a true adventurer. She decided that she enjoyed cycling after owning a bicycle for less than one year and so she registered for the tour. She bolstered everyone on tour and trusted the world to look out for her. Femke was a thirty-eight year old from the Netherlands. She would go on to win the tour's race. She was an impressive athlete who cared deeply for each and every rider. Everyone left a conversation with Femke feeling better than when they started. She knew herself, was true to herself, and she was a great ambassador of the Netherlands to the world. Jenny was a thirty year old British veterinarian who embodied spirit and athleticism. She truly loved testing her limits. Her talents included motivating everyone she met, working hard and partying hard. Finally Marita was an Irish "Bridget Jones" in her twenties who always seemed to find the lighter side to life. Marita's greatest regret so far on tour was not bringing waterproof mascara. She loved her makeup equally to extreme sporting challenges. Marita climbed to Base Camp, Mount Everest. Once she walked 50 miles on bloody and blistered feet. Throughout the tour, Marita would keep everyone cohesive through her event planning and sense of humour. Her motto on tour was "give them something to talk about so that they don't talk about each other". She was right. These four ladies would soon become my greatest support network. But today, we cycled unaware through tranquil and shyly curious towns teeming with industrious kids trying to earn money. Helpful elderly men and women greeted us warmly in their elegant and brightly coloured outfits. Finally, we arrived at our final destination: the zoo.

The Dongola zoo. Medusa's African vacation. Most cyclists came from countries which have a long history of the domestication and containment of their animal populations. In such countries, zoos are attractive because of the illusion of separation from this ideal. In other words, people are excited by the prospect of seeing animals in their natural habitat; a facsimile of "the wild". Since Africa living was wild and its animals untamed, you may wonder, what purpose do African zoos serve? None. So the Dongola zoo compromised and housed only animals made of stone or cement. Lifesize lions and alligators lurked in the grass, randomly spread across the entire zoo. We rested our bicycles on a fountain. A cement crocodile was eating a tasty turtle atop the fountain. We thought about settling in for a few minutes but then we discovered the one pitfall of the Dongola Zoo; it didn't boast our preferred attraction: showers. Had it been the penthouse in the Taj Mahal, we would have turned it down for the shack down the street with showers. Cyclists who have cycled hundreds of kilometers through a forty degree Wadi without showering in six days know all too well the healing and reviving nature of water. We were akin to those baptized late enough in life to remember their powerful rebirth. Showers cleansed your soul, along with all your dirty shammies, jerseys, bras and socks - which we usually wore into the shower. We would have settled for a shack, what we found was an unexpected paradise; the Candaca Nubian Guest House.

The Candaca Nubian Guest House was an eco-development run by a Korean man named Isa Kuri (Youngsoo Lee) who happened to be passionate about Nubian culture. Serenity blanketed the hand-made walls of the Candaca Guest House. Lounging on the patio surrounded by palm trees, this refuge was entirely handcrafted by Isa and his family. Using mudbrick to form stark geometric designs, Isa created a perimeter wall inlaid with representations of Nubian calendar circles. He painted his creation white with gold accents. Isa built a main structure housing a few rooms with modern beds and a long shower hall. Isa told us about the changes to Wadi Halfa over the past forty years. Apparently, the water had receded so much that the palm trees that lined the road creating shade and beauty had all but died. This explained why we saw so many abandoned houses along the road. They were simply too far from a reliable water source. As there were no beds left upon my arrival at the Candaca Nubian Guest House, I set my tent at the base of the inner structure and set off humming towards my seven-dollar-a-night rebirth. Isa, his two young children and his wife treated us like family from start to end. Therefore I was saddened and outraged to learn that Isa and his family were forcibly kicked out of Sudan the very next year without any explanation or compensation. They were not allowed to take anything with them but the clothing on their backs and a few books that they had used to homeschool their children. They were held in Khartoum for forty five days and then sent to Ethiopia. Unfortunately, many Christians living in Sudan experienced similar treatment at that time. The Sudanese government was as wild, hostile, unpredictable and ruthless as the animals not caged at the Dongola Zoo.

D-Day + 14
The one with the chicken massacre

Lesson learned in Luxor, I was modest in planning a Dongola rest day. With my showered laundry drying at the Guest House, I spent the morning pretending that I knew how to clean a bike and also eating an entire chicken. It was more exhausting than riding. The chicken man was the most popular man in Dongola. To the fowl population of Dongola, the day of reckoning happened once per year and was brought about to serve fifty pasty human beings adorned in lycra. The chicken man served whole chickens to every meat-eating cyclist on tour. I sat at a picnic table in front of the restaurant intent on people-watching but instead I instantly *became* the spectacle as I devoured my meal in mere seconds. A brand of poultry-induced-food-coma settled in and I became quietly contemplative of my host city.

Dongola is the capital of the state of North Sudan. It's history is steeped in Nubian, Christian and Islamic values. For many centuries, these value systems learned to live peacefully, more recently not. Evidence of this religious history followed Peter and I to the souq. Everyone working at the souq was friendly, warm and welcoming. In my experience genteelness is born of two routes; deep peace or deep fear. Some people, like many Sudanese, who have lived through unspeakable atrocities, profoundly appreciate peaceful times. They have internalized the unpredictability of life and feel the release of knowing how little they control. Others go the opposite route and strive to control everything. They live fearfully, as the unpredictability of life crashes all around them. In either scenario we were seen as a valuable resource to be cared for. To the peaceful folk, we belonged to a global network that could contribute to maintaining stability, to the threatened, we were a financial resource or a source of information that may prove valuable to authorities in some later version of events. As the saying goes "you catch more flies with honey than vinegar".

The Sudanese had a sense of humour as brightly adorned as their beautiful clothes. People expressed pride in their lives and livelihoods. In a Sudanese souq, you can do the unthinkable: make purchases without bargaining. No token, no scowl and the seller bids you goodbye with a friendly smile. We perused the scarfs, spices and all manner of household items, but I couldn't help wondering one vital question: Where in the world was all the shag carpeting?

D-Day + 15
The one with the great Sahara open air death museum

The next morning we bid Isa adieu. Ahead lay a challenging day which would ultimately lead to my worst decision yet. Foreboding headwinds greeted Bev, Nola and I as we cycled towards the town of Al Dabbah. We stopped at a local "Coke stop" for a quick break. It was there that I registered the first commonality between Egyptian and Sudanese men; when conversing with women, their first question always centers around marriage.

At this Coke stop "Will you marry me?" flowed out quicker than "What can I get for you?"

In cultures where marriages can be arranged and are often made without meeting your future spouse, everyone is in the running. Marital roles are so defined and enclosed by boundaries that the risky business of marriage is hidden, or of little concern. Thinking broadly about the eagerness of these young men to marry us, citizens of a different culture, it seemed quite optimistic and inclusive. Or fatalistic when you realize that women's rights extend no further than their noses in Sudan. The men at this particular Coke stop proposed in jest, were nice and cordial. We drank our Cokes, thanked them and set off towards the largest open-air camel graveyard museum in the world.

Camels invented the poker face. Camels would rather die than reveal their hand to their herders. Expert bluffers, camels will maintain their appearance of grandeur until the very last breath. When they go down, they take you with them. In Egypt, we all knew to avoid Camel safaris. We would secretly giggle when our paths crossed a camel safari, watching all the tourists walking painstakingly behind the unencumbered camels. Not only are camels supremely uncomfortable, they are also dangerous. One moment, a camel is chauffeuring you around the desert with zero signs of poor health, the next moment the camel is keeling over dead and you are riding its death to the ground. Many tourists have been pinned under dead camels, some died tragically. Every time I saw a camel I was reminded of death, however, in a few days that would change completely.

Since the early 1900s Sudanese camel herders have been marching their herds from Western Sudan to a village north of Aswan for sale. The camels are transported to the World's largest camel market in Cairo, Egypt, where they are sold for slaughter. It is estimated that over fifty thousand camels make their death march to Egypt annually. Modern transportation has seen a decline in herders willing to make the gruelling march. Still, camel carcasses line the route. When death comes to you in the middle of the Sahara desert, it triumphantly showcases your body. You lay where you fall, eternally exhibited in a death museum. Your display case is a strictly controlled environment. No water, no life to feast upon your remains, no decay. Well, little decay, over many decades. Dead camels serve two purposes. The first being route identifiers. The camels remained so intact that tour organizers used individual camel corpses as landmarks. The second purpose I was to discover the next day when my own carcass almost laid to rest in the great Sahara open-air death museum.

D-Day + 16
The one with the unthinkable

For once, the scenery couldn't draw me out of my head. Largely because I thought I would die. The morning had greeted me with strong headwinds and fifty degree weather. The heart of the desert burned red hot but empathized icy cold. The dead camels I passed seemed eerily like foreshadowing; warning me how quickly things could turn. With no shade in sight, I felt exhausted after the first seventy kilometers so I stopped, stretched leisurely and prepared my body and mind for the afternoon. For almost one hour I sat and watched most cyclists pass me. When I finally remounted, only a few riders were still behind me. Alone, I pushed my dehydrated weary body towards camp. I managed to cycle another forty eight kilometers under the brow-beating sun before resting yet again. Twenty-five kilometers away from camp, I waved goodbye to the passing lunch truck just as I heard my first "PSHHHH". Feeling sick and exposed in the hot afternoon sun, I got to work quickly fixing my flat tire. I quickly hopped back on my bike and pedalled furiously for less than a kilometer before hearing "PSHHHH". My brain felt like it was baking inside my skull as I worked furiously to change my second flat tire. I was running out of tubes and prayed that this one would hold. The flat, once again fixed, was tried and failed instantly "PSHHHH". I had one last tube, a quarter litre of water and twenty four kilometers to camp. I panicked. The lunch truck had passed and taken with it all chances of a water refill. I knew the next nearest cyclist was hours away. For the first time on tour EFI was thrown from my brain. I had a loftier goal: survival.

I contemplated my next move. My mind started simultaneously racing and trying to conserve, which felt like waging war on myself. I knew what dehydration looked like. During Phase Training with the Army Reserve I had witnessed numerous episodes of dehydration. From soldiers collapsing in ditches during ruck marches to one particular soldier's eyes rolling back into his head while his body convulsed after a long hot day of doing section attacks. I knew to look for telltale signs of dehydration. Was I still sweating? Barely. Were my thought patterns erratic? Yes. In my current environment, dehydration could kill me. My survival depended on shade. I looked around desperately and my eyes came to rest on a nearby dead camel. The only shade for miles was the innards of a dead camel. Nothing had ever felt so real yet so far removed from any previous experience. Was I really going to climb inside a decaying camel for shade? Yes. I needed a bit of time to wrap my head around this moment but taking time was not an option. My brain became increasingly panicked and more steady by the minute. In pinnacle moments sometimes adrenaline manages to shift vital energy and the world gives you a little boost. While fixing my fourth flat tire, while eyeing that particularly robust camel, the world decided to play a turn.

"When we met light was shed, Thoughts free flow you said you've got something. Deep inside of you."

Suddenly, Third Eye Blind's song Deep Inside of You started playing on my MP3 player. Not everyone would be happy to hear the lyrics "deep inside of you" while eyeing camel innards but this was a positive planetary omen. I could not believe what I was hearing. Deep Inside of You was THE song I sang to myself over and over during Army Phase Training to get myself through long hot ruck marches while soldiers dropped out all around me from dehydration. It focused my mind off peril and onto the next step in front of me. I had to keep soldiering on. Fourth flat fixed, I said good riddance to the decomposing camel and pedalled furiously, willing my speed to beat any slow leak that may exist in my very last tube. I sang the lyrics over and over as I pressed onwards. I quickly ran out of water despite my best rationing. I noted the moment when I stopped sweating and focused my mind on the song so as not to panic. I cried without tears. And then, like a mirage, camp was visible. I collapsed off my bike, shaken to the bone and feeling well past the point of return. The medics came to see me and watched me drink six full water bottles full of rehydrant packets. Although safe, my illusion of safety had been shattered. I vowed that this would be my last solo ride until my primal survival instinct felt secure once again. So, late that night, when my mind and body finally calmed, I set about making friends. Much later, I learned that my fatal flaw on Dead Camel Day was not properly securing the tube valve before pumping the tube full of air. Tubes are weak at this connection, especially in extreme heat. What made the last tube hold as my pumping became less secure and more furious remains a mystery.

D-Day + 17
The one with the bulldozing camel

I woke up still feeling the sluggish and hazy effects of dehydration and hoped that cycling would clear my head. It turned out that cycling in fifty degree heat had the opposite effect. Cycling with Peter, I quickly started hallucinating, seeing cyclists where there were none. Then we saw an even stranger sight. I thought I may be hallucinating but Peter corroborated: it was simply another Sudanese gem. Countless people thought to warn me about the wildebeests that like to charge cyclists in Africa. This came about after one unfortunate YouTube video showcased a wildebeest colliding with a cyclist. Unfortunately, not one person cautioned me on runaway camels. As Peter and I cycled laboriously along a desert road, a camel charged just in front of us, narrowly missing us both. Gums flapping in the wind, the camel stopped and gave us a look that clearly stated "Just try it. I dare you.". Never ever mess with a camel who has lost his poker face. This camel had recently broken free from his herder and he had no intention of heading to Egypt to be eaten. He reached the other side of the road, turned around, and looked directly at us, menacingly. Alarmed, we took off fast. Animals are much larger when viewed from a bicycle.

Peter and I made it to the lunch truck unscathed. Voraciously eating a sandwich I gazed at two young boys playing with one bicycle. The bicycle had a broken chain and so one would sit while the other would push. Their joy was radiant and suddenly I was struck by the audacity of what we were doing. We were a tremendous demonstration of wealth in an impoverished county. I felt put off by myself. My privileged life had afforded me ignorance. I had the afternoon to consider the other side. We were infusing money into the heart of hundreds of impoverished towns and villages. We were providing interested locals a means to explore other cultures from their front door. I settled into thinking there had to be some good. I got back on my bike and pedalled off happily. Suddenly three men wearing jalabiyas tried to force me off the road. My sixth sense went into overdrive and I deeked around them, unwilling to see what they had in store. One of them lunged at me aggressively as I cycled past. The nearby villages were extremely impoverished. Locals lived in small mud huts without beds or proper cooking facilities. Shops stocked soda, tissue paper and lollipops. Although Sudan was said to have a growing economy, it certainly didn't show itself in rural villages. Life was continuously a harsh struggle. Nothing grew in the waterless fifty degrees heat of wintertime. Death was dealt to many people, animals and plants by dehydration and malnourishment. Even though I desperately wanted to believe in the good we were doing, when those three desperate men tried to force me to stop I knew we were the ones being audacious.

That night I sat with Marita, Femke, Jenny and Esther around a campfire. We laughed, quipped and joked about our experiences on tour. Most importantly, we bonded. From that night onward we became known as "the gang". Just like any effective gang, we supported one another until the last. We would make our grand debut the following morning.

D-Day + 18
The one with Zorro

The gang arose bright and early to get ready. Feeling increasingly confident in our bodies' ability to handle long hot days, we did not use this extra time to eat, stretch or hydrate. In fact, the gang had priorities. Today's priority was to draw fake mustaches on our faces using Marita's eyeliner and to tear garbage bags to create domino masks. We were to be a gang of Zorros. As today was our second time trial, many cyclists would be taking themselves very seriously on the road. Perfect. We cycled a grand total of one kilometer before stopping. Climbing and stacking we hastily created our "Zorro Pyramid Roadblock". Using our bicycle pumps as rapiers, we waved them madly at every group of cyclists who rode by. Most teams thought this was hilarious, except the Germans. Germans may be the only population in the world who can rival camels in poker. Their faces betray nothing. The stony-faced German team showed enough calculation and dexterity to impress even Zorro as they deeked around our roadblock at top speed and went on to win the time trial. Although their faces betrayed nothing, the German team later assured us that they found us quite hilarious. So did all the locals who stopped for a quick duel. The uniting power of having a sense of humour was utterly uplifting.

After the morning shenanigans a tremendous tailwind uplifted our spirits even further as we sailed into lunch at an easy forty kilometers per hour. From the lunch truck, all riders set out in a convoy through Khartoum escorted by Sudanese police. The traffic was complete chaos, though the police expertly shielded us from the worst. The police did such a great job that we had a chance to look around and take in first impressions of Khartoum without risking our lives. What struck me first was that Khartoum was organized into consumer districts such as a furniture district, a household appliance district, a butcher district and the largest district: a porcelain toilet district. Shiny white toilets lined the road while many consumers sifted through them. How they kept the toilets so white was a mystery. You could not get a full breath of air in Khartoum, dust took residence in your lungs and quickly became too rooted to simply be coughed away. It was worse than Cairo.

In Khartoum, most buildings did not exceed two or three stories. Every so often a monstrously big building would tower over the city boasting advertisements for mobile phone companies. Even in the most remote places in Africa, the basic necessities of life were water, food, shelter and cellular phones. Later on tour we would observe impoverished men and women, living in crumbling mud huts, huddled over an outdoor campfire, stirring their supper while happily conversing on their mobile devices. Community and communication rest at the heart of the truly happy. We were escorted straight to the National Camping Residence and set ourselves up for a rest day. How much rest we would be granted depended entirely on if we could stop our figurative wheels from turning. Looming in everyone's mind was what lay ahead: the most gruelling stretch on tour - eight continuous days of challenging riding in extreme heat. I reminded myself that mere mortals had accomplished the eight days before. Finally drifting off to sleep I could not shake the feeling that being a 'mere mortal' was about all I shared with these true athletes.

D-Day + 19
The one with blue and white equaling brown

In two thousand and eight I travelled to South East Asia with my sister Min. We learned two important lessons. First lesson: Min is the name of MANY male Asians. Second lesson: it is impossible to see absolutely everything a country has to offer. We tried to see everything in Vietnam, Cambodia and Laos. Our itinerary was planned to the millisecond. When we hit Thailand we lounged on a beach for a week seriously considering the irony of burning out while on vacation. In memory of that burnout my current goal was to bear witness and be mindful wherever I found myself. On this rest day in Khartoum, I found myself knee deep in dirty laundry and dusty kit. As I scrubbed away filth by hand in a bucket of soapy water, thoughts kept rudely interrupting my mindfulness: 'Laundry! Really?! Don't you know that there is a whole undiscovered city beyond the park walls!' After laundry, bike maintenance, tiger balming sore legs, eating, much needed alone time and saying goodbye to Peter who was turning green and being medevaced to Nairobi, I did finally leave. But instead of setting off on a grand adventure, I found myself headed to the Afra Mall.

Just outside the park, I hopped in a large van with Jenny, Carlos, Esther and Ian, a British cyclist in his twenties. Omar al-Bashir, Sudan's president was visiting and so we were quickly stuck in traffic. I inspected Khartoum in slow motion, while Jenny and I philosophized about life. Like Cairo, garbage gathered everywhere spilling onto the chaotic streets. Unlike Cairo, locals would meet your gaze and return the slightest hint of a smile. Their disdain for foreigners was less developed, which probably meant that there were fewer foreigners residing in Khartoum 'making a REAL mess of things'. Ever since my exchange with the lady in a burqa in Wadi Halfa, I was curious about the status of women. As a whole, Sudanese women struck me as more confident and vibrant than their Egyptian counterparts. A quick closer look painted a dichotomous image. North Sudan is one of six countries worldwide yet to sign the Convention on the Elimination of all Forms of Discrimination Against Women. Women are underrepresented in the workforce, underpaid, undereducated and subject to female genital mutilation at shocking rates. In two thousand seventeen, Sudan ranked as one of the poorest of one hundred and eighty-eight countries on the Gender Inequality Index. Egypt outperformed Sudan. I struggled to compare what I was seeing with what I knew. Were Sudanese women happier with a defined role, even if their role amounted to a prison? Did choices create chaos? In North America, with so many doors wide open, can anyone feel truly at peace with the one door they chose to walk through? Is anyone confident enough? Things are never as they seem.

Traditionally, Khartoum's labour force was divided by class and class was determined by tribe. This would change with time as over one hundred indigenous Sudanese languages and cultures came to Khartoum to melt together into one. Cultural loss would mean financial gain over generations. Ethnicity would be edged out in favour of simple classifications like Arab and Muslim. In this powerhouse capital, the edges were already starting to smooth. Finally, our small group arrived at the Afra Mall and almost immediately realized that we were all famished. After a quick shopping spree we headed to eat at the meeting point of the Blue and White Nile. Sandwiched between the two I quipped that only in Sudan did mixing blue with white yield brown. We watched a fat cow slurp the brownish water from both Niles. I will always regret my next move. I opted out of eating "hotdog pizza" in favour of mezze. Mezze is a grazer's paradise. As little dishes filled with scorched baba ganoush, hummus, couscous salad and marinated vegetable medley started to populate our table I felt confident in my choice of food. I promised myself that one day I would return to Khartoum to try their version of American food but in preparation for the upcoming eight torturous days, I knew that what my body needed most was soul food. After lunch, I headed to the local souq with Femke, Marita, Carlos, and Marianne. Marianne was a middle-aged Australian woman who always had a beautiful laugh and a positive outlook. Souqs in developing countries have many commonalities but each also has its own flavour. Sudan's souq boasted universal clothes, shoes, sunglasses and electronics but with a killer backdrop of awesome African beats. The souq swayed with rhythm as we weaved through the maze of shops. The music filled every spare inch of our brains, providing quiet relief from the ongoing mental jibber-jabber of what awaited us for the next eight days. Packing light, we made small purchases and returned to camp weary. The most gruelling stretch was coming. Would I make it?

D-Day + 20
The one with lying escorts

I woke up to the news that Cairo was in chaos. More than seventy people were killed and thousands more injured at a football match between Al Masry and Al Ahly football teams in Port Said. The tension in Egypt took very little to ignite. Once again, I felt like a deserter while parts of the country I called home were ripped apart.

I felt terrified of the upcoming eight days. My strategy was to join the racers in an effort to provide my body with enough rest time at camp to make it through. Seven 'young' women rode out of the city in peloton formation. A peloton is formed when cyclists ride closely one behind the other to encourage drag and reduce wind resistance. We were pedalling straight into a headwind so I felt thankful for the formation. Suddenly we were the lucky recipients of personal escorts, as a few men directed traffic, guided us out of Khartoum and generally WATCHED (being the operative word) for our safety. They were taking photographs under the guise of the local press. Somehow, we never doubted their authenticity until we almost got creamed by oncoming traffic. "SCREECH!" traffic swerved to avoid hitting us at top speeds. It turned out that the "escorts" who chose to accompany and photograph eight young women cyclists from behind may not have traffic safety as their priority. We were grateful for their help in navigating out of this chaotic city.

Once released from the oppressively sandy hands of Khartoum we were quickly back on desert roads, watching shepherds tenderly direct their flocks and men lounging while pretending to work on powerlines.The Sudanese workers greeted us warmly and thanked us for visiting their country. Children working in the cotton fields laughed and cheered as we passed. The

Sudanese animals seemed to know their agendas as we saw a few unaccompanied donkeys bearing water or hay, happily taking themselves where they needed to be. They were contributing members of society, unlike that one runaway camel! I had a particular fondness for rotund donkeys and I pictured every donkey speaking to me in Eddie Murphy's voice.

"And then one time I ate some rotten berries. Man there were some strong gases seepin' outta my butt that day!"

This game kept me entertained for hours. Long gone were the days of baking camel carcasses as we greeted our first corn field. Soon enough we would think nostalgically upon camel carcasses and HATE corn fields. For many years, corn fields would evoke a significant stress response, but for now, they were a welcome sight. Day one of eight concluded unscathed. Day two was waiting to slap us in the face the moment we awoke.

D-Day + 21
The one with fake plastic trees

I awoke to a commotion. From my tent I could hear voices screaming and items being thrown. The one hundred and fifty five kilometers which lay ahead would pose a significant problem for two cyclists who woke up bikeless. Sudanese thieves had managed a midnight heist despite the watchful eye of the police guards we had employed to protect us. More than likely, they had been helped by police eyes. I was a little miffed as the two bikes that were stolen were locked and the thieves went to great lengths to steal them. Buck lay close by my tent unlocked and casually tossed on the ground. Apparently, Buck was not worthy of theft, or perhaps nobody wanted to deal with his surly attitude. One of the stolen bikes belonged to Heiner, a Swiss man with a fantastic sense of perspective. He calmly said "There are worse things".

There were. Peter had to be evacuated from Khartoum to Nairobi after a life threatening illness and would not return to tour. Heiner wouldn't miss a day of cycling as Cinelli had donated a few bicycles to test on our most rugged days. Today's ride fit that description. The other bicycle stolen belonged to Robert, a Texan adventurer who led with his mouth and took on any challenge head-on. Robert was a competitive and voracious traveller and "zen" was not his modus operandi that morning. His voice was the one hurling expletives outside my tent. If Heiner exemplified water by subtly and gradually shaping his surroundings, Robert was fire racing to steal the most oxygen. Both had a significant place on tour.

We set off into green landscapes today and the calming effects were instinctual. The body recognizes an environment suited to life after passing through a desert. Happy faces on people and animals made the day a little gentler. We passed by thorny trees and bushes, I held my breath and luckily my tires did the same. We passed cotton fields and mud hut villages with ornate windows and doors. The streets were filled with sheep sellers and girls going to school in billowing white school uniforms. We had entered the land of chic donkeys with manes styled in mohawks, and angry camels ridden by courageous and foolhardy youth. Mini twisters of sand hopped across our path, casually reminding us to be grateful of the strong tailwinds pushing us to camp. A man wearing a shirt bearing the word "TIME" today plunged me into thought. Time; the most powerful man-made invention. This trip was freeing us from the incessant ticking of the man-made metronome and tuning our senses towards biological rhythms and their inclination to work with nature. Our days began and ended with the sun. Without measuring our lives in ticks and tocks, we were closer to quiet.

First Peter, then Nola. So many people with whom I loved to cycle had trouble early on tour. Train tracks are natural enemies to the bicycle wheel; one says zig, the other says zag. One train track, carefully concealed on the downhill, did fierce battle with Nola's bike this day, but not before flinging Nola headfirst from the battleground. She was concussed and taken away to be medically assessed. Poor Nola. We knew nothing of this while we waited at the bottom of the exceptionally long downhill for Nola, carefully considering whether or not to ride back up. Thankfully a kind stranger pulled over and told us before we began to trek uphill which would have increased our distance on a gruelling one hundred and fifty five kilometer day. This day, I was forced to retract my statement regarding nothing growing in Sudan. I cycled past field upon field of thriving plastic bags. Single-use plastic bags would tumble along merrily in the wind until suddenly anchoring on a dead plant or stone. Fields full of dead plants would boast hundreds of plastic bags waving in the wind. Goats had become so accustomed to this new crop that they munched away filling their bellies merrily with plastic and whatever vegetation remained underneath. This is an attraction that every North American willing to shell out five cents per bag at their local grocery store ought to witness. As the tour progressed we would realize that Africa was drowning in single-use plastics.

Our camp was adjacent to the Dinder River, the ultimate nurturer. The Dinder River meandered four hundred and eighty kilometers through Sudan until finally joining the Blue Nile near the town of Sennar. As the water flowed it gathered stories and worship in exchange for life; drinking water, washing water, shelter, relief. I smiled at a few young ladies slinging heavy urns of water on their heads before commencing their long walk to the village, at a few chatty kids bathing communally near the river banks. The mayor of Dinder province came to officially greet us. Media was there to catch our lovely dirty and sunburned faces as they brought forth local treats, water and Coca Cola - not to be underestimated; the things you would do for a cold beverage in a hot desert go far beyond anything you people living with a refrigerator can possibly imagine. The Mayor passed along information about their province. He was an excellent ambassador to his homeland. We went to bed happy but apprehensive for our first day of offroading on tour.

D-Day + 22
The one with proof required of bones

Having changed my tires from Schwalbe Marathon Plus to my mountain bike fat Nokian NBT, I was feeling confident in my bike. The question mark was my body. Off-roading was uncharted territory for my body, never having had to contend with it on Tour du Canada. I trained for Tour du Canada on Buckshot Lake Road, a hilly road near my cottage. I used to get off my bicycle and walk sections that I considered impassable by bicycle. This was logical for a Canadian tour where asphalt ruled the roads. This present day, we cycled over one hundred kilometers on seemingly impassable roads. The corrugation shook me so much that when I finally stepped off my bike I felt my organs bouncing to a settle. It felt like spending a ten hour day in forty-five degree heat sitting on an overloaded washing machine. When we tried to speak to one another, we sounded like we were speaking into a fan. My bum started plotting its revenge. The good side was that I relocated some long lost rock climbing muscles, my forearms pumped repeatedly as I gripped the handlebars for dear life. The roads were not only impassable, but highly dangerous.

We, the gang, skirted railroad tracks and we started our ascent over a large bridge towering hundreds of feet above water. The bridge had a tiny protective parapet which was really more of a tripping hazard than a safety net.

"Bwwob bwwobbubwub."

From behind we heard a motorcycle getting closer. Suddenly the motorcyclist was right beside us aggressively bullying his way between us. Feeling exposed and shaky, I slowed right down so as to not plummet from the bridge to my death. There is no feeling more vulnerable than being challenged by a motorized vehicle while clipped into your bicycle. The bridge felt like some magical pass from the Middle East into Africa. Everything changed after that bridge. We passed through villages straight out of National Geographic with red mud conical huts, souks, and schoolgirls giggling to one another. Young children running around half naked would stop dead in their tracks and wail. To them, our white skin made us terrifying ghosts, some did not believe that we had bones. This is more than reasonable when you consider that Sudan has a median age of under nineteen years old so many Sudanese children are brought up by other children. Convoys of women dressed in vivid orange and carrying small mountains of long grass on donkeyback rode past us and waved. Trucks with people hanging off every surface rode past. Kids raced our bicycles and gently touched our skin to feel for bones when they caught up. The music was energized with a beat that rattled my heart into knowing the dance steps. At one point I looked up to see a herd of bulls headed directly towards me and I knew I was safe. Moments started to feel magical.

The magical feeling was short lived as this Africa welcomed me ruthlessly, with thorns. Flat tire number one came shortly after lunch and with thirty kilometers to camp. The gang waited for me to change my tube but I missed the perpetrator: a huge thorn. Consequently, flat tire number two came shortly thereafter and Jenny and Marita decided to carry on to camp. Esther, being a champion, stayed by my side. Flats three and four came in quick succession and my last tube was inside my tire when flat five graced us. This was it. I would lose EFI. Luckily, before I threw in the towel and mounted the lunch truck to camp, L.S came upon us. She loaned me a tube large enough to fill my fat tire. As I fixed flat number five, Esther put her bike down and we heard the now all too familiar "*PSHHHH!*". Both her front and rear tires deflated.

All we could do was throw our heads back and laugh uncontrollably. Thorns play roughly with thin large tires, piercing their way through the tubes, which was a tough lesson to learn on such a long hot day. Esther embodied loyalty and resiliency in friendship and I will always remember this as the quality that saved my day. We celebrated our long anticipated arrival at camp with a selfie and a quick dip in the muddy nearby watering hole. Donkeys eyed us suspiciously as they lapped up our now murkier water. We fell asleep exhausted and awoke to a sweltering fifty degree day.

D-Day + 23
The one with the donkey shower

The day began well for the gang. We cycled over packed sand through small villages. We stopped to speak with young students en route to school. Once they had entered the mud "school" hut we heard them yelling their lessons loudly by rote. More than one herd of camels enveloped us as we cycled along the dirt path. We chased cattle, lambs, goats and donkeys. Laughter erupted as we witnessed a young boy asleep on his donkey-taxi being carted home - presumably. In the fifty degree heat, the tour staff organized a refresh stand with water before the lunch stop. It was a wise decision as our medical staff was stretched thin tending to numerous heat-related illnesses. Establishing the refresh stand required supplanting over fifty local cattle from their resting spot. After a quick stop we cycled straight into a cornfield. If you ever cycle off-road in fifty degree heat, let it NOT be beside a cornfield. Stephen King foretold of the human sacrifices taken by cornfields in his novel Children of the Corn. On this day in Sudan, children did not drag us from our bikes to be sacrificed in cornfields but the extreme corrugation certainly did. Corrugation is a feature of all well-managed cornfields. Defensive corrugation protects against flooding, offensive corrugation is the result of rock-hard, dry, cracked soil. Today's corrugation was waging a fiercely offensive battle on our minds, butts and souls. We felt like guitar strings being plucked from our seats and then released to vibrate during Stevie Ray Vaughan's hard rock guitar solo only to have our feet break from their clips and our bodies flop to the ground as he continues playing with the remaining strings. The corrugation slowed us to speeds of four to eight kilometers per hour, which made the torture last an eternity. Our eyes strained and dried reading the ground, unwilling to blink lest we miss our next move. Our thoughts slid out of our bouncy castle heads and were quickly followed by tears. Our sunburned knuckles turned white under the strain of holding on for dear life. Before the day was done the cursedly corrugated cornfields and extreme heat took more than one rider's EFI.

Beaten and tenderized, the gang made it out the other side with our energy effectively sapped. It took us far too long to realize that we hadn't passed any flagging tape. Staff navigated riders through Africa using neon orange flagging tape usually tied to street signs, trees or bushes, sometimes left under rocks or on dead camels. Though cows and goats enjoyed the occasional munch on this foreign orange "vegetable" and at times we would pass children wearing the flagging tape like Rambo around their heads, usually there were not many roads to choose from and the route was clear. It had been over ten kilometers sans flagging tape and the gang felt less than confident in our decision-making skills since our brains had been bouncing and baking inside our skulls all day long. We decided to follow bicycle tire treads left in the sand, not considering that the bicycle was a primary source of transportation in Sudan. Finally we got confirmation that we were on the wrong path: the locals we passed started looking at us strangely.

It was perfectly justifiable to question our sanity, we were doing that ourselves on a daily basis. But this look of incredulity was alarming and foretold doom. You see, we were slow riders. By the time we passed through towns, forty other faster cyclists had already ridden past. It was the quick riders who were stared at with incredulity, we were usually old hat or target practice. As such, we knew these locals hadn't seen any other riders. We were in trouble as we had just cycled six kilometers downhill in the wrong direction, to a small town called Maudet. "Maudet" was aptly named as I immediately felt exactly like the French translation: cursed, damned, wretched. Had we made it through the gruelling cornfields only to lose EFI in Maudet? The gang tried to interrogate locals, who preferred to question us with rote English Lesson Number One:

"How are you?"

We sat in quiet defeat watching boys with homemade bows and arrows take shots at rocks and stones. A young boy of four or five sat beside Esther and took such joy in copying all her movements and expressions. The thing was, Esther looked happy. I wondered how this was possible when we were all about to lose our EFI a mere ten kilometers from camp, so I moved in closer to her conversation. A local man was trying to gesture where the best photography locations were in Maudet. Esther was still soaking in Africa and trusting in her journey. Her goal was loftier than EFI. Many days on tour I found myself in awe of Esther's beautiful outlook on life and this day was no exception. The rest of the gang sat with the entire village and pouted, watching the sun start to set as we contemplated the death of our EFI.

Then the impossible happened. We suddenly located a working cellular phone. Somehow we recalled our tour leader Sharita's phone number. Then we called Sharita and described our nondescript surroundings well enough for her to show up half an hour later. While this seemed like a miracle, we did not yet know Sharita very well. She embodied Africa to the point that its entirety is written on her soul. Not only could she triangulate to anywhere, she fully understood the processes of everyone inside her continent. To me, Sharita was Africa personified. Like hope at the bottom of Pandora's box, Sharita swooped into Maudet at five-thirty and immediately directed us to camp. In order to make camp, we would need to cycle our defeated bodies over ten kilometers, mostly uphill, in half an hour. We bid adieu to the entire population of Maudet. We strained our muscles past the point of exhaustion and made it to camp just in time to watch the sun go down, EFI intact. For the remainder of Sudan, staff began marking the ground with sugary Tang instead of the neon orange flagging tape. Wobbly-legged, the gang collapsed at camp with nothing left to give, until we set eyes on the only thing cyclists love more than rest; a shower. A Donkey Shower to be precise.

Holly was exceptionally entrepreneurial. She also had a unifying way with people, crossing cultural barriers as if they didn't exist. She somehow convinced a local man to bring his donkey and water cart to camp. We took turns sitting partially clothed in a plastic bucket. The man directed his donkey who was pulling the water cart, then using a large hose cyphoned water onto our heads. This exceptional spa cost one Sudanese pound. As the water poured over my weary body, I knew beyond a doubt that this Donkey Shower was the most heavenly and transcendental shower I had ever experienced.

D-Day + 24
The one with the Sudanese party

The gang awoke to the promise of a piddly eighty-four kilometer day off the beaten path. Little did we know it would be agonizing. This was to be our last full day in Sudan and true to form, Sudan would send us off with both extreme highs and extreme lows. The morning was promising as we rode with Ian and Marianne on gentle dirt roads through picturesque towns. We entered a new village and we were quickly ushered down a small side street into the heart of the village. We dismounted in awe. Close to one hundred stunningly vibrant women and children were singing, dancing and beating hand drums. Their clothing was bold, bright, beautiful and in stunning contrast to their flawless dark skin. At first I thought we had happened upon a wedding but, as there were no men present, it soon became clear that they were celebrating us. They were exuberantly trilling and encouraging us to join in. We were served a hibiscus drink and shown the inside of town. Here were glorious women, whom we considered to live in abject poverty, giving freely what they had to us; their guests. I was incredibly moved and saddened to think that my own culture has drifted so far from these nourishing roots. Their communal bond allowed them joy and happiness beyond measure. How did we get to a point of not knowing our neighbours? Of locking front doors? Of creating parking spaces at the expense of porches? No wonder mental health issues continue to rise at alarming rates in developed countries. We have annihilated the concepts central to humanity: togetherness, community. The women were unforgettable ambassadors to a country who recognized blessings deeply. This pure sense of joy could only come to a heart bolstered by familial community. I will never forget these women. Women can be an unmeasurable source of unity around the world. We are to be celebrated. The gang arrived at lunch confident and refreshed after such an uplifting morning. We ate sandwiches and relaxed in the shade. After lunch, Sudan forgot to turn off the oven. We started baking in fifty degree heat. Then we headed straight towards endless cornfields. The roads we travelled were overcooked, to describe them as corrugated would be flattering. Deeply cracked, scorched and broken roads lay under tire, which we navigated at fewer than five kilometers per hour in the midafternoon heat. With nothing but endless cornfields on either side, our minds could hardly keep entertained and the voices started to take over. Our bodies started to commit mutiny and the leader of the revolt, our derrieres, protested loudly with each bump. For the third day in a row, our bodies took a vicious beating. With every inch of our bodies tenderized, there was no more shifting we could make to become comfortable. I later learned that many cyclists walked the cornfield roads. It may have been quicker to walk through some of the incredibly rough patches. We stopped for shade anywhere and everywhere. But we quickly discovered that we were running out of water. Praying for a refresh stand kept us going but my mind started panicking as the kilometers stretched out without any sign of relief. At least a panicky mind left no room to listen to the demands of other body parts: my one and only thought was water. All I could do was try to mentally coach myself through. I alternated between cursing the road and coaxing myself on, sticking to this refrain to avoid mass panic. Right when I thought I could hardly take anymore, two things happened simultaneously: I got a flat tire and I caught a glimpse of the refresh truck a few kilometers away. So many times on tour I had walked the thin tightrope of EFI, about to topple over when suddenly the ground shifts and I am miraculously balanced again. I was so dehydrated that I considered riding on my rim to the truck. Knowing that it may destroy my rim I disembarked and walked. I was as close to mentally unstable as I had ever been in my life. Not willing to stay too long at the refresh stop for fear of a gruelling afternoon I rode off with Ian and Esther, who were both on mountain bikes with suspension. Having neither a mountain bike nor suspension, I quickly overheated trying to keep pace with them. To cool off I stripped down to my underwear and lay in the shade. Jon joined us en route looking as if he may die.

Since the beginning of the tour, Jon had changed dramatically in appearance. Jon became gaunt, his eyes drooped, his skeleton poked out at alarming angles and he was increasingly confused. Being unwell, Jon coughed all day and night and refused to eat. Esther and I stayed with Jon all the way to camp to ensure he made it there alive and then spoke to Sharita. She told us that every year one or two men refuse to give up their EFI, pushing themselves beyond reasonable limits to attain their goal. One man had even died from a heart attack after the medics repetitively asked him to stop riding. Soon enough, Jon would decide to stop riding. This decision may have saved his life.

Our last camp in Sudan was near a very Harry Potter-esque baobab tree. Underneath the tree we changed our tires back to the skinny but tough Schwalbe Marathon Plus. This was a good sign. It meant that although torture awaited, it would be of a different brand than cornfields.

While we were changing our tires, a sectional rider named Clara said to me "You are tough, it is very surprising!"

I was tough, but not always brave. People interchange the two all too often. I was not brave enough to race, nor to keep pace with the quicker cyclists. Quite content to achieve my goal, I did not push my limits very often. Though I certainly didn't present as tough, I was made of dogged determination. That night in my tent, feeling proud of my accomplishments, I bade goodbye to the beautiful, haunted, genuine, and DRY Sudan. Ethiopia brought the promise of beer!

Ethiopia

D-Day + 25
The one with beer fishing

Marita wanted to marry Professor Edward J. de Smedt, inventor of the modern day asphalt. But if he wasn't available, any of the hundreds of chinese labourers paving roads in the vicinity would do. Derriere delight! We were cycling on smooth pavement again and even strong headwinds could not sweep the smiles from our faces. To mark the momentous crossing from Sudan to Ethiopia, the gang decided that a theme day was in order. We cut plastic water bottles and duct taped them to our helmets. We duct taped our bike pumps alongside representing snorkels and wore life preservers purchased at the Afra Mall. Collectively, we were Scuba Steve, the fictional character portrayed by Adam Sandler in the film Big Daddy, a costume which was quite ironic as we would have done nearly anything for a bath. Somehow we convinced Pål, a thirty-seven year old Norwegian sectional rider, to wedge a stick into his helmet and we attached a beer can on a string to the stick. We may have lured him with immediate membership to the Scuba Squad. Pål led the way and we followed, "swimming towards Ethiopian beer". Still on the Sudanese side of the border, we cycled to the lunch truck without a single local asking us the questions three. Dressed as we were, they were likely terrified of our answers. After lunch, we were the last group to cross the border so the lunch truck prepared to go with us. Staff handed the Sudanese children numerous bags of leftover food as perishables were unwelcome at border crossings. Pure joy lept from these kids as they quickly ran away together to feast. I could not remember ever radiating as much joy as those kids. Perhaps I never had. Could it be that the less you have the more you feel? Was this the secret behind Sudan's generosity; that divesting yourself of things makes you happy? Could this be driving the minimalist movement in wealthy countries? This germinating seed of thought was my parting gift from Sudan.

Goodbye dry detoxifying Sudan, hello wild Ethiopia. The prospect of alcohol lifted our spirits as we sat in customs trying to act official but looking ridiculous. I was particularly worried as I had a seven month visa to Ethiopia; one month longer than they usually allowed tourists to visit. Months earlier, at the Ethiopian Embassy in Toronto, the seven month visa had sounded like a great solution to a logistical problem. Now, I was praying that the 'illegal' visa would not become a logistical nightmare at the border. Luckily, it was not. They were so dazzled by our outfits that I am fairly certain they did not read the date. I breathed a sigh of relief; I would be allowed to continue the tour.

We passed over a fairly arbitrary line drawn in the sand and suddenly the rhythm of life had changed dramatically. Borders hold tremendous power in dividing humanity. More often than not this division is destructive but for us cyclists, it was exciting. Metemma was the Ethiopian border town. Aptly named for the Arabic term meaning "the place of cutting". The label designated the end of the Muslim countries, and within a few feet of dirt a whole new world awaited. Ethiopia, one of the world's oldest nations. Ethiopia, a world which held a thirteen month calendar and separate clocks for day and night. Ethiopia, the only country in Africa with its own script. Ethiopia was ready and waiting for us, it would soon take us by storm. For the moment, it ended our drought.We rolled into Ethiopia in high fashion and entered the first bar for a beer. There is no better elixor than the first sip after a Sudanese drought. We watched as younger kids were being coached by older kids to pilfer items from our bicycles. Instead, we gave the youth PVM energy bars and they ran away happy; much to the chagrin of their failed coaches. I could immediately tell that the kids were edgy and full of attitude and mischief. They were focused, goal-oriented and intense, which was alarming after the kind and gentle Sudanese youth. As we rode through town, a giant roar erupted. Fourteen riders beckoned us to join them outside at a local bar. After two beers I was completely drunk. We wobbled our bikes all over the road and into camp while loudly singing songs from Top Gun. I passed out, feeling worn, dehydrated, hot and sore but also healthy and happy. The next day, we would start to climb.

D-Day + 26
The one with reverse frogger

Ethiopia greeted us with a day of endless climbing. The mountains teemed with children who raced alongside us; wild with mountain lust. Imagine superimposing Lord of the Rings with a misty Vietnam war movie and you will arrive on our first day in Ethiopia. Like Lord of the Rings, every moment was serenely beautiful. To the left and right we watched hazy scorched mountain tops holding onto the toughest of greenery. Paradoxal. Just as the environment boasted stunning jagged rolling beauty it was to be met with a cautiously suspicious eye as it forced us into extremely harsh climbs and dangerously steep descents. Like a Vietnam War movie the people were dual, lighting up to greet you only to throw stones at your back as you pedalled away. Ethiopia is the African country with the second largest population and the Ethiopians all seemed to dwell by the side of the road. The concept of pedestrian right of way was well established as many walked unexpectedly onto the road without looking for oncoming traffic. Ethiopians also have one of the lowest life expectancies in the world. We tried speaking very loudly to alert pedestrians to our presence but it did not help. A few riders flew over their handlebars in a desperate effort to avoid colliding with locals. Locals also stood in the middle of the road, unpredictable. They waited to smile, touch, talk or lunge. Naked children holding sticks would run by yelling "You! You!" as we prayed that their sticks remained just out of reach from our wheel spokes. The cattle were slightly more street savvy. Hearing the comedic tragedy of cattle symphonies mooing, I stopped my bicycle to let a herd of cattle cross the road. Suddenly the herd split in half with the back half granting me the right of way. In gaining the right of way, we were at least higher than the cattle.

The locals were beautiful but their eyes betrayed hardship. With years of famine written in their genes, their look was one of tormented strength. We were in the birthplace of mankind and the generations showed in their deep pooling eyes. They had fully embraced the unknown. They knew that change was the only constant. They embodied this fact. One moment their eyes shone with extreme softness and the next, they flashed with extreme hardness. Women and animals were truly beasts of burden here, carrying heavy loads of wood and sticks up and over the mountains. The huts lining the roads were made out of wood and sticks, resources rarely found in Sudan. Although more durable, wood was much heavier and bent the woman carrying it in half. Women did all of the heavy lifting in Ethiopia.

I arrived at camp feeling exhilarated and alive, fresh full of mountain air. I set up my tent at the precipice of the mountain, took a quick moment to enjoy the view, then walked to the local pub with Ton, a fifty-nine year old from the Netherlands, Mike, a middle-aged Canadian rider, and Carlos. Ton bought everyone at the pub a drink in appreciation for "not throwing rocks". I sat down on a small stool with my beer. A little boy was pulling faces and imitating everything I did in jest. Youth was youth everywhere, a sense of humour innate. The kids had all styled their hair into small circular mohawks and proudly wore wooden crosses around their necks. Ethiopia's population was over sixty percent Christian. The adults also wore crosses. The adults took turns riding our bicycles while the kids recited their limited English vocabulary. We returned to camp feeling very endeared. This feeling was not to last until the next night.

Most nights, when darkness had fallen, I developed the ritual of wandering off to be alone. I bathed in the sounds and breathed in the stars. This ritual brought stillness to my soul before the next riding day. I soon understood that one was never truly alone in Ethiopia. Kids and adults were always hidden nearby, watching, planning. In Ethiopia, you always had the sense of being watched, because you were. The tour organizers would section off the perimeter of camp with orange flagging tape to keep locals out. This concept put me off. It felt like we were on their land claiming some form of ownership. What right did we have? Tour organizers knew what we were about to discover; without the orange flagging tape we would have woken up naked outside with our belongings pilfered by the greatest heisters of all time. As human noises finally gave way to crickets I found myself wondering what I missed from home. I missed nothing. I have a tendency to travel through life in the present. This was developed as a mechanism for coping with the frequent relocations thrust upon our family by the military. Army brats know all too well that you can't take the past with you. Over and over we would say goodbye to all our friends with promises to keep in touch. I was blessed to have had many wonderful friends throughout my many relocations. There were many. By the end of University I had relocated over a dozen times and attended eight different schools. At first, I tried my very best to maintain contact by writing letters and chatting for hours on the telephone. As one move led to another, these promises proved unsustainable. Though I cherished and valued my friendships beyond measure, time constraints wouldn't allow me to properly invest in the present with so much of my focus remaining in the past. So I lived in the present and I missed nothing, which felt like empty happiness.

It was the right time for empty happiness in my life. I promised myself that one day I would feel the fullness of permanent relationships. I would have someone to miss.

D-Day + 27
The one with lost belongings

We had arrived at that last of eight riding days and Ethiopia felt like a series of manic moments before death. I set out alone, as this day was to be full of climbing. I did not think I could keep up with the gang on hills. The geography of Ethiopia inspired intense peace and serenity but it was all an impossible illusion. I spent the day on edge and on THE edge. I was prey to the beautiful mountains with their sharp steep climbs requiring the granniest of gears to go just seven kilometers per hour, for a total of thirty-six kilometers uphill, or two thousand five hundred and two meters up. I went up. Up switchbacks, up roads. Past crazy women trying to get me off my bicycle, past kids walking alongside, grabbing at me and making me feel particularly vulnerable and slow. Up, up, up, and more up. Up past rocks being launched by the children on cliffs. Up past a young adult that told me that I "needed a different motor" - how true. I gave everything I had. Suddenly I could see downhill and it was a beautiful dangerous sight.

The long downhill to lunch proved treacherous. Kids yelled their now tedious refrain of "You! You! You! You!" and threw sticks and canes trying to land them expertly between my spokes as I sped away at forty kilometers per hour downhill. Animals and people walked out in front of my path as I sped down. Adults by the side of the road swung objects at me. By lunch I was frazzled emotionally, physically and mentally. I felt fearful of riding alone. So I joined the gang, determined to keep up. Small militias of children pretended to push us uphill while opening our back bags, trying to steal our belongings. They threw rocks at us when we got away. Riders lost many personal items this day, some of which were later recovered somehow by Sharita. Though the uphill was completely exhausting, we couldn't stop for a reprieve. The moment we thought the coast was clear and stopped, dozens of little children would come forth from their hiding spots to ambush us. We ended the day with a two kilometer climb straight uphill in Gondar. Legend had it that a buffalo led Emperor Fasilides to this area in the seventeenth century where a venerable elderly man told him he could locate his capital city. Emperor Fasilides decided to build up, a decision rued by many cyclists. So we climbed one last hill. In all my life I have never felt so done. I made it. Barely. When I reached camp I was physically, psychologically and emotionally empty. My body shook for hours after completing the ride. I was so layered with dirt and apprehension that I hardly recognized my own face in the hotel mirror. Yes, the HOTEL mirror. I treated my poor abused body and soul to a hotel room and laundry service. I ordered all the food allowable without getting dirty looks. We would have two rest days in Gondar to unrattle our entire beings and give oil and rest to our granniest of gears.

D-Day + 28, 29
The ones with dislocated shoulders in eskista

Gondar, lovingly nicknamed the Camelot of Ethiopia, had a rich history dating back to the twelfth century. Many royal castles and forty-four churches lined the streets begging the question of whether the mountain we had climbed was in fact a time portal to another era. History blanketed the entire city. In 1632, this land enraptured Emperor Fasilides enough to cause his generationally nomadic DNA to settle. Gondar quickly became the capital of Ethiopia and remained so until 1855. I would have loved to seep in Gondar's history but we had an agenda. We were headed to our first bicycle donation platform: Kebele 03 Elementary School. Since nineteen ninety four schooling was free for Ethiopian students between the ages of seven and fourteen. Nonetheless, many students would never attend due to financial hardships. Schooling itself was free but there were many hidden costs such as uniforms, textbooks and transportation. We were lucky enough to be in a position to help. Twenty-five dollars USD afforded a uniform and a backpack full of school supplies. Around a dozen cyclists stood before the hundred students. The school leaders greeted us with a traditional coffee ceremony. Ethiopian claim ownership over coffee through the legend of Kaldi and the magical bean. Around 850 AD, an Ethiopian goat herder named Kaldi noticed a magical bean that enlivened his goats to the point that they were partying all night long. He took a risk and presto-chango, coffee was introduced to the human palate. The coffee ceremony was a significant symbol of friendship and "Well come" as a nearby sign warmly greeted us. The Ethiopian coffee ceremony was unique in the countryside as coffee was served with salt, popcorn and roasted peanuts. Three cups was the polite amount to consume and they believed that the third cup possessed heaps of blessings. I was brushing with the law and fate in turning down every one. As a former coffee addict, I visualized the slippery slope back to eight cups per day. When a Taurus proclaims that they will break an addiction cold turkey, you believe them. If you verbalize doubt, they will make it their life's mission to prove you wrong. This happened December 5th, 2004. Having endured classic migraines and general malaise since joining the Army Reserve three years earlier, I was beginning to deduce that Tim Horton's coffee may be the culprit. As soldiers well know, vices can be a best friend. Smoking to keep the gigantic mosquitos at bay in Gagetown, New Brunswick. Chewing tobacco or Spitz to fend off boredom. Alcohol to fend off the cold and coffee to keep awake. In 2004, I convoyed with military members from St. Catharines to Burlington Ontario, a forty-five minute drive. We stopped four times for coffee. So, on December fifth, I decided to cut coffee cold turkey. At the time, my finance thought this was an impossible goal, a doubt which spurred me on for fifteen years and counting. He never did have faith in me.

The teachers rallied to get the students' attention and I was dumbfounded by their unusual method. They waved sticks and threw rocks at the young learners. Effective though these strategies were, these were the exact same behaviours we cyclists had been taking so personally. It wasn't personal; it was cultural. Eventually, the students lined up to receive our donation of approximately fifty uniforms and backpacks and two bicycles. We went on a quick school tour. The classrooms were painted a calming blue and sparsely decorated with long shared benches and tables. One small chalkboard hung on the wall for upwards of fifty students. No paper, pencils, books or school supplies lay around. Students would come to learn in shifts, always prioritizing family work before school. There was a sizable soccer field and a wooden shelter for shade. The young learners seemed to love school and were joyful. Many had received their very first new clothes and books. We were ushered to outdoor bleachers and the students started dancing for us. It was the first time we saw "Eskista": the art of Ethiopian dancing. North Americans lead with their hips, Ethiopians lead with their shoulders. Imagine a peacock strutting his stuff to hip hop music. The dancers puffed out their chest and rolled their shoulder blades in time with the music. Their shoulders undulated at incredible speeds, seemingly detached from the rest of their upper bodies. They stayed perfectly in time with the music as they moved in sequence. Undulating the upper body rather than the lower took a fair amount of skill as I was about to learn later that night. Having always prided myself on being a dancer, at thirty-one, I suddenly felt too old for new tricks.

From the school, we set out to lunch. After the previous day's disapproving glances, we quickly figured out how to eat enough to satiate our fierce appetites without appearing gluttonous in a famine-filled country: restaurant hop and ingest injera everywhere. Injera is the national Ethiopian dish made out of teff flour. It tasted like a flattened Spongebob Squarepants dressed in sourdough. Injera came with a melange of various meat stews, legume stews, vegetables and a small side salad, enough for the entire family... or one cyclist. We feasted at more than three restaurants, then collapsed in a coma while our stomachs dealt with the tangy fermentation. Arising from our self-induced coma, we went dancing. The dance club was as dark and dingy as the best clubs in North America. The music vibrated every cell as we watched amazed at the dance floor. Dancers were strutting everywhere and willing us to join in. After a few lubricating beverages, we tried to limber our shoulders enough to not be laughingstocks. It didn't work for all but one: Peter. Peter was a thirty-two year old German cyclist who had dislocated his shoulder on one of the last riding days in Egypt. This dislocation must have widened his range of motion as he earned applause on the dance floor with his particular form of Eskista. We stood amazed as Peter kept up with the most enthusiastic of shoulders. This should not have come as a surprise, Peter was an ever optimistic cultural bridge builder on tour. Gaps close quickly through skillful dance.

D-Day + 30
The one with foreign invaders

We awoke to more than half the camp paralyzed with gastroenteritis. Workers always get sick on holidays as do cyclists on rest days. Double rest days allow extra time for the body time to identify, process and attack bacteria.

Ethiopia's particular army of foreign invaders were alarmingly violent and decapacitating. Many riders decided to remain at the hotel in order to pray to the porcelain gods for redemption, some even exiting EFI in the process. I was one of five lonely cyclists considered the "lucky ones". We were lucky enough to never feel sick but I couldn't help but contemplate the abuse that had cultivated our stomachs to be impervious to superbugs. Years spent eating military rations caked in mud, street food served from unwashed hands in Egypt, and my own terrible cooking had prepared my stomach for the worst.

I set off with the usual gang accompanied by Alaric and Jon. We were instantly rewarded with endless expanses of stunning scenery. We traveled in real time through thickly forested picturesque postcards and the day even felt somewhat downhill. There was magic in the scenery which encouraged faith in fairytales. We expected gnomes, goblins or trolls to leap from behind greenery. What we got were children lining the road in an elaborate game of Red Rover. If we were in a fairytale, the kids we met were collectively the Big Bad Wolf trying their best to topple us. Yelling their warcry "YOU YOU YOU YOU YOU!"

They created human roadblocks, launched rocks and sticks at us, and generally tried to control our journey. Forty-three percent of the Ethiopian population is fourteen years old or younger, which explains the generally devious nature of the country. We met a few steep hills and I suddenly felt deflated and unable to carry on a conversation. All my sensory feedback seemed normal but my physical output was severely limited. With one word Femke solved the mystery: altitude. We had climbed over two thousand meters above sea level, so high that oxygen was in short supply. I found my speed once again as my struggling lungs were overshadowed by my prideful legs capable of climbing to such heights. We sailed into Yifag pleasantly surprised by our first day back in the saddle after a double rest day.

D-Day + 31
The one with White-Neigh-YOU-YOU-YOU-Stoned

With another rest day in sight, we cycled sixty kilometers through rolling hills to Bahir Dar. We were joined by the Bahir Dar local cycling team at twenty kilometers to camp. They expertly fended off cars and kids which lightened our mental load immensely. The welcoming party was extremely timely as I kept contemplating how my body's recovery rate had slowed tremendously from one day to the next. My body was clearly still in the repair shop after the challenging eight day stretch and could only be used gently. We arrived at the residence in a relaxed state of mind and thanked the cycling team for all of their hard work.

Bahir Dar, the Ethiopian Riviera. Bahir Dar had a distinctly European flavour to it's African beat. Palm trees lined wide clean streets offering shimmering glimpses of Lake Tana. This capital city felt organized in a manner befitting a postcard. How could this influence be possible when Ethiopia was the only African nation not colonized European colonial forces? Being frequented by French, Belgian and British travelers in the 19th century, as well as being occupied by the Italians in 1936 - 1941, Bahir Dar learned early to capitalize on tourism. This well served our current mission. With a large part of the day ahead of us, the gang headed to the market to find costumes for the annual party always held at the residence's bar. This year's theme was to be a Whitney Houston Tribute. With a little intrepidness you could uncover true gems at even the most understated of markets. That day, we found all of our costumes and more at the Bahir Dar Market. It was all too easy, too conformist. Our costumes pieced together as follows: Marita was a White goddess, myself a horse, Esther and Jenny were rock-throwing Ethiopian youth and Femke was a stoner. Collectively, we made "Whit-ney YOU-YOU-YOU stone". Others had found similar gems. Rob dressed as Kevin Costner from The Bodyguard, while Ian, Holly and Steve, a fifty one year old South African, donned bed sheets as robes and posed as Whitney herself. Steve had even created a wig out of cotton balls. By early evening we gave the residence bar our best seal of approval while drunkenly dancing without inhibition. Although Bahir Dar had provided a night of relative normalcy for most cyclists coming from first world countries; a drunken costume party, it felt miles away from anything authentic.

D-Day + 32
The one with hippo bait

To make up for the previous night's sins we went to visit monasteries on Lake Tana, a tour organized by the Bahir Dar bicycle club. With a price tag of zero dollars who could resist! Little had I known that sickness was upon me. My stomach may have been impenetrable to foreign invaders but it had a significant design flaw: motion sickness. Unawares, I climbed aboard the small wooden boat shored at the entrance to the Blue Nile. Entons Eyesu Monasteries was our first destination. Lake Tana was only fourteen meters deep and milky blue, a mysterious blue that lulled senses while sparking interest in what lies beneath. I would soon find out. Five minutes after departure I was waving my face over the side of the boat as my stomach emptied at an alarming rate. I suddenly realized that I was a living PEZ dispenser to the marine life below as they ate my offerings with joy. With my face but a foot from the surface, I prepared myself for what could emerge from the water's depths. Hippos. Africa had hippos. North Americans wholly underestimate hippos thanks to Walt Disney. The infamous "Walt Disney hippopotamus" was bumbling and jolly. It would seem that Walt accidently mixed his ferocious rhinoceros with the harmless hippopotamus. While rhinoceri are so visually impaired that they would be lucky to see their own glorified snouts, let alone prey, hippopotami are territorial, vicious, and kill more people in Africa than any other animal. I worried about an ultra-territorial hippo leaping suddenly and eating my candy-dispensing head. Mercifully, we arrived at a small island, head intact, ready to trek to the monastery. We trekked up a path of loose rocks past growing coffee beans, half naked children and vendors of religious paraphernalia. Finally Entons Eyesu came to view.

Entons Eyesu is a medieval orthodox monastery originally built in 1314. It is famous for housing the peaceful coexistence of nuns and monks without hanky panky. This is easily enough understood when you consider that the entire monastery is painted with biblical scenes of a graphic nature. In one painting a man's hands are sheared from his body as blood spatters out, in another a blade is thrust deep into a sinner's abdomen. These vividly painted reminders would throw a wet blanket over anyone's libido. The paintings were as visceral and real as Ethiopia, beautiful yet edgy. Unafraid to flaunt the unpredictability of life. We knew this well as life on tour was unpredictable.

Just this day our chef Jon had been airlifted to Nairobi in a tremendous amount of pain. The next time we saw Jon, he was in Nairobi, forty pounds lighter and sans appendix. Who knew what the next day would bring?

D-Day + 33
The one with Andrew as "Shit Hot"

We awoke apprehensively to a one hundred and sixty four kilometer day, beginning ungraciously with a fifty-five kilometer climb. We cycled out with local cyclists from the Bahir Dar club.

A few kilometers down the road the peloton passed us and Jenny commanded 'HOP ON!"

So we did. Before I knew it, I was swept to the middle of the peloton pack unable to escape and deeply in panic. I pedalled like crazy and suddenly realized that I was fast enough. The local riders were taking huge shifts at the front of the pack to break the wind for us. The kilometers melted by. After lunch, my mind no longer felt up to the stress of the peloton and so Andrew and I took it easy the rest of the way to camp. Well, most of my muscles 'took it easy' with the exception of my abdominals; I had never laughed so hard and for so long in my life. Andrew navigated the world with wit. He launched a witty retort to every barrage of "YOU! YOU! YOU!" and "Where you go?" I may have had the upperhand in Egypt, but Ethiopia was Andrew's turf. The kids found it hard to throw rocks accurately as they laughed uncontrollably alongside us.

We passed endless fields with flat-topped trees. Green hills the colour of the Grinch's toilet paper blanketed us warmly. Rock fences surrounded wooden houses with bright blue shutters and doors. Horses proudly passed us, strutting their bright red tassles. Women and children stopped us to have their pictures taken. Although I assumed Andrew was regularly stopped by starstruck fans, these people bore a different purpose. Having no mirrors in their homes meant that they rarely had the chance to see themselves. Picture display had a much higher resolution than water reflection. We entered what Andrew referred to as "a real basket weaving town". We stopped at a local Coke stop and suddenly Andrew was grinning from ear to ear.

He murmured "I'm shit hot at ping pong." and leapt from the table towards a ping pong table in front of the establishment.

It turned out that he was "shit hot" even on a warped table with a rubberless racket. Andrew quickly tore through the casual ping pong players of the town and so they brought out their big shots. He beat them too but not without a struggle. I looked around and realized that we had drawn a massive crowd and not the type of crowd we were used to. This was a crowd who had zero interest in pilfering our belongings. Andrew had forged a connection and connections were sacred in a nepotistic country. If they ever needed ping pong lessons, Andrew had shown his worth. Andrew had the pulse of Ethiopia and riding with him felt like what this tour was actually about.

D-Day + 34
The one with Esther's champion

In Ethiopia, all goodness comes with a price tag. Today we climbed. We climbed beautiful mountains. We climbed past vistas that enriched our psyche. We climbed. For hours, my legs got stuck in the nine to fourteen kilometer per hour zone. In fewer than twenty-four hours, this would be considered racing speed, but on this day it felt like an eternity. A monkey cheered us on enthusiastically from the sidelines. Forests of tall trees stood still like soldiers monitoring mischievous children playing some strange combination of hide and go seek and capture the flag (the 'flag' being our belongings). Small trees spiralled larger ones creating a giant cascading canopy of shade. Shade was revered here. There was no wiser place to be than carefully shaded at the base of an Ethiopian tree. From there you could be still and attract some of the most beautiful birds on the planet. Ethiopia is a haven for birding with its rare and exquisitely coloured and patterned avifauna. Even my unschooled eye knew to be delighted daily by the uniqueness of Ethiopia's birds so we sat and watched often. So, it didn't strike me as odd when Esther expressed the desire for a shade break. Looking forward to my amateur birding I almost missed Esther collapse under a tree shivering and blazing hot to the touch. That was the thing about Ethiopia, one moment you could be the image of health, the next you may find yourself in the fetal position wishing for death. With twenty-seven kilometers to camp, Esther was sore and feverish and severely in need of fluids. With regards to rehydration, Esther was in luck. Apart from birding, one of Ethiopia's greatest joys was juice. Juice bars were everywhere. Customers broused local fresh produce and ordered a tailor-made heavenly-layered elixir. Spriss juice has five layers of fruit including the ever so popular Avocado, Papaya, Mango, Banana, and Guava mix. Like a density column, each fruit preferred to hold its own and not to mix with its brothers above or below. It was the deluxe model of what most North Americans didn't even know to rank. We simply didn't know it could taste this good. With a mango and avocado juice down the hatch, Esther and I set off with Marita and Peter. What happened next said as much about Esther's karma as Peter's character. Peter, recently mended from his painful shoulder dislocation, physically pushed Esther's back, supporting her as she weakly pedalled uphill. Riding a lighter model, he offered to exchange bikes and carried Ether's bike across many gravel patches. Peter was always quietly working to bolster others when they needed him the most. I found myself quietly contemplating why I had not offered as much. It was difficult to swallow but my heart was still not in the right place. Esther was always quick to support anyone and here I was holding back. Although I would never deny a friend asking for help, I was in self-protect mode and not a proactive nurturer. I perceived myself 'fighting' daily to make it to camp and barely surviving. I wanted EFI. Although we all made it to camp that afternoon, I felt like I had let myself down deeply.

Nola was injured again. She had swerved to avoid children, hit a few speed bumps and flipped over her handlebars. Luckily, a World Vision truck came to her rescue and brought her to the tour truck. World Vision was everywhere. While most aid organizations contented themselves with self-aggrandizing posters by the side of main highways and offices in the larger cities, World Vision was the only organization present in the extremely remote areas. They were on the ground doing meaningful work in the poorest of villages. In an effort to release myself from feeling like a terrible human being, I vowed to one day sponsor a child through World Vision. I kept this promise, sponsoring Linda in early 2018. That same year, my infant son Emmett taught me a thing or two about nurturing. I am still no Peter, but what a fantastic role model.

D-Day + 35
The one with forward pedalling and backward movement

When you begin the day with twenty kilometers downhill, an eighty-nine kilometer day shouldn't take over seven hours. It did. After a leisurely twenty-nine kilometers, we descended on unforgiving roads that jealously demanded more attention than the serene vistas on either side. I was happy that the road was so demanding as it gave me no chance to think of what lay ahead: twenty kilometers uphill. We sped down hills flanked with cliff faces partially hidden by palm trees. Cacti jutted out straight from trees aggressively like soldiers on the raid. Their flat oval cacti compatriots, obviously the senior officers, lounged low to the ground and expanded widthwise showing off their fat. Families of baboons stared at us as if we were crazy. Donkeys barely saw us as they were so laden with grass and hay that only the tops of their heads poked through. We descended faster than the birds of prey that swooped ominously close only to suddenly veer off and nab a victim in the field. We may have smelled close to death, but thankfully these birds could still tell the difference. We went down past churches vainly created in a spiritual setting. Down, down, down, to the Blue Nile Gorge.

Locally named the Abbay River, the Blue Nile Gorge is the world's second largest canyon. With a depth comparable to the Grand Canyon, the Blue Nile is a generous monster. Eighty percent of total Nile waters flow from these Ethiopian Highlands in the rainy season. The rise of Ancient Egypt owed its legacy to this sacred place, for without this influx of water the fertility of the Nile Valley would be significantly compromised. Many explorers described our current location as "impassible". Historically, tracing the course of this Nile left a wake of destruction; transportation wrecked, lives lost. A nagging thought 'Would I witness history repeating itself?' The next twenty kilometers would take us up one thousand three hundred and sixty meters. On average that was over sixty meters upward per kilometer. Ethiopia was considered "the roof of Africa" as it contained over seventy percent of all mountains in Africa. This was the steepest, longest climb we would face during the tour and for me, in a lifetime. Click, click, click, I geared up to my granniest of gears mentally preparing myself for hours upon hours of sitting with granny, watching the world pass by at her pace. I took stock of my blessings: my health was perfect, my body was in good form and I was acclimatized. I started to push uphill. I rounded a corner to see Esther, who felt well enough to ride but ill enough to be passed by many slower riders, walking her bike uphill. Together, we had a shade break and then hopped on our bikes going at the backbreaking speed of six to nine kilometers per hour. We spiraled up switchbacks and roads so steep that we moved quicker than the load-bearing vehicles. As a great chasm started separating the quicker cyclists from the slower, a local man told Ciaran, one of our tour staff, that we resembled lost cattle, and that he needed a large stick to hit the slower riders in order to bring us back together. After a quick water refill with Ciaran, I got back on my bike and tried to pedal uphill...the street grade was so steep that I kept rolling backwards while pedaling forward. I was forced to do the unthinkable, pedal DOWNHILL, and use the momentum gathered to turn and pedal like mad to start climbing again. This was adding insult to injury.

We took a Coke break at the midway point and watched a chameleon wobble across the road as local boys approached him menacingly. We quickly named him Carmen and I picked him up on a stick to save him from his ill fate. He clung to me for dear life. I was going to place him high in a tree but then Gennesse picked him up and cycled him three kilometers to safety. We trudged forward and suddenly we were near the top. Esther and I decided to take in the view as it was spectacular. As we admired our accomplishment, a goat came over and licked the salty sweat from our legs. It took me three hours and fifty minutes to complete the torturous twenty kilometers. Many cyclists took three to four hours to complete the climb. Not Pal. Pal, had shown everyone up and gone ahead to set a tour record of one hour, seventeen minutes and fifty nine seconds. Pal was a legend, a norse God who had come to Earth to show us all how unfit we humans are. It was the ONLY explanation. Victory was sweet. Although the Blue Nile had certainly wrecked my body, my transportation and spirit remained intact. Why do people explore at great personal peril? Newness of appreciation. Appreciation for limits stretched, new discoveries and the art of rediscovery. That night, I rediscovered how soul cleansing a hot shower could be. We stayed at a Canadian compound of Doctors Without Borders, and they gave us access to their hot showers. As hot holy water dribbled over my wrecked body it restored enough strength to face another day in the saddle. This is why we explore.

D-Day + 36
The one with Salamo

The climbing continued as we finally reached our highest elevation on tour, three thousand, two hundred meters above sea level. Our reward was a gentle coast to camp which was situated atop a vast gorge. It was here I met Salamo. Salamo was a local boy who came under the guise of helping me set up my tent, only to peddle his wares in the most genteel manner possible. Supposedly, he lived at a nearby monastery, his mother having passed away. It was there that he made crosses out of rock to sell. This was his story, no matter how true, it made no difference. Salamo was soft spoken, polite and a calming presence. We sat a long while on the edge of the gorge and chatted about life. We were more similar than different. We watched the birds dance in the open space below as I considered my prejudice. In Ethiopia, I had expected to see gaunt, struggling faces. Poverty, hunger and desperation being the primary determinants. As misconceptions tend to knock you off balance, I struggled to make sense of the happiness, self-confidence and curiosity looking back at me daily. The children looked different from the Unicef commercials I saw on television. They looked healthier and happier than most North Americans I knew. Certainly they were quite healthy as they chased our bicycles at eighteen kilometers per hour on foot. Salamo put it all down to one important factor: community. People lived in a sense of belonging, at harmony with nature. North Americans had deviated too far to understand this profound joy. Salamo did caution me that we were only seeing the "rich" who lived by the side of major roads and that rural Ethiopia may paint a different picture. I hoped we would have the chance to see that side.

D-Day + 37
The one with Hitler

The downside to sleeping at the top of a gorge? Troops of baboons. Baboons are the African rooster. Shrieking with delight the moment the sun rises, waking us far too early. The baboons sounded like shrill birds singing falsetto. Salamo returned to help me tear down my tent and pack my bags. He left before I could give him a tip. The gang set off for the day. We rolled through many villages smelling vast amounts of dung. Mountains of cow dung were piled high beside donkey dung. For a little extra you could lavishly treat yourself to a donkey dung special mixed with rock and sand. Being exceptionally versatile, dung was used to line floors, walls and even for household fuel. Ethiopians used it for everything. It reminded me of Canada's love affair with duct tape. We arrived at the lunch truck, smelling a little worse for wear. It was there that someone kindly pointed out my resemblance to Hitler. This story began in Canada, during the planning stages of the tour. I went to my local doctor to buy the antimalarial Malarone, only to be told that it would cost one thousand five hundred dollars to buy enough for four months. Balking at this price I returned to Egypt and purchased the same amount of antimalarial medication for three hundred dollars. Slightly worrisome was the listed side effect of sun sensitivity, but the price was right. Being slightly gingerish, this was not my best decision. Not only did my skin feel like it was continuously being pricked by hot needles, but I had managed the least attractive feature imaginable: a white Hitler mustache. My sunburnt nose had saved my upper lip from burning. It was the last reminder of my actual skin colour. My upper lip was ghostly white, while the rest of my face was red. I was a discoloured Hitler. After getting her fill of laughter and pictures, Jenny saved the day by providing me with just enough Malarone to get to Kenya. In Kenya I would replenish her pills and buy enough Malarone for the remainder of the tour, for less than four hundred dollars. I will forever blame Canadian pharmaceuticals for my Hitler mustache.

After lunch, we convoyed to Addis Ababa with some local riders. Ethiopia's capital city, sat on top of the world at an elevation of 2,450 meters. More than eighty different ethnic groups converged in Addis Ababa making it a bustling and chaotic big city focused on economic, social and political activity. Feeling hungry and tired, we quickly settled on a nearby restaurant named The Cottage that night for supper. On our way home we casually noticed that we were the only people on the streets. We soon realized why as three pickpockets brazenly approached our large group. Sensing danger, a few riders pushed them to the ground as we hurried away. The pickpockets seemed so shocked that for a moment our response seemed unjust. Perhaps we were supposed to pick up a few rocks and launch them instead? Next we passed a young girl begging for money. When a local man gave her a few birr, some riders commented on why he should not.

He walked away mumbling "I hate white people".

That struck a deep chord. Through many years of travel I had devised a test that never failed to reveal how charitable a subculture was. I simply called it 'the neighbour test'. The test consists of two simple questions: How well do you know your neighbours? Do you lock your front door? Mistrust begins at home and permeates all aspects of the human psyche. Trusting people give more freely, without deep concern for being taken advantage of. They look for reasons to trust, to unlock doors for others. They continue to trust for the sake of trust, even when proven wrong. Mistrustful people live fearfully, thinking others simply want to take advantage of them. They protect their assets and rationalize their locked doors. Ironically, those who have the most tend to trust least. The world has taken care of them and yet they were less willing to take care of others. There are millions of justifications for why the less trusting route is logical but it simply doesn't work towards happiness. Unfortunately mine was a culture of mistrust. Although positive role models surrounded me, I had a hard time quieting the all-consuming question "What is their true motive?" I did not give to that girl. Perhaps she would have used money to buy drugs, alcohol, or some other life- ruining vice. That is not the point. I wanted to go through life trusting. Although generalizing to 'white people' was broad, my culture had certainly made this a challenging goal.

D-Day + 38
The one with restoration

Being jostled by the previous night, I opted for a quiet day of sleeping, reading, eating and lounging in front of the television. Addis Ababa was our third large capital city, and it felt much the same. Hustling busy people filled the streets as noisy cars spat out black fumes nearby. I did not want to venture. I needed to restore my energy for rural Ethiopia.

D-Day + 39
The one with the United Nations versus Ethiopia

I was under no illusion of being in shape. Everyday I parcelled out energy in small increments hoping to be able to sustain what little I had left for one hundred and twenty days. The gang stopped often to relax, which suited my leg muscles swimmingly. On one such stop, we found the exception to my relaxation rule: volleyball. A local school was outside playing volleyball and enjoying the fresh air. Without a moment's hesitation we were off our bicycles and right alongside them begging to join in. They welcomed us onto the court. We held our own with the more traditional volleyball skills of bumping, setting and spiking. However, the local teenagers had a deadly weapon: their toes. Balls spiked to the ground at sharp angles would be revived at the very last second by a sneaky toe expertly placed to set the ball back in play. Their feet could accurately set a ball for an attack. Volleyball was redefined as 'soccer with hands' and we posed no threat. Ethiopia easily beat the UN with the entire school watching. Happily humbled, we thanked them and set off again with tired and sore muscles.

As I cycled onward to camp something strange came over me: reverse-illness. I felt normal as long as I kept cycling but the moment I stopped for a break I was so nauseous and dizzy that I felt like I may vomit and pass out. No more breaks for me that afternoon. My impenetrable stomach had finally succumbed to Ethiopia. I made it to camp and following my animalistic instincts, I found a secluded hole under a tree in which I went to die alone. I curled into the fetal position and remained there for quite some time as my stomach decided to launch attacks. Miraculously, I started to feel better so I returned to camp. Plain noodles were on my menu and I hoped that the next day wouldn't require much sustenance.

D-Day + 40
The one with the great toilet tent heist

Thirteen hours of sleep muted the nausea and I was able to ride on. Children lined our journey, once again chanting the chorus "MONEY!

MONEY! MONEY!"

Some danced by the side of the road as we passed while others tried to yank us off our bicycles. A few riders, less empathetic after so many days in fierce battle with mischievous children, decided to tell the local police to do something about the children grabbing and yanking them off their bicycles. What the police decided to do was a public beating of the young boys. The riders didn't have the stomach for watching youth beaten with sticks so they came to their defense. The police laughed at them and walked away. We did not have the stomach for Ethiopia, literally or figuratively. The gang overshot camp as some children stole the finish line marker. This was foreshadowing. Camp was a trap. We were in a perfect ambush location. It was as if Earth had created a bowl and we were ducks all sitting inside and waiting to be stewed. Dozens of Ethiopian children sat on high ground surrounding us and waiting for their move. As the sun started setting, they pulled a feat that I'm quite certain no Canadian Forces recce element could muster. With over half our camp sick with gastroenteritis our two toilet tents were more popular than the Las Vegas Strip. Somehow, before dusk, the children had managed to not only find an unoccupied latrine, but to steal the canvas toilet tent from its very visible location and move it stealthily up the steep hills that surrounded us, without anyone witnessing the heist. This would prove to be one of the more useful items they would steal from camp, and they would steal many. Though Bryce's GPS must have brought momentary joy, the canvas of the toilet tent would live on for years to come, visible to future cycling tours as patches in cloth and houses. Children were not the only pilferers that night. Hyenas visited our tents scrounging for food and sounding like the jolly grim reaper. One found itself three feet away from my tent and I cursed myself for setting up next to the camp organics bin. Hyenas sound like gremlins being repeatedly hit on their funny bone. They sound like adults imitating irate babies. Luckily I knew Africa's golden rule: no body part is to be exposed from the tent if you value keeping it.

D-Day + 41
The one with the nearly victorious gang

The day started with a seventeen kilometer climb. Gargantuan banana leafs sheltered small huts to the left of us, trees with endless trunks skyward-bound were to the right, and there we were stuck in the middle dodging poo. Large birds of prey circled overhead letting feces fly in all directions. Finally, at twenty-two kilometers, we saw Jon and Juergen under shelter and decided to join them. Jon was an Australian rider with a great sense of humour. Jurgen was from the Netherlands, and he dictated the terms to life. His terms included smoking a pack of cigarettes per day, drinking with the best, cycling the world. He did all three astonishingly well. We sat and played with chickens under the sturdy bird-proof awning. The nearby boys looked like they belonged to an emo band with what appeared to be thick eyeliner on their upper lids. In broken English they informed us that at ten years of age, boys would get their eyelids cut three times and coal would be placed in the cut. Tribal ritual served as a tremendously important unifyer in a land where unity equated to survival. As we would see, Ethiopian scarring ceremonies were not uncommon.

Along came Doug. Doug was our South African bike mechanic. While many staff members had joined the tour in order to travel and begrudgingly got on a bicycle from time to time, Doug's first passion was cycling. He joined our race teams and rode on his rest days. He was also nominated as "sweep" more often than not. "The sweep" cycles at the back of the pack, painstakingly slowly, and gathers the slow, weak, broken or distracted riders. The sweep also helps with any problems en route. Due to our highly distractible nature, the gang rode frequently with the sweep. Doug's racing spirit hardly made him the ideal sweep, but he was a crowd favourite with his quick wit, positive humor and seemingly indelible patience. You would never know he was anything but thrilled to be spending the day cycling at ten kilometers per hour and stopping every five (though you could almost see Doug's muscles atrophy at this speed). The gang knew that we clipped his wings often. I could pretend that our motivation for what followed was to set Doug free, but I would be lying. Doug, with a mischievous smile and fun-loving nature was a prime candidate for trickey. It would be Doug vs. The Gang and we needed the entire town on our side to pull it off.

In Ethiopia, a typical greeting for weirdos on bikes was to drop everything and run immediately onto the street yelling "FOREIN-GEE!" at the top of your lungs while waving your arms madly. If there happened to be cyclists stopped nearby, the arm waving would turn into violent pointing in their general direction. This would never do. We let everyone in on our plan.

Doug entered town and we crouched down low in our seats behind the tall blue walls. The town followed our lead and crouched just outside these walls, not uttering a peep. Thankfully Doug was racing, a brief moment of sweet release before he caught the slowest rider. Otherwise he would have noticed an entire town crouching as if sitting on invisible toilets. Focused, he passed through town quickly. Victory was ours! We would sweep the sweep! Our victory was short lived as Doug returned within twenty minutes. Inge, a sectional rider from the Netherlands had spotted us by the chorus of "FOREIN-GEE" and wondered where we were when Doug rode up behind her. If there was one thing Doug liked less than cycling at ten kilometers per hour, it was backtracking for us. We rewarded him with the laziest day of cycling on tour. Together we stayed another hour enjoying the chickens and coffee then started to climb again.

At the top of the mountain we spotted the Sport Café and victory beers were ordered. Sitting on the balcony being watched by dozens of locals we decided it would be fitting to teach them "the wave," given that it was a sports café and we seemed to be the main attraction. The only sport advocated by this establishment was vase-chucking. The bathroom was littered with dozens of broken vases with used toilet paper shoved in the cracks. A cute guard puppy stood post. After another hour, we got back on our bicycles and bid adieu to the café. We got to lunch at one o'clock, just as it was shutting down. The afternoon would be a very different ride than the morning. Over the span of forty kilometers, the demographics shifted from comfortable to impoverished. Citizens were as likely to greet you as to throw objects at you, or at least to pretend to, which they found outrageously funny.

A chorus of "MONEY! MONEY! MONEY!" followed everywhere we went. Rocks slammed into the ground all around us and as rocks reached their breaking point so did the riders. One rider chased a few children through town and into the children's home, yelling at their parents when they ran and hid. That afternoon we stopped at a local fountain for a dip. We bathed in the fountain, cooling our tempers and cleansing our bruised egos. We knew our fuses ran short and it was high time for a change of scenery. Luckily, Kenya was just around the corner. Unluckily, the route to Kenya remained mostly unpaved.

D-Day + 42
The one with the peanut seller

It sounded like hyenas were being ripped apart near camp. That is how baboons argue. Everything 'baboon' is the opposite of subtle, arguments included. When baboons shriek at one another, the neighbours call the police. The gang left camp quickly to avoid being complicit. Within thirty seconds we were completely surrounded by children. Bumpy gravel roads allowed kids to walk comfortably alongside us, all day long. I was not trying to be rude or antisocial, but my brain could hardly form a sentence as it bounced violently off all sides of my skull. The kids didn't mind. In fact, they followed us everywhere. Including our frequent pee stops. It was common for a few tagalongs to get more than an eyeful as we squatted behind trees or bushes. Femke decided to increase the spectacle by standing half-naked, air drying and dancing in front of her audience. Jenny was stoned for attempting the same. One thing is certain; there is no land unwatched in Ethiopia. Some scenes simply stick in your mind. As I watched Esther cycling in her red jersey, surrounded by lush green vegetation narrowly dodging a white goat I realized that I was seeing colours for the first time. Colours are so vividly bright in Ethiopia that they seem to target your brain receptors differently. That, or I was experiencing the effects of brain trauma from cycling on such horrible roads.

At our first rest stop, a large man greeted us wearing a t-shirt that read "I'm a moody woman". The gang sympathized. We sat for a break at a small local diner. A vendor came by with roasted peanuts wrapped in paper. There are few greater treats for hungry cyclists than deliciously roasted protein and calorie-filled nuts. We bought one each. Marita was the first to unwrap her peanuts and she stood aghast at what she found inside. The peanut seller was wrapping his wares with math textbook paper! Marita launched into an attack.

"You won't need to sell peanuts if you use the textbook paper! DO SOME MATH!"

He hurried along embarrassed. So did others. It was the first time we were left alone all day. The rest of the day was spent climbing to camp on extremely bumpy roads that made me want to cry. I knew I could not afford the energy so instead I focused on effectively dodging the multitude of animals and children. Carla, a forty-one year old Canadian, was unlucky. A lady walked right out in front of her and she flipped over her handlebars trying to avoid a collision. She dislocated her collarbone and then got back on her bike and cycled her way to camp. Carla had the toughest of the strong wills on tour. She embodied the perfect balance of drive, determination and generosity of spirit. Arriving at camp with her collarbone very visibly protruding, Carla was still committed to the idea of riding the next day. Thankfully, staff dissuaded her as the next day we faced a new challenge: mud.

D-Day + 43
The one with crying

Baboons steal as well as they fight. A large baboon got my attention this morning by aggressively tossing branches from trees. Then he descended and began a most intense staring competition from fewer than fifteen feet away. I knew the rules, I didn't blink. Suddenly he lurched forward so I retreated blinking furiously to show my surrender. He grabbed my camel pack and retrieved the plastic bag containing my passport photos and Egyptian ibuprofen. The only logical explanation was that he wanted to traffic drugs to Kenya and needed an alias. He ripped the bag apart and was about to sample the drugs when a proactive Canadian working with a nearby NGO bravely shooed him away. His heroism left me feeling cowardly yet again. I would have a chance to redeem myself the next morning when faced with far deadlier wildlife. The gang set off apprehensively for the upcoming sixty kilometers of offroading. For the first thirty-four kilometers I pushed so hard that vomit permanently burned the back of my throat. Then came the rain. We decided not to stop for a break, spiralling a few into grumpy caffeine withdrawal. We hit the secondary dirt path and came to a dead stop. Mud; tire's quicksand. The more we struggled, the more we sank. Marita's front mud guard became clogged every few meters as did our brake pads. Coke stops were replaced with declogging stops and they were necessary every few kilometers. The only benefit to our terrifically slow speed was that we were able to really soak in Ethiopia. True Ethiopia. The one that exists outside of where the rest of humanity goes. The one that you only access via mud paths and gravel walkways. It all felt very genuine; nothing had been contrived. We passed through numerous traditional Ethiopian villages lined with wooden crisscrossing gates and huts sprawled everywhere. Little faces peered from every window yelling "FOREIN-GEE!" at the top of their lungs. Then, at one of our routine stops, we somehow lost Marita. We waited a while and then set off, thinking she may have ridden ahead. I never did find out where she went as the next time we saw Marita she was brimming with stories of her day. Predictably, cycling alone in Ethiopia was as hairraising as Egypt or Sudan. Kids continually tried to pull Marita off her bike, steal her possessions and swat at her as if she were a beast of burden. When a kid stole her camera, it was the straw that broke the camel's back. Marita threw her bike down in the mud, sat down and wailed. She cried until she heard a rustling and then looked up to see the thief poke his head out from behind a bush. He threw her camera back to her. She collected herself, then her belongings, got back on her bike and rode on.

That afternoon we stopped for a Coke and I couldn't stop staring at the locals' eyes. They had changed. They were edgy and aggressive with tones of deep void. It was a scary combination. When I mentioned this to Shona she pointed out the orange drink many of them were offering us. It appeared that the entire male population of some towns were inebriated and the hootch made for some bad drunks. Happy to be on pavement again we left quickly and passed over a bridge sheltering hundreds of men, women and children of all ages bathing naked together in the muddy water below. I remembered an old boyfriend teasing me as I dressed to go to the bathroom in the middle of the night, which was two steps from my bedroom, in case my roommate saw me naked. I was not a prude, just socially conditioned. I felt envious of the natural freedom enjoyed by the bathers below. The cycle to camp was peaceful with animals sheltering under trees, layered mountains growing maize, dry cracked riverbeds and rolling hills accentuated by steep drop offs. We arrived at camp and relaxed before our last full day in Ethiopia.

D-Day + 44
The one with Storybook Africa

I awoke to a tiny scorpion entering my tent. The general rule with scorpions is the smaller the deadlier. This was my moment of redemption for the baboon incident. Without panicking or calling for help I gently kept an eye on my little friend while nonchalantly tearing down my tent and packing it on the truck. Later that day I would wish for the sweet release of his sting. The word "Yabelo" sounded like an Egyptian swear word. It should have been. Getting to our hotel in the town of Yabelo would invoke many expletives. The gang started riding down a harshly cracked and corrugated dirt path. Our eyes strained to find the best route between small boulders that littered our way. The unforgiving road, mercilessly shaking our battered and bruised bodies, forced us apart as we focused our attention downward on the treacherous terrain. The absence of hearing the girls huff, puff and swear, told me that we had lost one another. Then thorns, wild turkey, geckos, cows, sheep and camels came out to play. I dodged them all, thankful for the sweet reprieve of not having to watch for people. I was in the middle of nowhere and I could only look down. When I stopped briefly to wait for Marita, I finally took in my surroundings. Termite mounds taller than trees flanked me on both sides, their dirt a deeper red than the soil of Prince Edward Island. Fields of white butterflies played tag nearby. I wondered briefly if I had taken a wrong turn and ended up in Kenya. Surely, they couldn't mean for us to cycle THESE terrible excuses for roads. Also, it felt like Kenya. The culture had shifted before the border. Women wore bright orange and red kangas tied around their waists, boasting many traditional designs. Long exquisitely beaded necklaces draped long necks sandwiched between massive earrings. This was a different Africa than the day before. This was storybook Africa.

I came upon Graham, a fellow Canadian, conversing with a local man. Graham had terrified the man's daughter. Upon first glance of the 'white ghost man', she dropped the bucket she had been slugging uphill and ran fearfully home. Together, we had a good laugh. Then we began climbing on loose gravel rocks. No matter how I shifted my weight, my back wheel kept spinning out over the rough gravel and I had a few sideways falls from my bike. Partway up the hill, I tried more than a dozen times to start cycling but without any momentum my wheels would spin so much that it was impossible. So I swallowed my pride and walked Buck to flatter ground. Getting back on Buck with great trepidation I struggled uphill, mentally coaching myself towards achieving realistic goals.

'One more corner. Make it to that tree. Just over that hill.'

Graham and I cycled the remainder of the day together in

conversation, which took some of my mind off the physical torment it was enduring. Being bounced around aggressively all day long took as much of an emotional toll as physical one. Just as my breaking point was being reached, we saw asphalt from afar. I looked at it lustfully and promised myself to never take asphalt for granted. The freshness of appreciation rejuvenated life and I made it to the hotel albeit completely tenderized and in serious need of a rest day. Yabelo was to be our final rest destination in Ethiopia.

D-Day + 45
The one with forced merriment

It was well within reason to believe that the road to Yabelo had swallowed us whole. Many cyclists had sustained injuries as their wheels skidded out from beneath them on the jagged gravel roads. This unforgiving land had a history of bloodshed. In the late 20th century a severe famine took hold. Yabelo, having been architected to support a much smaller population had ballooned through immigration from neighbouring countries. The ongoing deadly fight for resources in this region was showcased in 1992 when a sub-ethnic group of the Oromo people called the Borena Oromo massacred the Gabra, a Somali-Oromo ethnic group living near Yabelo over a severe lack of resources. Human Rights Watch remains vigilant in Yabelo though the violent motivations have shifted from resource scarcity towards politics. Though access to resources remained a concern for many ethnic groups surrounding Yabelo, for city dwellers a saviour was born under the name of avitourism.

We became aware of avi tourists through an unfortunate event. Our lodging had lost Internet connectivity. Being unable to spend our rest day online assuring loved ones of our continued survival we were forced to be social. To the extrovert, Yabelo was a haven. Not only was socialization forced, but there were plenty of English speaking white faces going around. Going around where you might ask? The answer: bird watching. Yabelo is one of Africa's lead birding destinations. Birds in Yabelo would give you lessons on the true nature of primary colours. They introduce your mind to a unique sound spectrum. They were the very definition of magnificent. Many cyclists forged friendships in Yabelo and learned a great deal about birds. Being an introvert, I spent the day healing, cleaning, writing and trying to locate the damnable hole in my thermarest. Sleeping on Kenyan lava rocks without an insulating layer sounded like tour's personal brand of hell.

D-Day + 46
The one with abuse

On asphalt and without a care in the world the gang backtracked a few hundred meters to a coffee shop for some caffeine and gossip. There was plenty of gossip after a particularly rowdy party the night we arrived in Yabelo. Needing to talk about something other than that epic party, we also made plans for the next day's border crossing. Then, refueled, the gang remounted and set off. Yabelo, now feeding from the teat of tourism, housed many rich, fat and seemingly happy locals. Somehow this made them less edgy. Instead of violently launching projectiles our way, the children settled for the more jovial bum slap. Youth would run up behind our bicycles and slap our derrieres as hard as they would their mules. We breathed a collective sigh of relief. Not only would we no longer have to contend with raining rocks but the kids would help propel us forward. Bliss.

Mega, a town of under ten thousand, was not named for an inferiority complex. It simply knew it's roots. Mega; a large dose. Ethiopia's way of presenting itself one last time before saying goodbye. Ethiopia was mega in every way. Mega-edgy. Mega-vivid. Mega-beautiful. Mega-gruelling. Mega-historic. Ethiopia existed on the edges of extremes, there was no soft ground to be found anywhere. Ethiopia was proud to hold humanity's longest history. Just before arriving in Mega, I stepped off Buck and went to visit the ancient ruins of a nearby military fort built in eighteen ninety-seven. Alone amongst the ruins, serenity flooded my body. This was an odd physiological response to a place of Italian invasion in 1936. During the Italian invasion Mega was a crucial communications hub. After the invasion, Mega returned to a quiet, remote sleepy village, a place of rest and serenity after battle. Perhaps my physiological reaction was not so misplaced, I yearned for this brand of tranquility. I desperately wanted to find a corner, curl up and soak in the atmosphere. With kilometers stretching ahead to camp, I got back on Buck and cycled into the town of Mega. Stopping for a quick drink, I knew this was goodbye. Goodbye to Ethiopia and to the hardest stretch on tour. Goodbye to the definition of extreme.

Kenya

D-Day + 47
The one with the miraculous Mad Hatter

It was the first of March. For the better part of two months we had been battering our physical and mental health. Had it made us stronger? To find out we would soon face the ultimate test: Kenyan lava rocks. To get there we needed to survive one last day in Ethiopia without losing our minds. On this day, In honour of March and our trampled sanity, we dressed as the March hare for the border crossing. More precisely; the Mad Hatter. We duct taped our bowl, plate and cutlery to our helmet. Esther painted fake mustaches on the gang while Steve, a fifty-one year old South African man who was known for his pranks and fun-loving nature, pimped out Jurgen's bike with a gazelle skull. He attached the skull so that the horns jutted out ahead and claimed that they were nature's aero bars. We set off together for the border. At our first rest stop, a local contingency decided that we were unstable. They were correct. Keeping their distance they spoke to us through a megaphone for half an hour. At our second rest stop, a local contingency decided that we were divine. They were wrong. Proceeding to wheel out a woman (whom we witnessed walking to the wheelchair), they claimed she was a paraplegic from birth and desired healing. As we cycled away, she got up from her chair to a loud cheer. These receptions were befitting seven crazy tourists. The last houses we saw in Ethiopia were pressed together using recycled cardboard with plastic bags shoved into gaps and holes. Gone were the tourists, jobs and money. Although the avifauna was regaling, the land had become too inhospitable for bird watching. This land belonged to the wild spirits, both living and otherworldly. We left Moyale, Ethiopia and entered Moyale, Kenya. We were not down the rabbit hole. Tribes don't always recognize arbitrary lines drawn on their earth and in this case, local tribes spanned countries. Ethiopian, Somali and Kenyan tribes lived in this fierce land. We defined the term"foreigner" understanding none of land nor custom. One thing was certain, it was time to retire our costumes as this was not a land for mockery. For the next three days, we would cycle the least hospitable roads imaginable and hope the wild spirits were on our side.

D-Day + 48
The one with Dedan's dust

The romanticism of cycling off road can only exist if your life isn't in peril. It was. We were on a road that brought an adult motorist to tears in his well-equipped car.

"Nobody comes here." was the reaction of a Kenyan cyclist who had joined the tour as a sectional rider, when asked if he had ever cycled these roads before.

When I first laid eyes on lava rocks I thought to myself 'Can the wheels of a bike go round and round over these sharp black volcanic boulders all the bloody livelong day?'

My bum shuddered at the thought. We had to cycle eighty-seven kilometers over two tiny tire ruts entirely covered with black menacing rocks, fist-size or larger. The gang set out to cycle the unforgiving maze, our eyes straining under the constant pressure of finding one 'safe' route. We glanced up every so often, on the lookout for curious giraffes, dik-diks and baboons strung along the path. Glancing, we would lose sight of our route and fall. Sharp, hot rocks threatened our every fall. We fell so frequently that we started classifying falls. "Sissy Falls" consisted of our tires spinning out in slow motion and us lacking the mental wherewithal to unclip our feet out before tumbling. The more prestigious "Captain Fall" happened when our bike slipped off a sharp rock forcing us to quickly topple over sideways. None of the gang members had any balance. Suddenly, we were passed by a cyclist with one leg. Dedan Ireri was a thirty one year old Kenyan cyclist. He had lost his right leg tragically as a child beggar in Nairobi when a car ran him over. Dedan found his passion for cycling and became a bike courier for Jamii Bora bank. In 2008, he qualified for the Paralympics in Beijing. Dedan was fast, focused and steady. Dedan skillfully weaved the impossible maze of lava with the balance and precision of a surgeon operating on a tightrope. We ate his one legged dust in absolute awe. Where the rest of us lumbered clumsily, Dedan floated gracefully by making the playing ground look effortless as only the most skilled of athletes have the ability to do. He greeted us warmly with a huge smile and a wave, as passion oozed out of every pore. Dedan was pure inspiration.

We rocked and rolled over volcanic lava and I wondered aloud whether internal organs could dislodge. Egrets flew overhead looking like toilet paper billowing in the wind, a sharp contrast to the red sands and black rocks under our tire tread. I marvelled at how the rules had shifted again. Kenya's spirit had a rhythm unlike that of frenetic Ethiopia. In Kenya, nature sang and swayed with a tangible beat that felt like the universal heartbeat. Whereas Ethiopia's energy had highs and lows, Kenya's felt steady. We cycled through lush forests all day before falling into "Water Hole Camp" to extract thorns from bikes, then bodies. While removing thorns I felt somewhat pleased to land my first tan of the trip. Upon closer inspection it was a ruse. Nature's fake tan: heat, sweat and red dirt. I was akin to the Red Elephants of Tsavo - the only red elephants in the whole world. I had encountered them on Safari a few years earlier. These vain elephants beat red dirt all over their bodies to hide their grey - they know their reputation and have to keep up appearances. For a brief moment I considered keeping my tan and going on a wet nap shower strike. Vanity aside, this sounded like a recipe for infection. Ironically, the water at Water Hole Camp was non potable. We discovered this fun fact by drinking it. Cramps and nausea quickly infiltrated the entire camp. For the first time on tour everyone went into town to buy bottled water. Then the staff informed us that our group was cursed. This was not ideal given that we were entering parts of Africa that dealt in black magic. Staff had already made more hospital trips on this tour than during the entire year before, despite our group being smaller. Just that morning, for example, Klaus skidded, fell and broke his hip. By the time we arrived at camp, Klaus was already in Nairobi awaiting an operation. We had a deluge that night as we fell asleep to nightmares of slippery lava rocks.

D-Day + 49
The one with emotional toying

Mud was as unhelpful as sand. The gang fixed four flat tires within the first ten kilometers. Feeling a need to suffer in silence I broke a rule I had made in Sudan and set off alone. It was a strange feeling to plow through beauty while agonizing. My years in the military had told me that the only way to get through such hardship was to shut my mind off and to press forward. Eventually I would die or get there and either way my mind wouldn't know the difference until it was too late. I tried to shut my mind off. Every so often the path would clear momentarily and I would glance up. This brave act would be rewarded with the truest form of beauty. The necessity to imprint it on my mind would jolt me out of my military trance. Then the suffering would restart as I tried to stop my thoughts anew. I saw giraffes munching on thorn trees covered in bird nests. Baboons enjoying family time, devilishly playing tricks on each other. Camels socializing with birds endowed with endlessly long beaks. In small houses with thatched roofs large families stared intensely at us, seemingly uncomfortable with who we were and what we were doing. Occasionally we saw trucks loaded with people on top cheering us on. Otherwise the only road traffic was UN, Red Cross and International Aid vehicles sharing these terrible roads. At times, a passable route simply didn't exist. I alternated between swearing and counting blessings. S@*#! Cooler temperatures in the low forties. F@*#! Zero flats. D#@$! Perfectly placed trees for shade every ten kilometers. Most of the time a herd of goats had discovered and monopolized the shade. The animals in Kenya were not as used to chaos as their Ethiopian counterparts. I startled donkeys, goats and cattle simply by riding by. At long last, camp was within sight.

There was one major drawback to repressing thought and emotion during the day's traumatic events. Once released at camp, my mind processed it all at once, poorly. Instead of feeling accomplished and proud I felt an overwhelming urge to find a protector. Also, I fiercely missed every protective figure in my life, from my parents to other close relations and ex-boyfriends. Then I became unjustly paranoid of vehicles approaching camp, sensing threats everywhere in my vulnerability. Finally I settled into a deep sleep and dreamt of past creature comforts: eating Fusion Sushi on my little red couch in Egypt, cuddled under a few layers of blanket. My mind searched everywhere for protection and comfort knowing full well that the next day would be even tougher.

D-Day + 50
The one with unfaithfulness to Buck

Today came with an EFI warning: leave early or get swept. Just before leaving camp one of my tires flatted. I had woken up early to maintain my EFI status and here I was destined to leave late. For a moment, I lusted over the staff bikes. They were temptresses, available for use and seducing me to cheat on Buck. What did they have that Buck didn't? Working tires and suspension. In the end I couldn't do it. I took one look at my Surly Long Haul Trucker and knew that we were in this together, for better or worse. Irrationally, I wanted Buck to have the entire experience alongside me. It turned out that by flatting, Buck had my back. As I changed the flat I suddenly realized that all the tire tubes Heiner had given me two weeks ago were useless. They had the wrong valve for my tire rim. Against all odds I had not flatted in weeks, including over five days of off roading and lava rock fields. Had I flatted, I wouldn't have been able to replace my tube. I would have had to hitch a ride to camp thereby laying my EFI dreams to rest forever. I was ever so thankful to have remained faithful today. Together we would continue to aspire towards EFI. Sometimes seemingly catastrophic situations carry the most beautiful blessings if you see them through to the end. Life wasn't always easy but I certainly felt attuned to the right path. Once again, Buck and I set off clambering over the coal black jagged furnace balls, surrendering to a violent day together.

I was meat trapped in a tenderizer, climbing up hills of lava rocks. At kilometer forty-six, I started bribing myself through every kilometer. I would set a target off in the distance and allow myself to quit once I achieved that landmark. Oddly, the road felt lighter and better once I arrived so I quickly set a new landmark with the same rules. And so the day went. Closely approaching my breaking point, the road flattened and the lava rocks subsided. That day, my guardian angel was Chinese. The Chinese were everywhere in Africa, grading roads in exchange for minerals. Unbeknownst to staff, they had recently tackled a section of our route. Had they not, my body would not have seen me through the day. Newly leveled roads allowed for peeking around and what I saw was beautiful. In the middle of this semiarid region I cycled past Lake Paradise in Marsabit National Park. Marsabit was a word cursed vehemently by all riders over the past few days as we cycled over the remains of Mount Marsabit, an extinct shield volcano. Now I stood in awe of Marsabit's Lake Paradise. It felt like Eve had heaved up that forbidden fruit and returned me to paradise from eternal damnation. A deep bowl of emerald water ran still at the bottom of the garden of Eden. In the wet season, lush vegetation curved up the two hundred meter sides of the crater, hiding leopards, baboons and buffalo. Water was life during the long dry season of Northern Kenya and this lake was giving.

With the town of Marsabit in sight, a local man named Ali met me a few kilometers from camp. He rode his motorcycle alongside me with his wife on the back. Ali was a talkative Born Again Christian who co-founded a theatre group aimed at bringing awareness of issues such as AIDS, female genital mutilation and other relevant topics to Marsabit. Mercifully, he showed me the route to camp and took my mind off the intense ache pulsing through every muscle, tendon and ligament of my body. Overused to the point of failure, my muscles died as I collapsed on the ground at camp. Suddenly I felt like I was at the pearly gates, as I was being greeted by nuns holding beer. We were staying at the Marsabit nunnery, and the sisters were quite savvy entrepreneurs. They knew their clientele well. Without moving one inch from our collapsing point, we drank away our pain and suffering.

D-Day + 51
The one with MooDonna

Although we had entered Kenya four days ago, I felt newly arrived. With my eyes cast downward attempting survival, all that I had seen of Kenya was lava rocks. I woke up in Marsabit with the strong urge to explore. My muscles had other plans, so a compromise was found. I lounged outside the convent with a group of riders, taking in the morning sun. A bull approached with the most spectacular set of horns, almost demanding worship. The bull had many devout cows and chickens following his every move. As I turned my back to comment on how cocky this bull appeared L.S exclaimed:

"Should this be happening?"

Sure enough MooDonna, the bull, had his head deep in our bread bag and was munching away on hundreds of lunch rolls. His mischievous eyes were peeking over the edge at us in defiance. L.S made an awkward attempt to shoo him away but stopped dead in her tracks once the bull stood his ground and stared at her. MooDonna, the bull was large and knew an inexperienced foreigner when she saw one. Just like the Ibuprofen stealing baboon, we were completely useless until a local nun ran over and shooed MooDonna away. MooDonna ran and her admirers bucked along behind her. Once again, Africa made us all feel like sissies.

Life without a calendar was truly a treasure. Time expanded, contracted and suspended with the rhythm of life, blissfully unaware that it was meant to be following a rigid schedule. As we rode into Marsabit we suddenly came face to face with Sunday. We knew this only because citizens lined the streets shouting "Hallelujah!" and singing gospel music. Christians and Muslims worshipped alongside one another. Perhaps they couldn't find a straight enough pathway through the lava rocks to draw metaphorically divisive lines in the sand. Additionally, people seemed to understand the value of slow spirituality. They took the time to process the sunrise and sunset. They learned to calm down and see the fullness of time. Our differences were pronounced when one rider became exceptionally irate at the forty five minutes it took her to receive a Nescafé. Even with nothing pressing our agenda, even with no calendar in sight, we somehow felt rushed. Spirituality won't be rushed and cannot exist in a soul driven by its next occasion.

Marsabit was a vibrant town. Small shops lined the streets boasting a wide range of connections and expertise such as Safari booking service hidden within a small paint shop, behind the SIM cards and toilet paper. Pharmacies requiring no prescriptions sold drugs alongside brightly patterned kangas, that light weight and versatile material used women as skirt, towel, head-wrap, pot holder, or apron. Every shop required a thorough dissection to uncover its buried treasures. Goats ambled nonchalantly through town. As we explored deeper, we suddenly found ourselves on the outskirts of Marsabit in a smaller subsection named Badessa. We walked the sand paths passing small communities of mudhuts, worrying about how much was in a name. We certainly didn't want to cross the people of "Bad-essa". In fact, the kids were thrilled to see us "mzungus" and cheered us on. Kenya, like Sudan and Ethiopia, seemed to be growing "plastic tree fields" at an alarming rate. On the twenty-eighth of August, two thousand seventeen, Kenya took global leadership in creating a law banning single-use plastic bags. Offenders would face a four year imprisonment or a forty thousand dollar fine. Sadly, this was the level of inconvenience necessary to stop the use of such bags. The Westerners shook their heads at these Draconian measures we could never hope to understand. Our garbage is tucked away politely from sight. We don't have to look daily at "plastic tree fields" or recognize the pure havoc our global obsession with plastic is having on the planet. Kenya also had a problem with crushed bottles. Ethiopian kids would literally brawl on the ground for the rights to a plastic bottle. Every cent that was earned recycling a bottle had an immediate effect on their quality of life. Conversely, the kids of Marsabit and Badassa were hardly motivated to make a few cents. Instead, they would crush them and leave them on the ground. Occasionally, one plastic bottle would find its way into a child's imagination and toy cars, planes and trains would be created. In the West, one of the many prices children pay for consumerism is the surrendering of imaginative creation. This learned behaviour translates into adulthood as the West produces a fraction of what it consumed. Travel; where bigotry ends and self-evaluation begins.

D-Day + 52
The one with Jesus failing

The morning began with Sharita giving two stern warnings:

"Do NOT F!@# with these people. If you stop to take a photograph, you will receive a spear through your head."

This first warning was bad news for Ming, a fifty-nine year old Taiwanese paparazzi. Tribes in Northern Kenya believed that the camera stole part of their soul. This particular riding day was renowned to be riddled with 'minor' problems such as spearings, shootings and cyclists held at gunpoint. The tribalism in Northern Kenya demanded respect and caution. The second warning broke even more spirits.

"This ride will be tougher than your last."

Brave faces broke upon hearing this and more bikes were piled on the truck as cyclists increasingly decided to sit this one out. After releasing the cyclists, Sharita confiscated Ming's camera and tasked a staff member to ride with him the entire day just in case he had a backup. She knew that a photography addict would not curtail his behaviour with a simple warning of death. Ming had taken thousands of photographs. Often Ming would get swept and driven to camp as the sun set, having made it a fraction of the cycling day due to his affliction. As enablers, we all reaped the benefits from his work when Ming generously shared his stunning photographs. We convinced ourselves that we had paid our dues by continuously changing Ming's flat tires when we saw him stranded by the side of the road (while he took pictures of us working). Ming would walk away from the tour with two titles: first Taiwanese man to complete the tour and first rider to NEVER change a flat tire. To earn the second title Ming had to be conniving. If he discovered a flat tire in camp, Ming would pump it up with enough air to ride one kilometer then flat again on the side of the road. The cyclist code forbids riding past a stranded cyclist, inevitably someone would stop and volunteer help and Ming would accept, camera at the ready.

The gang started the day by changing Jenny's flat and trying numerous times to stick Marita's new "Jesus never fails" sticker to her bike. Resorting to superglue, the sticker still failed. This was a bad omen. Sure enough we took a wrong turn out of camp. Luckily, a few racers whistled loudly and got us back on track. Our first challenge was over fifty kilometers of downhill. Paradoxical challenging downhill. Downhill was usually a time to savour the fruits of your efforts, this was no ordinary downhill. This extreme downhill had a viciously steep grade and required precision maneuvering around poop, rocks, crevices and sand. We feathered the brakes for over an hour trying desperately not to fly over the handlebars. At one point I hit a rock mosh pit of jagged large boulders and was flung in all directions but somehow I managed to stay on my bike. Many cyclists did not. Later that evening, the staff nurses would treat dozens of cyclists wounded in this section. Jay, an emergency room physician, mentioned how he peed blood for the next twenty-four hours. Kilometer after painstaking kilometer we cycled down, occasionally glancing up to see what we were missing. We were missing a lot. There was tangible power in this part of the world. Every element felt fully alive, charged with good and evil forces at play. We were surrounded and enveloped. The terrain didn't feel as if it belonged to humans. I reflected on how little in North America felt this free. We had tamed, domesticated and reduced many aspects of life in North America. This terrain would never allow itself to be tamed. In fact, it would require us to be wild and fierce. The wind toyed with us, delivering tailwinds strong enough to push us over our handlebars as we descended steep inclines and headwinds requiring herculean efforts to make it up hills. Nothing got in the way of the wind's agenda. We sliced through the wind all day long as it raged all over our bodies. It's soft and angry voice spoke to us, whispering doubt in our ear. It feels like the world was watching our every move. The tribal people also ooze elemental power. We saw our first warriors. Turkana warriors with beaded zigzagging bands across their bare chest, feathers in the shape of a mohawk sprouting from red dyed pleats. Paint from soil and animal fur menacingly lined their cheekbones and faces. Beads adorned their heads and bracelets gathered around their wrists. High crisscrossing socks accentuated a brightly coloured tunic. The women were dressed in bright kangas with neckbeads and beaded head ornaments that loosely resembled crosses on their forehead. Beaded ear extensions arced from the tops of their ears giving the impression of elf ears. Men and women both held a hardened steely expression and carried spears. Not a smile was to be found, but I was hit with a few rocks. We cycled through villages of stick houses held together with plastic bags or cardboard. Some inhabitants had surrounded their homes with small privacy bushes. In the stifling afternoon sun I rode with Shona and we found the smallest sliver of shade for rest. We agreed that part of the beauty of this trip was slowing down to a point where thoughts could be processed immediately. Thoughts speak loudly when their only competition is the sound of your breathing or heartbeat. Experiencing life through the senses happens fully when you slow to a cycle. Shona and I talked our way through life all the way to camp.

At camp, we were informed that there was a local wedding nearby and we were all invited. A group of warriors collected us. We were herded on the back of their truck and paraded us around town like freshly caught zoo animals. Newly on display, I kept considering how we must look, unkempt and smelly with our featherless boring hairstyles and ratty old beadless t-shirts. I'm quite certain they pitied us. This did give us the chance to dig a little deeper into warrior culture. We found out that Warriors do not go to school. School boys cut their hair for identification, while warriors grew their hair the entire fifteen years that they remained a warrior. It was a vocation. Initiation rights often included the slaughter of a local animal. Both warriors and non-warriors married between twenty to twenty-eight years of age and polygamy was well respected. We never found the wedding. I wondered if Akuj, the local sky god was blessing them, as today Jesus was in serious hiding.

D-Day + 53
The one with nostalgic bottoms

The decision was made to bus the next one hundred and seventy-six kilometers. This was a decision that the tour organizers did not take lightly. The clanism in Northern Kenya was disharmonious and violent at the best of times between the Borana, Somali and Turkana tribes. Violence had escalated in recent months and staff were uncomfortable with our chances of making it through the next two days unscathed. The road we traveled was referred to as "The Road of Death and Terror". We felt happy to sit this one out.

As we mounted the bus we giggled at Ming who was wearing bike shorts. He was the clever one. For twenty-two kilometers we jiggled slowly and violently over the same corrugated roads we had been cycling, solving our daily riddle of "Can motorized vehicles even drive these roads?" Barely. Every couple of seconds the bus would lurch and body parts would fly in all directions. The bus was slower than the bike and chaffed our behinds in all the wrong places. Everyone experienced shamie-envy as they watched Ming sitting comfortably padded. As we jostled around I couldn't help but wish for the millionth time in Kenya that the route would be steady enough for us to actually see. We were in bandit territory rife with tribal violence. The route appeared mostly desolate with the occasional warrior sheep herder. Through the orange tinted windows we saw dik-diks, baboons, warthogs and many birds of prey. A few ostriches decided to race our bus and effortlessly surpassed us. We dismounted at a camp in the town of Isiolo, the urban gateway to wild Northern Kenya and a city rife with pastoral violence. Though Northern Kenya had a deep history of inter-clan violence, particularly with pastoral and nomadic tribes, the problems were increasing. Climate change, poor governance and an increasing access to heavy weaponry were blamed. The day before our arrival was met with a lot of gun violence in Isiolo. The previous November a tour bus was attacked. The operator was shot and killed and one tourist was seriously injured. We were strongly encouraged to take the next two days and rest within the walls of our comfortable and serene camp. We wisely acquiesced.

D-Day + 54
The one with the crash

Mount Kenya, Africa's second highest mountain, was our first challenge of the day. The gang started the forty kilometers climb to an altitude of two thousand, five hundred meters. My left knee was screaming mad the entire way but I was no longer stressed by pain. "Resting scowl face" seemed fashionable with the locals we met along the route. In a split instant, they would go from looking murderous to the world's warmest if you took the time to greet them properly. The trees also appeared beautifully unapproachable. Thick thorns poked out everywhere giving the appearance of spruce trees covered in icicles. Birds flew by inches from our heads, nature's purest image of freedom. It was a fact that riders started gaining weight in Kenya. Shops like *Wilmer Wonka's General Store*, the *We Serve You To Grow* and the *Nice Café* were hard to resist. The *Plan B Highway Shop* knew its place as it was generally rundown and had bricks missing. We debated over which had the nicer accommodations *God is Able Hotel* or the *Butcher's Hotel*. Different target markets I mused. All businesses had one thing in common, they were painted vibrantly. They share the same bouncy rhythm that unified Kenya. At long last the gang reached the lunch truck at the top of our pass. A foreign bodily sensation came over everyone simultaneously. We were uncomfortable and it took me a moment to realize what it was...cold. Hot's wicked stepsister. Acclimatized to Egypt, I could function perfectly in heat, cold disarmed me completely. I needed a sweater but settled for a bottomless cup of Kenyan chai and a few chapati at a nearby restaurant. Claire, an Australian nurse on staff, joined us to complete our rider profiles.

Right before leaving Claire casually mentioned that we were still in Sharita's good books as she "likes riders who don't fall off their bikes and do leave her alone."

Famous last words.

A few kilometers down the road we had a massive gang pile up. Descending Mount Kenya at quick speed, a matatu cut in front of Jenny. Matatus were kenyan road pirates. These ubiquitous privately owned mini buses, acting as public transport, had a long history of criminality, recklessness, violence and gang connections. In the past few decades, the kenyan police started cracking down on matatu drivers, requiring basic passenger safety precautions and a less offensive setting. Still, passengers would cram into loud matatus and be subjected to rigorous driving, while portraits of famous and infamous people dangled about their heads, clanking on the slogans spray painted on the side bars. Jenny braked hard and Esther and I swerved. I did not swerve far enough and Esther got caught. Her front wheel hit Jenny's back and they both went down. Then Marita rolled over both of them and tumbled. I looked back to a mixture of body parts and bicycle bits and my heart sank. Was this it for the gang? The entire emotional spectrum came flowing out as we yelled at the matatu, grimaced at the bloody road rash, laughed hysterically and finally hugged one another closely. Many locals who had rushed to our aid were perplexed by our confusing display. Unsure of how to help one man imparted his wisest of words "Tomorrow is a new day" then lumbered off across the road. Thankful for no broken bones, we set off to camp, hopeful to remain in Sharita's good books a while longer.

D-Day + 55
The one with heads in toilet bowls

The equator was not an arbitrary line drawn in the sand. Planet Earth decided to wear a belt to hide her bulgiest bits. The sun weighed in. The town of Nanyuki was situated right atop Earth's roll of fat and home to the most infamous of lines. The inhabitants of this privileged town honoured the equator by lining it with toilet bowls. I wondered what the Earth would say to having it's Coriolis effect reduced to a party trick requiring audience members to place their heads in toilet bowls. Perhaps true party goers were already attuned to the Coriolis effect having spent a few too many parties with their heads already there. Nonetheless, we inserted our heads and watched to see if the water would spin in different directions to the North and South. The joke was on us. It turned out that the toilet bowls were more powerful than the rotation of the Earth. Although the Coriolis effect was real, it was all a ruse. We settled in together as a group for the quintessential equator photograph. The gang held hands and collectively leapt across North to South then got on our bikes and pedalled onward. As we cycled for the very first time in the South, we realized quickly that we didn't need tourist tricks to notice change as we were quite attuned to nature. Our first indication was the large termite mounds leaning in the opposite direction. Termites used the sun for thermoregulation and used the surface area of their mounds to maximize basking. The vegetation changed immediately from dry lava rock fields and thorns to dense rainforests, soft gigantic banana leaves and smooth red dirt. The Southern Hemisphere felt kinder, softer and more forgiving.

On our way to camp for the night we passed alluring signs like the *Hot Pot Hotel*, the *Angel Chemist* and the ominous *Highway Butchery* but had to stop to reward a restaurant strongly committed to stopping inflation named *1 Great Cup for 5 Ksh*. We stayed that night at a beautiful camp along the Sagana river. It had an outdoor pool, white water rafting and a bar. We had returned through Alice's looking glass to civilization and although I enjoyed sunning, swimming and drinking I already fiercely missed the Northern Wonderland we left behind.

D-Day + 56
The one with nothing

Just south of the equator, the sun had become a quick riser. The sun put itself to bed quickly at night and bounced out of bed fully awake in the morning without it's usual colourful leisurely morning coffee. We struggled to feel as awake after the previous night's festivities. I had an even greater challenge. This was my day of mental reckoning. The space one navigates on tour is not only physical, but spiritual and emotional. Cycling is very meditative as you release the mind to process and react to things in your life long ignored by it's more conscious bits. Your truth cuts through the noise and demands attention. I was extremely adept at the destructive skill of burying emotion and had a lot to process. One major trauma would be quieted no longer: divorce. In two thousand and seven, I went through a soul crushing divorce. Four years later and it was high time to deal with some residual issues. So, down the rabbit hole I went as tears showered and cleansed my body the entire ride. "You deserve someone so much better" were the words that had ever so politely asked me for a divorce. It still hurt to know that I was not worth original thought. It was not the obvious correctness of the sentence, it was the subtext. You dummy, you don't even care enough about yourself to get out of a relationship in which your partner thinks so little of you that he needs to use the first cliché that pops into his head while ending things. This lack of originality still stung. Cycling south I learned that emotion painted life's experiences. On this day, my emotional landscape stuck in a negative frame. I focused on my closing throat while climbing uphill and convinced myself that the entire day was uphill. My unhealthy mind could see only it's grief. I missed everything beautiful as I wallowed and processed. Then I got to camp in Nairobi and gained perspective.

It was tough to maintain a grumpy disposition as I reunited with four less fortunate cyclists who had been forced to leave the tour due to injury, illness and personal crisis. Peter, Nola, Andrew and Jon were back and their excitement was contagious. Although it had been mere weeks, it felt like years as attachment increases exponentially through shared intense experience. We celebrated together and I found a new frame. I was neither raw nor numb in Nairobi. I was healing.

D-Day + 57
The one with civilization

We awoke to news from downtown Nairobi. Somalis blew up a bus killing six people and wounding many others. Once again we were advised to stay close to camp. Violence was an ever-present threat in Kenya, as a result we would barely scrape the surface of this beautiful country. We had spent days on lava rocks seeing virtually nothing, followed by the bus transfer. We had been confined to camp in the larger cities by threats of violence. In total, we had experienced only four proper riding days of sightseeing and we would soon cross the border into Tanzania. We had missed Kenya, the heart of Africa. I felt profoundly sad as I knew what we were missing. I had visited Kenya the previous year with my friend Angie.

In 2013, I met Amma, Mata Amritanandama. I was living in Tokyo and practicing yoga with an incredible teacher named Paola. Paola inspired me to visit Amma, for which I am eternally grateful. Amma bestowed upon me two precious gifts which I unknowingly needed desperately: her embrace and a mantra. Both deeply connected me to the concept of oneness. My mantra and I have been on quite a journey together since and to this day remains my best way of turning inward while connecting outward. Amma serves and loves absolutely everyone and her selfless devotion is felt and worshiped worldwide. My friend Angie lived by these same principles. I met Angie in August two thousand and ten, when she came to teach alongside me in Cairo. Immediately I was struck by Angie's selflessness when faced with need. Angie would buy clothes and meals regularly for everyone in need on the streets of Cairo, the same people everyone else passed by without a second glance. She walked a longer route home everyday in order to leave food for all the hungry street animals. Also, Angie had adopted an entire extended family in Kenya. When Angie identified a need she took immediate action giving freely everything she had. So, years earlier, when Angie visited Kenya and met a lady with seven children who was in the process of dying, she adopted all seven. Then Angie organized for her new family to be safe and educated in their local community wanting to support "strong Kenyans in Kenya". She provided for everyone in the small village that took care of her children and also for Kasena and Mama Tom's family who overlooked everyone's well-being. She paid for medical bills, schooling, and the basic necessities of life for everyone who Kasena identified in need. Angie understood that not all of her money was ending up exactly where it should be and yet she put it all in perspective stating it as "the cost of doing good". Angie was as close to a saint as I knew and I hoped that her selfless qualities would rub off on me during our two week journey.

In two weeks we visited rural Kenya. The Kenya that exists when you offroad for hours through thick brush to finally arrive at your destination: a small village far removed from the main highway. This was the Kenya that believed in witchcraft and street vigilantism. This was the Kenya in which you couldn't walk barefoot for fear of burrowing worms, but you could sleep on a small mat on the ground. This was the Kenya of communing with nature, understanding the trickier aspects of community and of wheeling and dealing. Backs would break in support of family and yet they would ruthlessly throw a tire around your body and burn you alive if you wronged a member of the community. Kenya was spirited, lively and fierce. To grow strong Kenyans in Kenya was just how to lead the country forward. Angie knew it all along. We had caught glimpses only of Kenya as we struggled to stay upright.

The gang arrived at the Nakumatt, Kenya's superchain grocery store, the workers possessed a quality that relaxed most riders but put me on edge: domestication. Animals lose their fierce spirit once domesticated, so too do humans. The more comfortable, the more placable. There was a tangible emptiness in the sterile and orderly columns of the Nakumatt shopping centre while in contrast, the open air markets and street stalls were bursting at the seams with wares and warmth. The fiery spikes of negotiation and bartering were voided by people pleasing and easy consumerism. A numbness existed in blind fairness while emotions ran high in the more nepotistic of societies. Some beauty must have been held in the fight for resources, an unpredictability that fuelled the heartfire in the hurling of stones. I had come to idolize the wild human spirit above civilization. Although Nairobi felt like a nice mini vacation, sitting in a civilized café sipping decaffeinated coffee and treasuring every awakened taste bud, my soul missed rural Africa. I missed feeling the genuine spirit of the wild. A spirit that does not exist for people who can buy absolutely everything. Emptiness exists in too much order and you start to feel like a screw in the great machine of life. To feel human again, you need to feel closer to Mother Earth, closer to yourself, and understand that basic needs should not be overly comfortable. We would find this Africa soon enough.

D-Day + 58
The one with the dazzle

It was close to the halfway point on tour and twelve new faces graced the breakfast line. Their timing was impeccable as this was the first day we actually saw Kenya. Over one hundred and sixty kilometers of her. Even though a relaxed atmosphere permeated the South, Nairobian drivers seem to risk life and limb getting places fast. Cars would aggressively challenge matatus, and our cycling lane was their battleground. Numerous cars veered into the cycling lane forcing us onto the not-so-soft shoulder, which was oddly filled with speed bumps. Both cars and matatus hurled black soot as they left us in their dust. One car emitted so much soot that I was genuinely concerned it may be on fire. The pavement was unloved. Swimming pool sized holes randomly scattered the pavement for the first fifty-five kilometers.

Nonetheless, we found ourselves overwhelmingly grateful for a little more time to glance up.

Kenya was not at all homogeneous. The tribal look had changed drastically from North to South as did the flora and fauna. We went from dry desert to wet tropics, from camels to zebras, and from charged and harsh energy to feeling tranquil and welcomed. The one feeling that unified the country was it's bouncy rhythm. Like a character invented by Alexander McCall Smith, we passed a sign that read *Sister Blackies Print Shop*. We passed through endless valleys of savanna trees camouflaging small huts. A dazzle of zebras grazed by the side of the road. The gang dismounted and walked a little closer for a photograph. We noticed a foal being shielded by her mom. The foal had the cutest stripy underwear lining his bottom. If the mysteries of mathematics revealed themselves in nature, one would begin with the zebra. Zebras were perfectly striped. We passed through Maasai villages and everyone dressed in vibrant red shukas. The Maasai's shuka, referred to lovingly as the African blanket, was the red fabric often with black stripes draped over most Maasai warriors. Business-savvy detergent companies should clamor to film commercials with the colourful Maasai. Brightly dressed towns moved with such rhythm that they resembled seas of tropical fish being painted in fluid strokes while all the colours of the storybook jumped from the page simultaneously around them. Women wore kilograms of beads all over their bodies. Long-legged men jumped high in the air. These men and women had chosen to be Maasai. They decided against education and married young, often before hitting double-digits. Babies graced parents in the mid teens while life expectancy was around fifty years. I wondered: Was everything more beautiful when enjoyed over a shorter time period?

Students in uniform walking to school in a remote village in Northern Sudan.

School backpack donations at Kebele 03 Elementary School in Ethiopia

A camel slowly decomposing in Wadi Halfa, Sudan.

Curious villagers greeting us at the side of the road in rural Sudan,

The Donkey Shower, Sudanese entrepreneurship.

The little boy who loved pulling faces (directly beside me) and his mischievous
friends in rural Ethiopia.

The soft spoken, polite and calming Salamo showcasing his art.

Hardworking Ethiopian women.

A goat enjoying a salty sweaty snack after the Blue Nile climb.

Discovering the "New Happy" as we departed Ethiopia.

An unwelcome sight for all cyclists.

Culture clash. Young Maasai warriors meet festive tourists on St. Patrick's Day in Tanzania.

The live dunes of Namibia.

Tribesman sitting outside a local shop in Tanzania.

Siblings supporting each other and greeting us warmly in Zambia.

Tanzania

D-Day + 59
The one with graceful ageing

Crossing into Tanzania, I felt relieved that the gang had forgotten to dress up. Even our most elaborate and colourful costumes would be looked upon as dirty rags to the impeccably dressed locals. Tribal lines didn't give two hoots for colonial borders. We saw the same Maasai of southern Kenya in northern Tanzania. Bright red and vivid green shukas covered their bodies. Machetes took the place of spears while menacing scowls remained a source of pride. Sagging was beautiful. Holes wide enough for a three year old to golf a hole-in-one stretched earlobes and lips, while heavy beads and plates dragged both towards their knees. Travel had taught me a thing or two about the concept of beauty. North Americans were obsessed over an extremely narrow stereotype dictated by Hollywood and propagated widely and wildly by the media. I remember my Egyptian friend telling me that I had the hips of a twelve year old boy. Although my body type was strong, leanish and passable in North America, I was hideously small and unattractive in Egypt. Then, in fewer than twenty-four hours, I went from an extra small to an extra large. How was this possible? I moved to Japan. Suddenly I wasn't skinny enough to fit ANY clothing, my arms were way too long and my feet gargantuan. Adding layers to Japan's complexity, Sumo wrestlers were sexy superstars. After three years of living in Japan, I knew it was time to come home when I started lusting after a few Sumo. We were so brainwashed by cultural beauty that it could take a lifetime to redefine the concept oneself. Through living abroad beauty had become a spectrum, but sagging really threw me. Maasai earlobes and lips resembled shrivelling tapeworms dangling helplessly. If I could accept beauty in sagging, then I could do the impossible: age gracefully in the North American culture that fully strips the elderly of dignity. I failed, the dangly bits were unsightly.

For two days we had been asking if every lump and bump in the earth was Mount Kilimanjaro, the highest mountain in Africa. Today, on the halfway point of tour no questions were asked. Our mouths hung in awe at the resounding YES. The snow encrusted peak resembled a cloud. Snow, in Africa. Nothing was more majestic. The gang stopped to bask in mountain magic. While sipping chai and munching chapati we warriors watched. Passing locals hardly glanced at Mount Kilimanjaro. Another niggly aspect to beauty was how quickly human eyes cease to appreciate commonday artistry. Mount Kilimanjaro was a work of art taken for granted by it's closest audience.

Heading towards Arusha, we were rewarded with a stunning downhill. Candelabro cacti and bright purple and orange flowers lined our journey to camp, and to our double rest day. Arusha would be a launching pad to the Serengeti and the Ngorongoro Crater. The gang wasted no time in organizing a safari and then celebrated at the camp's pub. That night would turn into a party of epic proportions, with every cyclist owning their own version of events. What was commonly heard by all was Graham yelling at Ciaran "Get the)!(@ out of my tent!" as Ciaran drunkenly mistook Graham's tiny bump of canvas as his own in the early hours of the morning.

D-Day + 60
The one with hyenas

Observed in their natural habitat, cyclists sleep in until noon on a rest day. It was four forty-five in the morning and I was about to disrupt my first natural habitat of the day. Safari day was upon us so I ran around waking the hungover beasts. Joyce, our safari tour organizer from Tropical Trails, had promised that Stephen, our driver, would arrive at six to take us to the safari camp. Miraculously, Marita, Esther, Alaric, Raphael, Andrew and I all managed to look half awake and ready to go by six. We waited. Normally, "No hurry in Africa" was the gang's mantra, except on safari day. We did not yet know how closely Tanzanians kept time. Luckily, they kept time closer than their Egyptian counterparts who would have "Insha'allah" showed up at all. Forty-five minutes later Stephen raced in brimming with predictable excuses of traffic jams and mechanical failures. His act was almost Oscar-worthy until he saw our "extra person", Raphael had decided to join us at the last minute, and then Stephen decided to go for the gold.

"There aren't enough seats! What will God think of me?" Stephen's brow furrowed so deeply that it appeared his face was being sucked into the abyss of his dramatic thoughts.

Mercifully, his "God" was reconciled at the thought of pocketing the additional fee we would be paying to bring Raphael along. Finally, we set off towards the Ngorongoro Crater.

Somewhere in my subconscious I registered the mystical lush forests on either side of our ride with baboons peering around many bushes, but my consciousness was not allowed freedom of thought. Consciousness was being hijacked by my metabolic dictator. I was not alone. Every cyclist needed at least two breakfasts. Hearing our stomach's protest, Stephen stopped for breakfast and proudly doled out a few slices each of tomato, cheese and bread. Quite possibly, tourists in Africa chose to eat modestly for a variety of good reasons: respect for scarcity, consciousness of poverty, hot temperatures chewing effect on hunger, a stomach rebellion or simply trying to look Instagram worthy in photographs. However, most tourists did not burn an additional five thousand calories per day. This breakfast would not round one edge off our metabolic tirade. Stephen looked like he was a tourist on safari as he watched us voraciously tear through every morsel in sight. He dared not cross us the rest of the day.

We arrived at safari camp around noon. Having been up trying to corral people since the early hours I decided that a little alone time was in order to refresh my spirit. So I wandered. To most, it may be common sense not to wander alone in the bush at a safari camp but with two months of close communion with nature, I had the false belief that Mother Nature was on my side. Also, the locals were doing it. How dangerous could it be? Very. Though we were at the top of the crater, some wild animals fancied themselves athletes and trained by climbing the crater walls. Andrew popped out of nowhere and pulled me close. Fewer than twenty meters away we saw what I could only assume was the world's largest bull elephant. Academically, everyone knows elephants are large. We see elephants from afar at zoos and circuses and think "How mighty!" But the eye is an easily tricked organ, especially in relation to distance or security bars. Without both, elephants are mind blowingly ENORMOUS. One stomp of the foot and you would disappear enormous. I swallowed my North American naivety and decided that nature had no alliances. Together, we hurried back to the safety of camp where we met three spear yielding Maasai warriors. It quickly became clear why the locals were unafraid: they were expert spear throwers. Looking ahead to Botswana's Elephant Highway we decided that we needed professional spear throwing lessons. Had the Maasai seen us within the stomping range of the bull elephant and thought a dead tourist is a useless tourist? Or did they just want a good laugh? Either way, they obliged. We also obliged, providing comedic relief as spears landed everywhere except the intended target. Only Alaric seemed quite expert, landing the spear upright in the ground right on mark. He was a natural African athlete.

We all ate supper together hidden under the canopy of a huge tree and struggled to protect our bounty from the circling eagles. In Canada, birds remained in their realm. As masters of the sky, birds looked ill at ease when forced to ground for grubs for worms. Canadian birds are vulnerable, skittish and flighty. African birds oozed self-confidence and were expert predators. They made no attempt to be endearing and they certainly didn't sing for their supper. Like a ballistic missile, eagles overhead would athletically swoop and steal supper. Our metabolism's daylong hate speech was overpowered by the grit and determination of the African eagle. We lost many good morsels that afternoon.

Dusk was when animals traded their Clark Kent glasses for Superman capes. Having spent all day lulling their neighbours into a false sense of security, at dusk they attacked without mercy as their true spirit preyed on. Day infused nature with the sillies, dusk was the quiet and dangerous calm before the storm of night. At dusk we started our journey into the Ngorongoro crater. As we started the long journey down we passed small villages risking nature to capitalize on tourism. Stephen informed us that all villages within three hundred meters of the main road shared the profits of tourism equally. This seemed at odds with the survival of the fittest mentality within the crater. Perhaps being towards the bottom of the food chain, man had realized the key to survival in Ngorongoro was togetherness. Scientists rebuked the designation of crater. Craters exist atop a volcano but Ngorongoro had imploded, it was a caldera. Ngorongoro was an onomatopoeia answering Will Ferrell's call for more cowbells. It boasted an alkaline white lake teeming with a sea of pink flamingos coloured brightly enough to be spotted from the top of the crater. Moving specs of animal life filled the flat bottom of the caldera. Candelabra cacti the size of houses welcomed us as we made our decent. Vines hung playfully as I pummelled my chest to the tune of "Jana Tarzana!" The air felt energized. Then we met the gatekeeper, a wildebeest. He appeared transcended from the child's book "Where the Wild Things Are". His hideousness was comical. His face, only a mother could love and she was nowhere in sight. If you dared pass the greeting committee you were rewarded with a panorama of zebras and buffalo scattered amongst more wildebeest, just to keep the beauty manageable. A roly-poly zebra rubbed his neck on a tree nonchalantly as we passed. We drove past an entire warthog family. The youngest hoglets were frolicking in mud and then running single file to catch up with Mom who was on her knees to bring food closer to her chronically open mouth. Daddy warthog couldn't be bothered with such foolishness lumbering around in the mud, trying to find his purpose. All forms of deer crossed our path including the bushbuck. Although Disney muddled the rhinoceros with the hippopotamus, they got one mammal dead right, the hyena. Slumped, menacingly satirical, awkward, dangerous, gangly and unpredictable a hyena reared his ugly head and started chasing a zebra, just to be a jerk. This was strange behaviour for an animal which notoriously hunts in packs. Even the zebra seemed alarmed and confused by the hyena's erratic behaviour and jumped quickly out of the way. The hyena kept running, passing the zebra, seemingly on a mission. Then, we noticed between thirty and fifty hyenas coming from every direction and coalescing. Stephen drove quickly, there had been a kill. We drove to the collection point. The lioness was walking away from her prized carcass. Stephen explained that much like flies can ruin a great barbeque, so do hyenas. The lioness, feeling full and annoyed was leaving the spoils to the scavengers. Hyenas literally crawled over one another in a fury to rip flesh from the bone. Their faces were red with blood and bloody flesh was flying in all directions. Every once in a while, one hyena would tear off a prize piece and madly make a getaway with bloody meat hanging from her mouth as she was being chased down by dozens of other hyenas. They are the vampire mammals – once they smell blood they are single-mindedly on a mission. Tenacity is a hyena's strongest characteristic. Their eyes were as ferocious and intense as a lion's claws while attacking their prey.

We moved on and immediately spotted a large rhinoceros and some hippopotami. We drove past the alkaline lake and all of a sudden the flamingos took flight. Black and pink alternated metronomically as they flapped their wings and soared. Flying left then right they created a swirl of so much colour it looked like an invisible painter was broadly stroking pink on his canvas in the sky. As we left the crater we saw a herd of elephants eating thorn bushes by the side of the road. They seemed harmonious and the perfect send off from a truly remarkable place. When we got to camp, it was full of fellow riders. We had dinner together and went to bed early.

D-Day + 61
The one with a lake on fire

We woke up early, had a massive breakfast, then Stephen drove us to Arusha National Park. Our metabolisms quieted, our eyes were free to roam. Three giraffes were munching away on thorn bushes. If you had ever experienced the unpleasantness of being licked by a giraffe, my condolences. One could empathize with Sigourney Weaver when a giraffe opened his mouth. Horror movie producers could have saved millions on special effects if they knew about the giraffe. The experience went something like this. First, the victim is greeted with a fifty centimeter purple monstrosity oozing slime. Then the rough leathery slurp deposits a thick unwashable saliva all over it's poor victim. The rash caused by the harsh sandpaper like tongue quickly sucks in the thick saliva and mars the victim for weeks to come. Giraffe saliva coats thorns and renders them harmless as they descend through a giraffe's digestive system. Giraffe saliva takes it's coating role very seriously and clings for life to whatever it coats. My advice: stay away from affectionate giraffes.

We arrived at the park and were greeted by black and white colobus monkeys simultaneously grooming one another and searching for food. I thought to myself 'How many maintenance-averse groomers would change their tune if bite-sized candies were hidden all over the body?'. No wonder monkeys were so well kept. Two albino baby baboons frolicked by rendering our hearts to mush. Stephen stopped at Lake Natron, the far bank looked to be aflame pink. Handing us binoculars we spotted thousands of lesser flamingos fraternizing with their pat. There was nothing 'lesser' about these flamingos other than their slightly smaller frame. These flamingos were sober socializers, sturdier on one leg or two. They owned their colour name (flamingo pink) and branded it widely to parents who were comfortable with female stereotyping. Their bodies aligned beautifully when taking flight, as if they were privy to the deepest geometric secrets. Lake Natron was the only natural breeding ground for the threatened lesser flamingo and so hosted over two and a half million. The reason Lake Natron was such an ideal flamingo home was that it hosted seasonally formed evaporite islands which served to protect the young from predators. If stress manifests itself through the skin, these flamingos were beautifully relaxed as they glowed brightly. Speckles of red broke through the pink creating a red-blood lake as viewed through NASA satellite. We stayed for over an hour, wishing to bottle the relaxed sensation. We would need it for the upcoming eight-day cycling stretch. Stephen drove us back to camp. He had certainly grown on us after our unfortunate first impression. We had grown on him as well and he decided to tail us a while longer. This was lucky as in two short days his assistance would prove invaluable.

D-Day + 62
The one with rest

We rested.

D-Day + 63
The one with cultures colliding

Day one of eight just so happened to be Saint Patrick's Day. In honour of her primary patron saint, Marita had planned a celebration. Priority one was meddling with the kitchen staff until breakfast was green. Then she enlisted our help with decorating the lunch truck with orange, white and green sheets and balloons. Last, with the extra material from the lunch truck, we made colourful capes and decorated our bicycles. Buck was unimpressed. The gang, joined by Ian, Jurgen, Alaric and Jon painted each other's face with glitter, shamrocks, fake green mustaches and a green button nose. Finally ready, we set off.

If car horns did speak, today drivers rightfully chorused the question mark. It was well worth it to be wearing a cape. The cape was a safety blanket on the roads of Arusha. In a city where matatus took driving lessons from

Nascar, the capes made us appear larger and forced traffic a little further away. Marita had more festivities up her sleeve as she taught us a sea chanty at our first rest stop twenty-five kilometers from town. The Pirate Song, a popular nursery rhyme in Ireland, went like this:

When I was one, I sucked my thumb, the day I went to sea.
I climbed aboard a pirate ship and the captain said to me:
"We're going this way that way, forward, backward, over the Irish seas."
A bottle of rum to warm my tum and that's the life for me!

There were two problems with Marita's chanty. First, it was accompanied by gestures which were hardly conducive to riding a bicycle. Second, it was overpowered by the Bongo Flava that followed us everywhere. It stood to reason that some of the best music in the world would come out of a country whose every move was rhythmic. Tanzanians walking down the street looked like they were dancing to an invisible beat. Crowds swayed together. Rhythm and beat was learned from birth and so it came as no surprise when Tanzanians melded and improved American R&B, rap and hip hop music creating Bongo Flava. Bongo Flava followed the Tanzanian heartbeat. Citizens danced to Bongo Flava as if their body movements determined the next beat. If genetics hummed a tune, in Tanzania it would be Bongo Flava. Bongo Flava made our sea shanty feel domesticated. Nonetheless, it was Saint Patrick's day and we would follow the Irish.

At fifty-three kilometers we saw a new kind of warrior. Three young men were on the side of the road looking outrageously menacing. They were dressed fully in black. They had white patterns painted on their faces and two humongous billowing feathers extending from a headpiece near each ear. They scowled from feathery ear to feathery ear. There was a very good reason for their scowl. They were pre-Maasai. Youth who join the Maasai were circumcised (or re-circumcised if they joined already circumcised, ouch) and then spent three months dressed in black, likely to hide the blood, ostracised from the tribe before being accepted. Sadly, an estimated five percent of young boys died from this tradition. The women were also cruelly mutilated. Although the young three were dressed to look menacing, they appeared frightened young boys when we drew near. Perhaps they wondered what terrible bodily harm we were made to endure before being dressed so foolishly. I felt sorry for them having to endure such pain and wished we had some Irish Bailey's to offer up as a painkiller. A few kilometers down the road, we found our Irish Bailey's at the lunch truck. Shots were handed around which '*warmed our tum*' all the way to camp.

D-Day + 64
The one with Super Sharita

In Military Phase Training of two thousand and one I had my first encounter with mental warfare. After ten exhausting days living on the wet ground, covered in dirt, sweat and grease, staff descended as angels from heaven telling us to "get our shower kit", we were being bussed forty minutes to base for a shower. We pranced gleefully to the yellow school bus and dreamed of scouring hot water cleansing our souls. As we arrived at barrack we suddenly received a shock. The bus did not stop. It continued on past our lodgings and took us forty minutes back into the muddy field for another exhausting four days. Nobody spoke on the bus ride back and more than a few soldiers were close to tears. This cruel ruse broke more than a few spirits. On another occasion, staff, who counted the success of a morning job by how much vomit lined the route, ran the platoon the usual ten kilometers then proceeded to run past what had been our normal stopping point for the previous two months and into an additional three kilometer run. Only a few hundred meters into the three additional kilometers, almost half the platoon collapsed into the ditch. This was a good lesson on how strongly the mind holds expectations. Sometimes it was best not to know what would happen next.

On this riding day, nobody knew what would happen next. This was a new route for staff so relatively little information was disseminated at our rider meeting. We did not know that we would climb over fifteen hundred meters. So we set off in optimism, imagining the road flattening after every turn. We met the off-road with a warm smile. Tanzanian dirt roads were far superior to 'dodgy pavement'. Dodgy pavement was the gang's term for paved roads so potholed and broken that the asphalt felt like steering a toboggan on black diamond moguls. Hard-packed and smooth, these roads allowed me to look around and soak in my surroundings. I was rewarded with green mountains extending far above the blanketing clouds. Endless fields of sunflowers bracketed a road of deep red dirt. Wooden houses were set in plots of land surrounded by well-groomed gardens. Tanzania was extremely picturesque. In every watering hole there were dozens of naked bathers washing alongside black cows. Weaponless kids welcomed us warmly.

This was Iraqw territory. The Iraqw were an agro-pastoralist tribe known for their friendliness to foreigners. They had a great sense of humour, laughing uproariously at us struggling to push and pull our granny gears uphill on dirt. The Iraqw valued education and spoke excellent English. We were so taken with their English that we did not notice the diversion they were so skillfully creating. As a few Iraqw lectured us on the trustworthiness and kindness of their tribe, someone stole L.S's bicycle from the lunch truck. The police were trying their best not to look sheepish. This was a set-up. Little did they know but they had messed with the wrong tour leader. Sharita was upon them instantly, poking at their souls with hot cattle prods and threatening every fiber of their being. She found her informant within minutes. Sharita and Stephen took off in hot pursuit of the thief down a cattle path which ultimately resulted in L.S's bike being returned in one piece. We never learned the fate of the thief and we knew better than to ask. Being instrumental to the success of the mission, Stephen had secured a spot as local hero and stayed on tour for a while to come.

D-Day + 65
The one with serenading

Traditionally, this eight day section had been considered one of the toughest. Often it rained, transforming beautiful dirt roads to quicksand. The off road sections of Tanzania were a wolf in sheep's clothing. Luckily, the wolf stayed fully dressed for us. Not only did the heavens keep to themselves but our Chinese guardian angels had been hard at work paving over one hundred kilometers of the route. As a result, camp unanimously voted this day as the finest on tour. Tailwinds breezily pushed us past sunflower fields, endless rocky outcrops, light blue lakes, mountains and valleys teeming with vibrant flowers. It was like we were effortlessly sitting on a celestial conveyor belt, getting the deluxe tour of heaven's offerings. Stress was stripped clean off our shoulders. Esther, Marita and I rolled into a small shop that reeked of kerosene, that indelectable smell that triggered salivation for freshly baked chapatti, mandazi, and delicious chai. If you ever wonder what happened to all the well constructed floral patterned plastic thermoses from camping trips in the 1970s, rest assured they are still put to good use. Kenya and Tanzania serve chai exclusively in these large thermoses. Holly showed up and we ate and drank for over an hour, then pedalled to the lunch truck. Full beyond capacity, Esther, Marita and I settled in at lunch for a two hour nap.

Groggily, we awoke and got back on our bikes. As we were last from lunch, we would be riding with Katarina, the tour's public relations staff member and today's sweep. Tailwinds welcomed us and pushed us a few kilometers to town. A local man ushered us to the P.H. Dinery and sat with us as we ordered beverages. Our local tour guide seemed to take a liking to Katarina and he started serenading her with some homemade Bongo Flava.

"I will take you to my love pad, uh-huh, uh-huh, you are like black tea, spend time with me, oh yeah, oh yeah!"

As his beat progressed he threw in some quotes from Little Wayne and Rihanna. We heard Rihanna everywhere in Tanzania, the country was infatuated. I wondered if Rihanna knew what a market she had with the Iraqw tribe. I later learned that Rihanna donated bicycles, time and resources in support of education in both Tanzania and Malawi. She gave back to the people who loved her most. We bid adieu to our new musical friend and set off for a leisurely and uneventful ride to camp. Bliss.

D-Day + 66
The one with the spot changing leopard

Some riders were descendents of gatherers, collecting images and experiences as they leisurely cycled down the continent. Others were descendents from hunters, racing to accomplish their daily mission of arriving at camp. Alaric was a hunter, who on this day hung his helmet in hopes of trying his hand at gathering. Racers were allowed a few days "off" to see the sights, heal, or fix mechanical problems that arose en route. Alaric picked poorly, deciding to cycle with the gang, a group of veteran gatherers who had spent sixty-seven days perfecting the gathering skill set. The gang knew exactly how long to relax at various points throughout the day without recklessly jeopardizing EFI. The gang knew how to suddenly rest and relax the high adrenaline of cycling, and how to get back on a bike after the utmost in relaxation. We trained our bums, heads and hearts to enjoy every moment.These were not easy skills to master. It was foolhardy to think a racer could drop seamlessly into our world and Alaric was as woefully unprepared as we would have been racing. He got titchy after our first long rest stop and we lost him the second as he took off racing, unable to lounge another second. Alaric's need to go fast was just as primal as was ours to go slow. I began to understand something I previously hadn't, if racing was in your blood, wouldn't you prefer racing in beauty? I had often wondered why racers chose this tour, instead of racing closer to home, when sightseeing was not a possibility while racing. Surely some beauty soaked in even if your eyes were fixed straight ahead.

We cycled passed goats frolicking in all directions like caffeine brimmed ballerinas learning to grand jeté. Cows brawled, leveraging with their humps. Perhaps both animals learned their actions from the multitudes of drunk and disorderly men who sat about the towns drinking hootch. Moonshine and potent home brews had taken over entire generations of males in many parts of Africa. Cyclists were also not the model of sobriety, stopping to 're-hydrate' frequently. On the way to lunch Marita stopped by the side of the road and picked a sunflower for Noah. Noah was a valued staff member and the kind of guy who radiated joy. His smile would warm the devil himself and may even convince the devil to look on the brighter side of life. Noah's humour and gracious attitude toward life was exemplary and needed especially on 'dead-camel-esk' days. We bought Noah some mandazi at a local shop, and Marita secured the sunflower to her backpack. The sunflower had the same sunny disposition and penchant for travel as Noah. It voyaged expertly not losing a single petal all the way to the lunch truck. The gang presented him with the small token and Noah radiated, as usual. It was small moments of kindness on tour that would affiche themselves the most firmly to our grey matter. Noah's smile would warm us all for years to come.

D-Day + 67
The one with the dance party

Often legends retire after great feats. This is to preserve their legendary memory without tarnish. But the truly inspired don't give a rats ass for public opinion, they do what they want, when they want, for no obvious reason and always with passion. Sharita was an inspired legend, and on this day she rode her bicycle for the first time on tour. The gang first saw Sharita while we took a break high on a rocky outcrop. She had a follower in close pursuit. Although Sharita had started her journey on a well equipped tour bike, she quickly found the seat too plush and somehow finagled to exchange bikes with a local man. He was dutifully riding behind her to the lunch truck. Like disciples, the gang raced down the rocks and onto our bikes in hot pursuit. Hitting record breaking speeds the outcome looked positive until we encountered our Achilles Heel at the twenty-ninth kilometer: chai and chapati. Sitting at an outdoor table we were quickly joined by Shona, Bev, and Bob, an American Vietnam war vet who lovingly referred to chapati as "that pancake thing". Bob was a strong and practical cyclist who had his own way of doing things. He had strong opinions but also an open-mind, forging many friendships by making time for conversation with the locals the entire way down Africa. We left the café knowing Sharita was long gone. Therefore, we were surprised to find her missing at the lunch truck. Soon enough a motorcycle drove in close with a bicycle attached to it's rear. Another brought Sharita. Sharita knew how Africa was meant to be done. Africa's unpredictability outweighed everything and needed to be reminded who was boss. Unquestionably, the answer was Sharita.

A few kilometers from the lunch truck, the gang cycled through a small town vibrating with some serious Bongo Flava. The rhythm was bouncing around in our souls so we got off our bicycles and pretended to be interested in electronics to hear more. The locals were onto us. Three men were watching. One had a silent and perhaps fake ghetto blaster around his neck and he was swaying to the music. It was irresistible. We swayed alongside him and suddenly we were swarmed. Hundreds of locals came to dance or watch our dance circle which formed outside the electronics shop. One older man barely weighing one hundred pounds came towards the center and started shimmying his lower extremities and gyrating his hips so much that I can only assume it was his African response to Elvis. We tried our hand at some local dance moves and nobody laughed. This town was certainly a community that valued individual expression. Barriers broke quicker than a forty-two week amniotic sac and we were introduced fully to the African heartbeat. Everyone experienced the mysticism of oneness, as the music seemed to come from within each dancer. Then Sharita, Katarina, Annelot and Noah drove through town. We had never seen the staff truck halt so quickly as Sharita popped out and entered our dance circle, camera in hand. We knew then that we had accidentally discovered how Africa was meant to be done. It was Sharita-approved. We danced for over forty minutes to the local groove but eventually we had to get back on our bicycles. This dance party remains my fondest memory of the tour.

As we cycled away Martin, the lucky staff member on sweep, eased our sadness by teaching us the Jambo song:

"Jambo, Jambo Sana, Habari Gani, Mzuri Sana.
Mageny, Macariboishi, Tanzania, Hakuna Matata.
Serengeti, Hakuna Matata"

The song came in particularly handy at a rest stop in the afternoon when a man made us sing for our supper. He handed us maïze as a recompense. Tanzania was opening his arms widely and we were relaxing into them.

D-Day + 68
The one with the brakeless stop

Inspired by the non-consuming dance party we decided to have a few calorie-free stops. We climbed a few trees. We stopped at a bridge to splash in the water – well most of us did. I was not fearful of much in life, but when a personal friend started seizuring, had brain surgery and a stroke due to a parasite collected by swimming in the Mekong Delta it convinced me to steer clear from unknown swimming holes. I stayed dry on the outskirts talking with a few local fisherwomen and kids. They proudly showed me their catch which strongly resembled toilet fish.

Toilet fish became a known species in two thousand and eight, while travelling with my sister Min in South East Asia. We headed to the Tham Kong Lo Cave in Khammouane Province, Laos. The cave was a thing of folklore, not written in guidebooks but passed orally between foolish and intrepid travellers.

"It is like the River Styx meets Lord of the Rings." raved one traveller.

"The best place I have ever seen in all my travels." exclaimed another.

To get to the cave, we begged our friend for a handwritten note in the local language stating something to the effect of "Please help these idiots, they will need it."

To get to the village we rode on the back of tractors and donkey carts. We were put up in a small house stilted from the ground to prevent flooding. Our hosts knew neither English, nor why we were there. They laughed at us as we tried to communicate using the language provided at the rear of Lonely Planet's Guide to Laos. Clearly our intonation was lacking. They were kind and served us fish for supper accompanied by a long strange bean growing in pods on a nearby tree. These pods tasted more fishy than the fish and I kept wondering if we were being poisoned for insulting their family by accident in broken Lao. When my stomach rumbled and I asked to use the loo I was greeted by an audience. Right beside the toilet was a white styrofoam aquarium of fish, the fish we had just eaten. Toilet fish. Knowing a male's ability to aim their most precious appendage, I wondered how many yellow drops had sullied the toilet fish water over the years, then almost threw up. Our hosts did not try to kill us, even if they had wanted to there was simply no point, we were about to do that ourselves. The next morning our guides met us at the cave entrance armed with narrow wooden boats outfitted with small motors and battery operated headlamps. We hopped on board cheerfully then noticed how unstable the boat felt. Nonetheless, we entered the seven kilometer cave, immediately regretting our decision. The ceiling of the cave was vaulting three hundred feet high with cracks that created cascading waterfalls spread sporadically throughout. It looked like water gushed from the night's sky as we could not see the ceiling of the dark cave. Suddenly our guide yelled and our boat almost capsized as we hit an underwater stalagmite. Not being a tourist destination, no route was carefully planned out, no safety measures were in place. Reality hit all at once, our legacy would be winning the Darwinian award. We were floating on the unknown, in an unknown direction, and if we dunked, which was a REAL likelihood, the C batteries illuminating our route would die immediately. We would be treading water for seven kilometers through the cave's current in absolute darkness with tremendous waterfalls pushing our bodies under for stalagmites to use as pinballs. In other words, we would not make it. It was too late to go back to safety so we surrendered to Hades as he directed our fate between the underworld and the world of the living on this very real example of the River Styx. As you can guess by the fact that this travel memoir was written, we made it out the other side and thanked Hades for not wanting us. A few years later, Tham Kong Lo Cave was mapped, lit and organized to be a tourist attraction. Our experience could never be recreated, the same undomesticated beauty was never to be seen again. Hades had been evicted.

I hadn't seen toilet fish since our adventure in Laos, but here they appeared in Tanzania. I touched their squirming scales which made a few locals clap in joy. One of the women gestured to listen to my music so I put on Shakira's Waka Waka (This time for Africa) but she did not know it. As we were leaving one of the young boys hopped on Esther's bike and took off pedalling furiously. Esther hopped on the boys bike and trailed him in hot pursuit. It was not easy. Esther zigzagged across the road and struggled to gain ground on such a beat up single gear bike. Finishing his joyride, the boy came back and dismounted. A few moments later we saw Esther riding in fast and yelling "Look out!". The bike had no brakes. We evacuated the path. Friction and gravity eventually got the upper hand as she slowed to a stop many meters away. The boy laughed uproariously and then showed us the secret to stopping. He rode forward, quickly took off one flip flop and stuck it in the spokes. It flapped away as it hit each spoke and stopped the bike relatively quickly. Wonderfully resourceful!

D-Day + 69
The one with the award

Even though I had cycled over five thousand kilometers, I was a complete amateur. The evidence was everywhere. Not only did the international men and women in lycra race past me daily, but the locals scoffed at our lack of bicycle command. They passed us effortlessly while balancing crates of Coca Cola and textiles on their bikes, lunch sacks on their heads and four of their best friends standing casually on any tiny protruding piece of bicycle frame. Cycling was a primary form of transportation in Tanzania. It was no wonder. Soft orange dirt layered with packed sand made riding a bicycle feel like floating on cloud nine.

Even though the cycling conditions were sublime, my body was unimpressed. It protested in many small ways. A small skin breakout here, a swollen elbow for no obvious reason there. Strange fingernail bed patterns here, a hip that would suddenly and strangely lurch there. The gang arrived at camp amidst cheers, but quickly discovered they were not for us. The camp was hosting a local soccer tournament and the entire village had come to watch. For the first time on tour we held zero fascination, and the feeling of unimportance comforted me. I was never much one for fanfare. Fanfare did come later that afternoon at the rider meeting when Sharita had an unexpected surprise. An impromptu awards ceremony. She handed out a few awards to riders who "left her alone and didn't fall off their bikes" then she gave the gang an award I still hold more dear than my eventual tour completion medals: "Spirit of TDA". Sharita explained "What your group does is how Africa is supposed to be done". I glowed with pride. She mentioned how we were what this tour was all about; community. Our playful interaction with the world was important because Sharita told us so. Africa's embodiment told us so. We felt it in our hearts. Humanity's greatest evolutionary ally was not seriousness, the careful study of useful traits, but playful - nature's creativity yielding unexpected results.

D-Day + 70
The one with Africa's foul mood

The fanfare went to our heads and the gang got ballsy on day eight. All the fabulous Tanzanian riding days had blurred our frames as we missed two important details: today was a MANDO day (exceptionally difficult) and Sharita had mentioned an "epic climb" in a rider meeting. Proud of our award, Esther, Marita and I set off cycling with our newly validated light-hearted attitude. Our first stop was fewer than ten kilometers from camp as Marita and Esther struggled to tune the transistor radios hanging around their necks. This

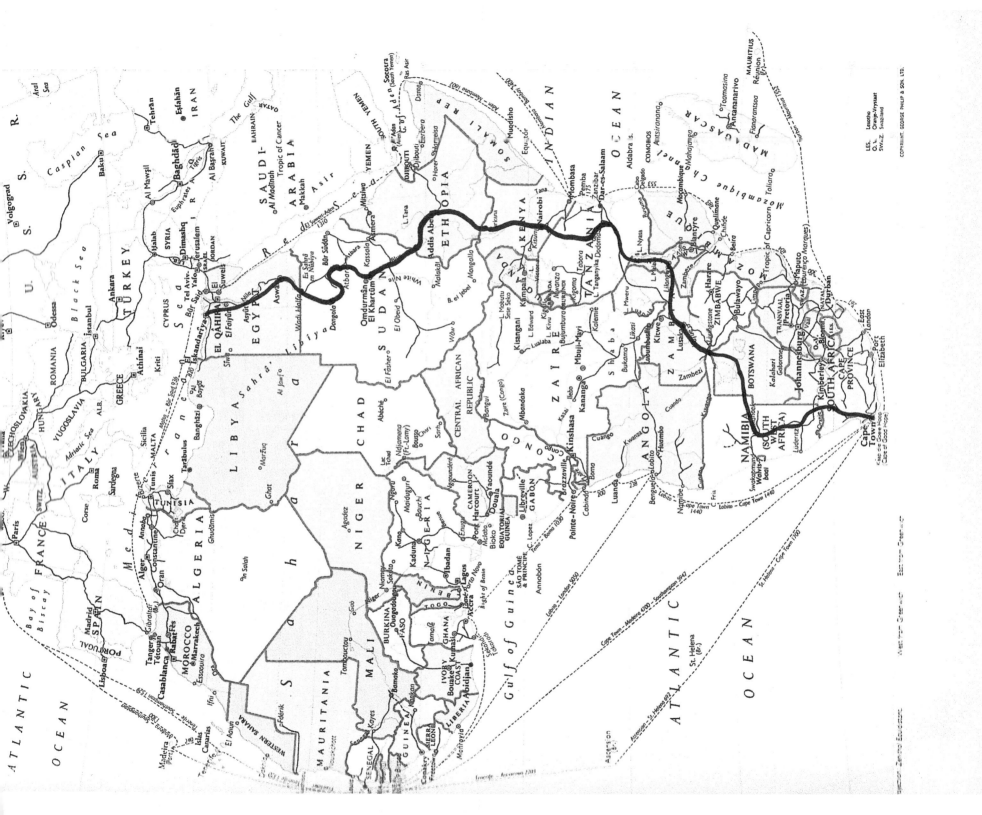

should have been our first indication of mountain interference. Radios crackling, we cycled on and found our first small river twenty kilometers from camp. This being only a measly one hundred and eight kilometer day we decided to take a nature break. Marita and Esther were joined by L.S for a leisurely swim and joked about how splendid it would be to be swept by Doug and ride with him for the day.

Many aspects of our morning lulled us into a false sense of security. Firstly, the morning was full of climbing which falsely reassured us that we were gaining ground on the two thousand four hundred meter high point. Second, the off road was good. Not quite better than dodgy pavement as rocks splayed everywhere, but we were able to maintain a respectable pace. Oblivious to what lay ahead, we stopped to have a nice chai and chapati in honour of Rosemary, it was Marita's mother's birthday. Unfortunately, it took us a long while to find chai in the village. Some nice local eventually led us down an alley into a very basic room that existed behind all the storefronts in some sort of parallel universe. It had two tables, eight chairs, a cup holder on the wall and a square hole where a window was missing. This local coffee shop served up some of the best chai we had on tour, so we savoured every long minute of it. Then we had another, along with more chapati and mandazi. We decided to quarrel over the bill for way too long and left far too close to lunch time. We felt glad when the road continued uphill, perhaps this climb was deemed epic as it lasted all morning? Not so. Very suddenly the road worsened and we hit the wall of headwind which only exists at elevation. My bike stopped in a ditch and I clipped out just in time to get a leg down before toppling over. We caught up with Manuel, a sectional rider on tour, who was in a complete frenzy. His derailleur was completely off and he was trying to cycle using only one gear, very unsuccessfully on the new steep incline. Where bodily problems are ignorable, mechanical failure is not. You can do it, but you are completely helpless without your partner. We tried to help unsuccessfully - Manuel needed a bike mechanic. Manuel eventually decided to run his bike over ten kilometres to the lunch truck. He made it there thoroughly exhausted and unable to complete the day, adrenaline and frustration eating away at his energy stores the entire time. At the lunch truck, we told ourselves we would leave by one o'clock. At one, I discovered my flat tire. I pumped up my tire convincing myself that it was a slow leak so that we could leave more quickly. I was starting to feel frenzied now. Things were stacking up against us quickly and I realized that EFI meant more to me than I allowed myself to consciously recognize. Immediately from lunch we started another massive dodgy climb on red dirt paths into a strong headwind. The gradient felt akin to climbing the Canadian Rocky Mountains, but the route was unpaved and treacherous. We had to dart off road to let vehicles pass so that we didn't accidentally fall into their trajectory. Feeling quite victorious after the first great climb we stopped and I pumped up my near flat tire again. At that moment, we had our first true look around and surrendered into the beauty; we were so high that the sky had distinct shadings of blue. Deep rich blue lined the base of the mountain while we were in a light green sky. Every colour on the spectrum existed in between. The clouds were so close that we felt we could reach out and touch them. We had to stop a few times for photos.

I got another flat. I was worried.

Marita did her best to comfort me stating "Jana has her pre-exam face on. We'll make it. We are at the top there, there is nowhere higher than there."

She pointed to the top of our current mountain pass. This was a very reasonable assumption. It was the only seemingly passable mountain peak. Nonetheless I pointed to a steep peak far off on Loleza Mountain.

Marita replied "There is NO WAY to get up there, we are fine."

Honestly, she was right. It did not look possible, we could barely even see the peak over the clouds. I relaxed a little until Sharita showed up. We were alarmed to see that she too had her "pre-exam face" on. At first, we stopped her at first to quip about the steep hill we had just climbed. Her reply made my veins run cold:

"You haven't even started the epic climb yet."

Our hearts stopped. It was three in the afternoon and we had fifty kilometers to go with an "epic climb" thrown in that we had not yet begun. Sharita told us of the massive off-road climb that lay ahead with some of the dodgiest roads to date. She told us if we did not leave immediately and push harder than we had ever pushed before, we were sure to not make it. The thought that it was close to April Fool's Day passed through my mind but her face betrayed no hint of humour. Sharita was serious. So we hopped on our bicycles and pedaled quicker than ever before on tour. I caught a flat tire five kilometers down the road and decided immediately to change the tube. Sharita stopped again and watched us, I could tell she was worried and rooting for us to succeed. We were three of the last four girls who still had EFI on tour. It would have been a crushing blow. Thanks to Esther's help, I changed the tube quickly and willed my legs to pump wildly. This was no April Fool's Day joke: the climb was EPIC. Long, steep, and jagged we pedaled through switchbacks. Glances of beauty and a seemingly never ending climb. I didn't even know I had it in me to pedal the way I was.

Doug was shocked by my climbing stating "Aren't you slow on hills?"

I pushed with adrenaline the first half, then became VERY scared as I started to experience extreme, uncontrollable exhaustion. The type where your brain feels threatened by your body. Warning signs leapt from my legs to my brain signaling failure in the form of extreme cramping. Like giving birth through your legs. I wasn't certain that my legs would make it, they came within a hair of collapse. I cycled over rocks and ditches in a state of madness, being driven by sheer will and drive. I cursed the man-made invention of time. My entire body was screaming after eight days on the bicycle and I was too panicked to even bargain with it. Suddenly, I caught Wossen, a sectional rider. For the first time I felt a glimmer of hope that I would make it. Even though every cell in my body was under extreme duress the beauty surrounding me spoke to my gathering spirit and I stopped occasionally for a desperate picture. Sharita kept showing up at various points throughout the climb, and although I'm sure she would deny the fact, she wanted to be there for us in support, should we need her. Finally, the unlikely happened - we made it to the top. It felt like weeks had passed since our quip to Sharita about the bump we had climbed earlier that day. The top was the most stunning scenery on tour. We were above the clouds looking down at endless valleys and small towns. The clouds beneath us were softly raining or gushing out waterfalls on the towns beneath. I had a quick scenic pee. We still had sixteen kilometers downhill and it was five in the afternoon. Sharita still looked incredibly worried. The downhill consisted of the roughest road of the day. Not rocks but boulders littered the road and shook us silly. My chain fell off after going over a bump and I went off the road completely, almost colliding with a large boulder. That was the moment I realized that I was past the point of making good decisions on the bike and I was a menace to anyone around me. I stopped trying to keep up with Esther on her mountain bike and I took off alone at my own pace with no additional distractions. I shook until every organ felt loose, Buck shook to his breaking point. EVERYTHING was worn and exhausted; my legs from pedaling, my hands from gripping the bars and steering to find the best route, my neck was seized and I could no longer turn it without blindingly sharp pain. My ankles hurt, my knees screamed and I didn't know how much further I could go on. Once again, my spirit was incredibly close to breaking. I was worried about permanently damaging my neck and then I narrowly missed the wipeout of the tour. There was a bike-sized deep hole between the offroad section and pavement. It swallowed Mike a little earlier. Getting off Buck and crossing safely to pavement I seriously considered throwing myself on the ground and kissing it wildly. It was delectable, I knew I had made it. To add one more layer to the hardest day of my life it started to rain. In a few kilometers, I saw camp and started shaking all over. Steve came out to give me a big hug, so did Andrew. They were likely propping me up as I was a complete wreck. I was wild with the adrenaline of survival. Everyone was so happy to see us as they were worried that we would not make it, as it was past six o'clock. Even Sharita looked relieved and gave high praise.

"Well done."

It meant the world. We had earned survival in the EFI club one day longer. It had been the second largest climbing day on tour with over two thousand meters of elevation, AND on the off road AND off the heels of seven days of cycling. How had we not taken the day more seriously? We had been ballsy and now Africa had reminded us of who was in control. Exhausted to the core, I fell asleep at the supper table in the MBeya hotel. As I transferred into a hotel room for the night I wondered how close I had come to finding my outer limits. So close I could reach out and touch their walls. It was the energy given by Esther, Marita and Sharita that day, which extended those walls just enough to arrive. I owed this day to them.

D-Day + 71
The one with healing

It was comical to think that I used to feel guilty about resting on rest days. This rest day in MBeya was devoted to the essentials. I loved every sweet moment of the quiet life. Everything I owned was damp so I set it all up in the sun. I washed and dried every article of clothing including my helmet and gloves. I aired out my sleeping bag. I ate. I wrote. I looked at Ming's pictures. I relaxed to the sound of rain pouring onto the roof of my room as the call to prayer sounded in the background. I was finally alone. I need to be alone to heal. I needed to wash away the previous day in order to start fresh. I would soon discover that the word 'fresh' did not exist in Chewa, Malawi's official language.

Malawi

D-Day + 72
The one without farts

Before departing MBeya, the gang dressed as Tanzanian hipsters. We wore our best fedoras, swung transistor radios around our necks, wore baggy shorts and lots of bling, pulled our socks up high and taped around our legs and arms. We tuned our radios to some serious Bongo Flava, thanked the pavement under our bike wheels repetitively and soaked in our newfound freedom to look around. The first clue that we were headed towards humidity was the lady we passed carrying a machete on her head. We were in a tropical paradise with lush vegetation for as far as the eye could see. Tessellated tea plantations felt optically spiritual while the leaves on nearby trees and plants made us feel infinitesimal. We cycled by a cabbage patch that made me giggle. I kept imagining plastic dolls popping up haphazardly with a tattooed derrière and a birth certificate in hand. Somehow I felt a little morbid eating the delicious cabbage supper prepared by our chef later that night. Women were outside working wherever we went. Kids played happily nearby, practicing handstands and acrobatics while death-defyingly carrying their smaller siblings. School-bound teenagers in bright red uniforms waved at us while travelling by foot, bike or donkey cart. Brick houses with thatched roofs resembling nice Canadian chalets were built into the side of hills and mountains to enjoy tremendous views. The clouds played with the mountain tops and we felt on top of the world. I was enjoying the serenity when a monkey wrenched me out of my stupor by running directly in front of my bicycle as I was speeding downhill. Luckily, he was an agile monkey. His quick leap made for an unexpectedly spectacular moment rather than the tumble of tour. At the base of the hill we saw a transport truck in the ditch. The driver was nowhere in sight, hopefully unharmed. Within a few hundred meters we came upon a large street sign that boldly pronounced "END OF THE DANGEROUS ZONE". Desperately, we wanted to believe.

So, when five imitation hipsters came barrelling into town doing their best Tom Cruise imitation and singing "Highway to the Danger Zone" the locals took notice. Although English was scarce one local man sat with us and ordered chai and chapati on our bill. Another approached us gesturing if we needed him to fix our bikes. Both seemed to think something was dreadfully wrong, our brains or our bikes.

At the border crossing we stopped for a *Konyagi* – Tanzania gin-akin. Celebrations were in order as we were officially halfway through our ten countries. This was a bad idea. As soon as we crossed the border a fierce competition ensued for what could raise our temperatures and expand our blood vessels the most, alcohol or extreme humidity. It felt like we were drinking heavily in an invisible hot tub. There was a reason that Malawi had passed "Malawian Air Fouling Legislation" in 2011, making it illegal to fart in public. Humidity spread scents like a living wet blanket and nobody wanted to be permanently dutch ovened. We were headed into the eye of the storm as our final destination was lovingly called "Humidity Camp". With the border crossing, the roads became desolate. Of the thirteen million Malawians, fifty-three percent lived quite below the poverty line. Cycling to camp we barely saw a soul because they were all at our camp already. Humidity camp was ALSO lovingly named "Camp Hefty Theft", in which unwatched items were swallowed at dusk. Tour staff had organized a local security guard to prevent theft, but he had his own agenda: eat as much as he could get his hands on and interject our lesson on Malawi's profile with enthusiastic details. Twice redirected to watch the tents for theft, twice he pulled up a chair and sat in on our meetings amiably. Needless to say a few items vanished in the humidity that evening.

D-Day +73
The one with dehydrating sardines

In the night, our tents sunk three inches into mud. Our muddy wobbly water-bed would have been quite luxurious if humidity wasn't such a heavy blanket. It felt and smelt like being inside a dog's mouth just after he nibbled on a few pieces of his own feces. I escaped my tent and regrouped. My cleansing efforts in MBeya were completely in vain as every single belonging was drenched and disgusting. Odor waged war on my brain. Sweat smelling like sweet acrid papaya drenched my nasal hair and refused to dry. With an estimated fifth of this land-locked country being water, nothing dried in Malawi. As we cycled from camp in oppressive heat and humidity I felt unusual. My body sensed danger in this moist breeding ground for bacteria and viruses. My endorphins ran off in search of dry land and opened the floodgates for panic and despair. Nonetheless, we forced ourselves to move quickly and raced to the local grocery store. Sharita had ordered us to do so. Or else starve. The choice was ours. For the next two nights we would stay at Chitimba Camp on Lake Malawi. Although they easily housed and fed over sixty guests, they could not meet our voracious demand for food. According to Chitimba Camp's previous experience with Tour d'Afrique our sixty-two staff and riders would eat as much as over two hundred 'normal people'. They couldn't keep up with demand. So that left us with the local grocery store, which seemed to have known we were coming.

American brands lined their shelves at American prices. I quickly surmised that with so many locals suffering below the poverty line, this grocer made his living on this day alone. I stocked up on CornFlakes, yogurt, chips and Malawi gin. Our appetites whetted, Marita, Esther and I got back on our bikes and headed toward camp. We lost our appetites within a few kilometers as we breathed in the remaining moisture of drying sardines. I remember wondering how they could ban flatulence but keep the world's stinkiest little fish! There they were, on the beach for as far as the eye could see, thousands of sardines sunbathing on wooden racks. They would have been beautiful but their silvery sheen was outdone by their absolutely putrid odor. Somehow, young children and their parents were blissfully sleeping in the shade underneath the sardines as dozens of youth frolicked in the surrounding sand. When life hands you dehydrating sardines, get the heck out of dodge by any means necessary. Which is what Marita and Esther did, commandeering a small wooden boat unconcerned that it was already filled to the brim with exuberant youth in various stages of nudity. They jumped, toppled and tipped into the refreshing water, laughing uproariously as I watched enviously from the beach wondering if the odor would wash out of both skin and lycra.

At camp, I decided to find out. Cautiously, I dipped into Lake Malawi, the fourth most voluminous freshwater lake in the world. Although Lake Malawi looked like a tropical paradise surrounded by green tabletop mountains, birdsong, palm trees and perfect sand, the water told a different story. It was warm and yellow; urine-filled bathwater. I exited feeling slightly less clean. Yet Lake Malawi held the world record for number of fish species, with over one thousand thriving in the murky depths. Instead of swimming, I settled on some beach volleyball and snacking, two of my favourite pastimes. There was a campfire on the beach which set the mood perfectly for Malawian Moon Cake. Mercifully, I declined.

D-Day + 74
The one with paralysis

Malawi is where magic goes to hone it's craft. Witch doctors proudly display their credentials roadside, in ever-present tug-of-war with the natural world. Mysteries hang thickly in the air, ready to streak past innocent bystanders. The cure for the vision is an Illusion as Malawi toys with man's favourite homemade concept of time. In Malawi, where dimensions are revealed in every humid droplet, drugs have to up their game. By living so closely to the mystery, Malawians already feel other-wordly. Their drugs need to boost an engine already running at full capacity. To outsiders, Malawian drugs were paralytic. Literally. The night before a few intrepid cyclists had eaten Moon Cake. They remained at the outdoor picnic table over twelve hours later. Because they were so relaxed and enjoying each other's company? No. They couldn't feel their legs. They had sat for the majority of the night, waiting for sensation to return, lapsing in and out of time. Their sense of time did not fully restore for days thereafter. Malawi was powerfully intruding in every sense.

D-Day + 75
The one of resourcefulness

Our twenty kilometer climb from Lake Malawi was an individual time trial. Riders left at intervals and our completion time was recorded in the race timings. You would think after seventy days of cycling, my legs would have developed a few muscles. You would be wrong. Three things suggested otherwise. First, I was passed by many cyclists. Second, I was passed by a nine year old boy on a single-speeder. But the most telling of all, I was passed by a monkey. This monkey obviously wanted to show off his true blue derrière, so blue that it looked as if he had spent the day sitting in a robin's nest. Every so often he would stop and wait for me to catch up. That was considerate. With taunting like this it was no wonder the cattle appeared suicidal. They lined steep cliff edges without even enough space to turn safely. These cows obviously fashioned themselves as dexterous goats, not knowing that they were in actual fact chunky clods about to plummet. The cows peered at me as if I was crazy, which made me laugh out loud. Finally I arrived at the top. Everyone was lounging on the ground grumbling about moisture and Moon Cake. It was very natural to be miserable in humidity. In the dry heat of the desert, nothing lived. The only real threat was dehydration and that could be controlled (the illusion existed nonetheless). In Malawian humidity, everything lived. A lot of what lived was microscopic and wasn't friendly. It was entering our bodies with each breath, often flooding our brains with strong scents and tastes. We couldn't even hold the illusion of control, which led to large amounts of grumbling. So we pushed on to lunch, hoping for the day to pass as quickly as possible. At lunch, we witnessed Bob's ingenuity first hand. A cap on his tooth had come loose so he had bought superglue from the grocery store. He was in the process of supergluing his cap back on his tooth. Bob didn't question things, if they made sense he just did it. Bob was an admirable doer. Bob would keep supergluing his cap in place for the remainder of the tour. He left Cape Town still in possession of the cap. Victory was his.

D-Day + 76
The one without the Lorax

Viphya Forest, the largest man made forest in Africa, needed The Lorax. In the morning, the gang cycled past Viphya's devastating deforestation with fields that were once dense forests, now reduced to vacant stump cities. Malawian exportation prices of lumber were comparably so cheap that forests were being depleted at a rate as high as 2.6 percent annually. In two-thousand seventeen, the Malawian army was called upon to protect Viphya from illegal deforestation, as water supply was finally threatened in Lilongwe, Malawi's capital city. It took a humanitarian crisis to stop practices that were clearly so unethical. Trees lay rotting in fields. To further debase, we cycled past two men pleasuring themselves while looking directly at us. This was not the same Africa. It was devastating and we had to witness it in slow motion as we cycled uphill for one thousand nine hundred meters.

Malombo, a local cyclist, had decided to join us for the morning. He was one of ten children, hoping to marry later this year. He told us that he only wanted two children so he could care for them properly. Malombo informed us that North Malawi was very divided from South Malawi on the issue of the dowry. In the North, the bride joins the groom's family so it is considered much better to have boys. In the South, the groom joins the bride's family so it is considered better to have girls. I wondered how this example of dynamism within a country may help to balance the rigidity of other cultures. We cycled past gigantic white mushrooms for sale, women carrying wood and water on their heads, drunken men. Up into smells of acrid hashish, moldy cheese, decay and sweat. The smells of town.

Feeling the need for an immediate rest from our emotional morning, the gang stopped in town even though it was only two kilometers to the lunch truck. Malawi was best explored olfactorily so we followed our noses into the labyrinth of huts, markets and awnings in our regular search for chai. The markets were full of various types of fish, tomatoes and many other ripe vegetables. The children looked at us apprehensively as we walked through the maze to the carefully hidden and best smelling shop. Jackpot! A kind lady served hot chocolate in orange plastic cups and chips piled high with cabbage and tomatoes. There was a full salt lick placed on the table and fabulous African beats poured from a nearby ghetto blaster. A man came to tell us that a truck with "friends" had stopped. Esther and I hurried out of the maze to greet Sharita, Ian and Bev, who were surprised to see us emerge from the depths of the small village, hot chocolate in hand. They joined us, everyone adored this little unassuming spot. Sharita even paid for our meal, which was unexpectedly appreciated. Two kilometers down the road, second lunch was as wonderful as the first. That night at camp the Malawian sky decided to put on it's red dress and dance. The intimacy of the Malawian sunset is a passionate affair. Colours pull, push and drag each other all over the dimming night's sky. I watched the dance from start to end.

D-Day + 77
The one with derrière rabies

Cycling over one hundred kilometers per day just wasn't cutting it anymore. The chai, chapati and mandazi were having their way with our bodies. The gang was plump. So we decided to throw a little extra fitness into our daily cycle. At ten kilometers we put our plan into action with a curbside abdominal workout and handstands. We crawled onto one another and held rather acrobatic poses, working our way through pnf stretches. This was way too much 'visual stimulation' for Texan Rob, who came back with a video recorder in hand. Ten kilometers down the road, we stopped near an incline for more abdominals and tricep dips. Rob and Ming joined our workout, but decided that their hips needed flexing and extending a little more than their triceps. Watching them was the best abdominal workout as we laughed uproariously. Texan Rob led us in some open-air yoga commanding us repetitively to "Salute the Mother Sky". Getting back on the bike was delightfully painful after so much laughter.

Ancient mariner rhymes had no place in the land of black magic.

"Red sky at night, sailors' delight. Red sky in morning, sailors' take warning."

Untrue. Despite Malawi's best sunset the previous night, this sky looked ominous. You might be wondering: how is it possible that eighty days had passed without mention of an ominous sky? The answer was unbelievable: this was our first inclement day. Experienced staff stood amazed at our good fortune with the weather. In tours past, rain would come for weeks, rendering pavement slick and off-roads barely passable. Our eighty day dry spell was highly unusual. I had heard that before. I was starting to take it personally. On Tour du Canada in two thousand and four we experienced less than twenty-four hours of rain in seventy-two days. That was highly unusual. So far we had cycled in fewer than two hours of rain on Tour d'Afrique. Reasonably, I surmised that I must have a guardian angel who likes to keep things dry. But

Malawi wasn't the land for angels, nor dryness. It preferred angels' racy, wild, and fallen counterparts. It poured.

The gang pedaled quickly into a village and chose an ideal storm watch location, a bar with a view. Unfortunately, there were two drunk men making things a tad uncomfortable so we moved into an adjacent room with a pool table, some great music, but sadly no view of the temperamental sky. Eventually, Doug swept and found our hiding spot, then convinced us to get back on our bicycles. We conceded unenthusiastically to ride in rain.

As soon as we set off Doug hollered at me loudly "Does your a*& have rabies?"

I was frothing through my shammies. My pioneering skills were lacking, I hadn't rinsed all the soap from my hand washed clothing.

We got to the Kasungu Inn completely drenched but on a mission. The next day was April Fools and we needed a live chicken. Pessimistically, I thought it was a hopeless mission as we had only twenty minutes and no idea where to start in Kasungu. I was proven wrong yet again. Freezing and drenched, we travelled around town doing our best to imitate a chicken. It worked. We were led down a back alley through a labyrinth of stalls and walls towards a coop with one poor chicken and two roosters shoved inside. Amarula, our newest member on tour, cost six hundred Malawian kwacha. We snuck him back to Marita and Esther's room at camp and waited until the clock struck three.

D-Day + 78
The one with the chicken plant

It was three-thirty in the morning, the gang was poised and ready outside Sharita's room, chicken in hand. Named Amarula, the chicken played along quietly until he saw a nearby cat.

"Cluck! Cluck! Cluck!"

Amarula sounded like a pacemaker sitting on a Royal Flush. Esther managed to open Sharita's door and crept in quietly with Jenny and Amarula in tow. Sharita suddenly shifted in her bed, which startled the pranksters into throwing Amarula into the room and running for their lives. Esther tripped on

Amarula and lurched forward banging and breaking her toe on cement. Safely outside, they caught their breath and we set phase two into motion: we tied doors and tents together. The gang waited in the truck forever. It was worth it. We heard the telltale cluck of Amarula and out she emerged with Sharita. Doors and tents were pried open slowly as we all had a good laugh to start the day. As we turned our attention to the riding day we realized that we too had been had. Ian had locked all our bikes together and hid Esther's bicycle altogether. So it was a slow start.

Departing last, Sharita approached and asked "Where's my chicken?"

We rescued Amarula from the guards and brought him to Sharita's Hilux. In a bid for freedom, Amarula made a run for it. Amarula was extraordinarily agile, it took ten people half an hour to corner her back into the truck.

Sharita bemused and disgusted by this spectacle had started to drive away, so Jenny ran after the Hilux yelling "WAIT! WAIT!"

The Hilux stopped and the door opened. Amarula hopped in decidedly, and took off on an adventure.

Gabriel did not like his name. He changed it to Tyre Mike. Tyre Mike was our local riding companion. He rode many kilometers beside the gang chatting about local customs and culture. Tyre Mike took us to the local supermarket in a tiny village. Having no power, the store was entirely illuminated by candles on the aisle floors. There was something magical about shopping for laundry detergent by candlelight. We spent all our money and bid Tyre Mike adieu.

At lunch we found out that Amarula was gone. Having spent the entire morning working out the specifics on how to keep Amarula happy and healthy on tour, we were gutted. Amarula had jumped out of the Hilux and Noah told a local man that he could have her if he could catch her. The local man gave Noah maïze then ran around for thirty minutes trying to catch her. Defeated, we cycled slowly into Lilongwe drowsy with the fatigue of an early morning pranking session. A few kilometers from camp there was a gloriously large grocery store. We stopped to pool money but quickly realized that candle romanticism had cost us everything we had. Marita told us to wait with the bikes. She entered penniless and came out with bags of chips, ice cream bars and chocolate. 'What sort of store gives grocery bags to kleptomaniacs?' I pondered as we dove mouth first into the salt and sugar. Marita was not a kleptomaniac but instead a legend. While none of us considered the possibility of a major grocer working on credit, she had. She simply asked if she could "pay later" and they had agreed. Optimism was always an option as she lived by her mantra "If you don't ask, you won't receive". In this moment of binging, Marita was elevated to the status of a goddess.

D-Day + 79, 80
The ones with one month blues

Lilongwe was our sloppy goodbye kiss to Malawi. Days were hot and damp, nights humid and restless. We had a little more than one month remaining on tour and I already felt lost in limbo. Experiences change you to corresponding degrees and this journey had been a series of many intense experiences. I felt hugely changed. Would people recognize me when I inserted myself back into 'normal' life? Would tour life be washed away with the first hot shower? Would I be able to retain fierceness of appreciation and remain closer to quiet? These questions did not bounce happily around in my hot humid head, but fixed to the moisture and remained heavily for two straight rest days. I was in a slump. A slump aided and abetted by the oppressive dampness of Malawi. It was hard to think positively when daily bacteria culture grew exponentially on every belonging. When nothing dried. When you could never properly clean. I felt thoroughly used and dirty in Lilongwe. I was looking forward to crossing into Zambia.

Zambia

D-Day + 81
The one with yellow fever

We awoke superheros for surviving moist Malawi sans grave infection, and decided to wear our underwear outside of our cycling gear in true superhero fashion. We wore our St. Patrick's day capes and superhero masks purchased in Lilongwe. Marita was Lavatory Lady beating all lavatory disease and saving Africa one pee tent at a time. Esther was the Arsonist, drying all things wet with her fire (lighting all things on fire – including Andrew's hair). Jenny was Little Miss Sunshine drying up humidity and Femke was The Flying Slime, I can only assume for all the 'slime' exiting our noses on a regular basis in sickness-filled Malawi. We dressed up Martin as well, as he was certain to ride with us as the staff sweep. I was Captain Africa, forward looking to a new Africa that awaited just across the border. Good riddance Malawi. It was not that Malawi wasn't remarkable. It was arguably the MOST remarkable country on tour with it's voodoo, black magic, witch doctors and electrifying energy. Malawi was a journey into backcountry Africa, untouched by modernization. It was utterly vivid. It was that Malawi threatened my EFI in visceral ways. I clung to EFI more strongly with three quarters of the tour completed. I felt that I was playing the odds with my health daily by breathing in Malawian hot, wet, living air. I got increasingly more filthy and with no means of proper drying I felt like I was toying and taunting disease, then lying in wait. I was a complete fool not to relax and be swallowed by Malawi. Malawi had so much to teach me but I was too protectionist. I wouldn't listen to Malawi's ancient wisdom.

We superheros quickly found our first crime. In the night, someone had written in permanent marker "Taking a bus is for p@#!$(&, real athletes bike Afrika" on the side of a touring bus staying at our camp. We knew the tourists who rode this bus. We had been following their route at much slower speeds for a while. Sharita was livid. I showed Sharita the teacher's trick of using a non permanent marker, writing overtop of the permanent, then erasing to remove the writing. She was still livid. Fully aware of who the one true superhero was on tour we decided to leave the case in her outraged hands and cycled quickly away before those hands decided to strangle anyone nearby.

The huge tailwind did nothing for our capes but helped with the one hundred and fifty-three kilometers that stretched ahead. We cruised effortlessly at thirty kilometers per hour. At our first rest stop, a local man sat with us. So we dressed him in our extra superhero apparel, then bought him tea and bread. The bread was deliciously fluffy and crunchy. We drank humongous cups of tea with the entire village onlooking. Locals were so intrigued that a mob followed us everywhere – including into the bathroom. Marita grabbed her slingshot and pretended to shoot rolls of toilet paper into the small ablutions hut. Esther almost lit Jenny's shammies on fire. The local kids were puzzled but amused. This very uniting sense of humour would later grant Marita permission into Zambia.

At the border, we realized that once crossed all leftover Malawian kwacha would be rendered worthless. Marita had millions. She had requested her parents send her some extra cash and ended up with a large fortune in Malawian kwacha. Undeterred, we headed back into Malawi on a spending spree. Some of the millions went to drinking our share of Carlsberg Special Brew. As we tried to drink away our losses, we completely lost track of time and soon enough a local man showed up at the bar; Sharita had sent him to fetch us before the border closed. Good thing, we did not want to anger the officials we would need onside to permit Marita passage. The Zambian border officials were sticklers for proof of Yellow Fever vaccinations. We were sternly warned that if we did not provide proof of vaccination, we would not be admitted into Zambia. Marita did not have her documentation – of course. Marita never worried about the details, she trusted in the journey. As they discussed what would happen to Marita, another officer entered the conversation and started laughing uproariously. He thought our costumes were hilarious.

He said "You look funny."

To which I chirped "That's because she already has yellow fever, she's crazy!"

We all had a hearty laugh and they stamped her passport. The real price of entry in most places is a sense of humour. I felt a twinge of happy regret leaving Malawi. I knew it's true flavours would only be released through steeping and we hadn't afforded the time. Mercifully.

Immediately, Zambia felt like it had more of a pulse and less of a constant hum. The nature was similar to Malawi, topical, but somehow it all felt more organized, groomed. The humidity was getting tolerable and I felt relieved. Zambians were known to be fast. They had just won the African Cup in football and the energy was still abuzz throughout our camp. I hoped cyclists weren't considered training camps for Zambian runners. None of us could handle another Ethiopia.

D-Day + 82
The one with the lorry

Zambia was the beginning of a racer's paradise. Racers really found their rhythm daily with over one hundred and seventy kilometers of pavement stretching lustfully ahead in the mornings. They hunted each other, focused and driven, arriving at camp early enough to rest well before the next hunt. Zambia was less of a gatherers dream with so many kilometers looming ahead demanding full exploration. Gatherers would pile into camp late, muscles aching without enough recovery time before hopping back on the saddle. On this first day in Zambia, I cycled my longest ever. One hundred and seventy-six kilometers. Oddly, it was the fifth of April. For some karmic reason, momentous life events always graced me on the fifth of April. Every year I took special notice of firsts, important life experiences and events on this day. A break-up here, an email from a long lost friend there, someone ALWAYS happened on this date. But I was mistaken. The fact that I would cycle my longest day was not April fifth's event, instead someone would try to kill us.

I was not the only gang member feeling apprehensive, we all made an effort to get an earlier start. It was not meant to be. We cycled two and a half kilometers before Andrew told us that Jon had taken off in the wrong direction. So, we waited for Sharita to drive by and informed her of Jon's mistake. We set off again accompanied by a sectional rider named Saskia. Within a few kilometers, her saddlebag fell off and she returned to camp. We waited for a very long time for Saskia to return until our nerves finally got the better of us and we decided to ride on. It was a late start greeted by headwinds. They yelled in our faces to take the day seriously! Then whooshed into tailwinds just as we were feeling a slight competitive edge. The winds criss-crossed all day long, more emotionally changeable than a pubescent teen. Wearingly, we climbed a slow gradient for hours. Esther was feeling ill so we pedalled slowly through every long kilometer. We took a brief rest in the morning to take in our new surroundings. Immediately, I noticed that faces appeared kinder and gentler. Scowls were replaced with engagingly bright smiles. You never knew what was behind a facial expression in Africa. In northern Africa, scowls hid kindness, in southern Africa, smiles hid menace. We saw their true spirit the very moment they got behind the wheel. Traffic would close in on us as if we were prey. Trucks would have two lanes to themselves, yet pass within an inch of our bodies and bikes. One giant lorry literally tried to kill us. He was oncoming, thankfully we saw him. The lorry dangerously darted across all the lanes of traffic aiming for a head-on collision with the gang. We screamed and quickly veered into the ditch to avoid colliding. He drove by exactly where our bikes had been. He was not kidding. Had this lorry been behind us, we would have never been able to avoid him. Human life seemed less valued in Zambia.

Shaken and defensive we had very little fun the rest of the day – we just pressed on. Very few rest stops presented themselves and so at one and a half kilometers to camp we finally relaxed and stopped for an orange break. While savouring the delicious roadside treat Sharita drove up beside us and laughed.

"Is this an *I have had enough break*?"

It most certainly was.

D-Day + 83
The one with the Accident Prevention Police

Morale was up. Mark, our tour chef, had prepared the one food that could single-handedly wash away all of Malawi's residual scents and uplift spirits for over one hundred and seventy kilometers: bacon. Delicious bacon. We sat happily munching away as Jenny fixed her flat, unconcerned about the magnitude of the day looming. We should have been concerned. Lorry drivers were making a sport of riding us off the road. One won the terrible prize as he hit Marita's camelback and missed her head by two centimeters with his

158

mirror. It was terrifying. It was not racism. We watched locals scurry from the roads as trucks zoomed passed. Locals who dared to ride bicycles scuttled from the road the moment they heard the lorry's roar. We were meek and vulnerable. Suddenly, a fast-moving car pulled out right in front of us and nearly caused a major collision and the second gang pileup. "Accident Prevention Police" was emblazoned on the side of the car in bright lettering. The irony was not lost. At one point, Jenny's chain fell off and she tumbled onto the road. She was unharmed and EXTREMELY lucky that no lorry was passing in that moment. One mistake or mechanical failure would quickly cause death in Zambia.

We needed a rest from the emotional stress of trying to stay alive on Zambian roads. So we took a moment at a small local shop and took in our surroundings. It was no wonder that bacon was so plentiful as roadside pigs were everywhere. The Zambian goats were tri-coloured and particularly stylish, their locks in direct competition with the ultra-cool and unique designer hairstyles atop every Zambian woman's head. At ten kilometers to camp, we found our second rest stop. Jennifer asked for music and the owners brought out a huge speaker and played some reggae. Although we were quite used to Bongo Flava, the music had such rhythm that we couldn't help but move in time. The music attracted all the nearby children and they started dancing, really dancing. Their moves would have made Elvis Presley blush and they were under ten years of age. We got up and joined them, showing off our more modest dance moves. The entire town got a good laugh. No matter, the dancing rejuvenated our spirits after two long and stressful cycling days.

Camp was near a neat little town and on the water. We ventured into town to buy eggs for an Easter celebration plan we had been hatching for the next day. Stalls and stalls of dried fish, straw hats and baskets lined the road. Everywhere we biked we saw evidence of the resourcefulness of Africans. It is a lesson the West would be fortunate to learn.

D-Day + 84
The one with the egging

We faced over one thousand seven hundred meters of climbing, another challenging day in Zambia. Additionally, the gang was chai-challenged. Our favourite caffeine boost seemed to stay behind at the border. We searched high and low but our forage for tea was futile. Coca Cola had replaced every drink, including water. I cursed Zambia when two months later a dentist peered into my mouth and exclaimed "What did you do! I saw you six months ago!" before capping all four of my molars. Thanks Coca Cola.

It quite literally took a village to raise a child in Zambia. Children ran everywhere together. The community looked out for them. Every mother has at least one baby sucking at her breast, or carried one securely tied to her back. Youth would often carry their younger sibling around. Even kids as young as four would strap their little baby brother on their backs before heading out to play. Parenting felt very organic. Communities felt genuine.

Suddenly an Easter miracle happened: we were offered Jolly Ranchers. Jolly Ranchers did not grace the shelves of tiny supermarkets in rural Zambia. In fact, I hadn't seen a Jolly Rancher since leaving North America. But here we were in Zambia being offered our choice of colour, by Genny, whose face was whiter than ours. Genny was a pallid American woman in her twenties working in rural Zambia with the Peace Corps. She was going mad. We met other Peace Corps workers in Tanzania who felt quite at home in their larger urban lives. Genny was off a beaten path, literally. She was incredibly isolated in rural Zambia and had lived the past two years knowing that every single person she encountered, needed something from her. She was truly exhausted and needed a reprieve. Jolly Ranchers somehow brought her closer to home. She would sneak away to eat them so as to not feel guilty, and we happened upon her self-soothing nostalgia with rectangular hard packed sweetness. Jolly Ranchers were Genny's lifeline until her parents came to visit in a few months, I almost felt guilty accepting a few. She told us about life in rural Zambia, about the inconsistent work she did from nursing to cleaning floors, about helplessness and poverty. I could tell that it took all her willpower not to lose her mind. I hoped Genny would not run out of Jolly Ranchers before her parents' visit.

At the lunch, the gang found our eggs hard-boiled and ready for decoration, thanks for Noah. We set to work decorating each egg festively. Departing a little late from the lunch truck, we were happy with our work. The afternoon rewarded us with a long downhill through tall grass tunnels. Glimpses of pure beauty peeked through the tunnel every now and again. We giggle as we passed an enterprise legitimately called the *You Look Honest But*

I Still Can't Trust You shop. This epitomized Zambia. We rode into camp excited for the Easter Egg Hunt but suddenly realized that the riders had already eaten our eggs! Earlier that morning, we had asked Raphael to plant eggs around camp. He was usually amongst the first to arrive at camp and so we reasoned that he would have an advantage in hiding them before riders arrived. He did. Riders couldn't believe their luck as they hungrily waited for supper and found a multitude of decorated hard-boiled eggs. Pack of vultures. They had almost ruined our game. We quickly hid more eggs and announced teams using our newly commandeered "spirit Board" from the lunch truck. The rules were simple, team members needed to locate eggs and smash each egg on their team leader's head. They got a point for each raw egg they found, they could eat the hard-boiled. Many villagers showed up to watch the hunt, laughing when someone got egged and a few took part in cracking eggs on our foreheads.

D-Day + 85
The one with the Easter sermon

It was Easter Sunday and one hundred and four kilometers on pavement felt like a miracle. It was such a blessedly short day but the gang departed camp divided; Jenny and Femke speeding, Marita and Esther enjoying every slow moment. I was somewhere in the middle, needing some time alone. I took a long break to refresh and Marita and Esther caught up. Cycling along the main road, Marita caught sight of a tourist road sign so we detoured to the local hot spring. What we found was the communal laundromat. Eighty degree water spewed from a head-sized hole while men hunched over the rocky outlet roughly cleaning their clothes. In the spirit of Easter, one man took a break from domestication, advanced towards us and preached Christianity. He was particularly focused on baptism and how total submersion was necessary for salvation. We started eyeing the head-sized hole with suspicion. Did he mean to dunk us? We decided NOT to find out and cycled away in haste. Our morning procrastination paid off when Noah revealed a juicy roadside mango at the end of lunch. Mangos needed to make a splash to be enjoyed thoroughly. We devoured the mango enjoying the sensation of velvety sweetness dribbling down our chins. We plotted. Every year, staff organized t-shirts to be made for all members. The gang had a special request. Our greatest accomplishment so far on tour was not cycling six countries, but impressing Sharita. To us, Sharita was Africa. We designed t-shirts that commemorated Amarula the chicken and fossilized Sharita's gospel of "Shim-ba-la-bim!" The front boldly claimed "We impressed Sharita". Then we purchased a shirt for Sharita that read "I impressed the gang". Thinking we were quite clever, we rode happily to the Chainama Hotel in Lusaka for a rest day.

D-Day + 86
The one with dry belongings

Zambia was Malawi's drier cousin, but still a fun-loving lush. Low hung humidity had made morale uncomfortable. In the spirit of the tropics, nothing had dried since MBeya. Every article of clothing was damp and disgusting. When we awoke in Lusaka, we awoke to sunlight. Not rays weakened and divided by moisture, but pure unadulterated rays of warm light. As soon as we stepped out of our tents we knew something had shifted. Suddenly, we were dry. I basked in the sunlight for hours, then set about cleaning every single thing I owned. Everything dried and it felt redemptive.

D-Day + 87
The one with the crocodiles

Leaving today everything breathed new life and felt aligned. We sailed down the road effortlessly as kilometers passed by unannounced. In the first fifteen kilometers the gang changed six flats but nobody seemed to mind. We saw a row of picnic tables under a large awning near a small river and decided to take a break. In my newly elated state, I uncharacteristically decided to take a dip. Just this once. Then something happened which ensured I kept this promise to myself.

Visibly panicked, a man raced towards us yelling "Get out! GET OUT!"

We stared at him unconcerned until he yelled two bone crunching words: "Hippopotamus! Crocodile!"

This was the moment we learned that hippos and crocs loved to cruise the rivers of Zambia. This was also the moment we raced out of the rivers of Zambia. I found it ironic that the one body of water I decided to trust was the least trustworthy of all. Not to be defeated, we decided to have a tea party at one of the picnic tables and watch for predators from afar. Tea, not being the choice of Zambians, took one hour to make. We didn't mind waiting in such a picturesque spot.

Just as we cycled past *The Most Excellent Hotel* the rain started. Unwilling to concede our feeling of 'dry' we deeked into a labyrinth of nearby stalls. Youth who had never seen such pasty white complexions, started crying. Some ran away scared. We waited for the rain to stop in the excellent company of maïze and mandazi. The maïze cost me a dance. Locals enjoyed watching us try to find our rhythm. Much like a toddler taking first steps, to them we were clumsy, off-balance and totally invested in the process. Dancing and humour were both excellent Zambian currency.

D-Day + 88
The one with the storm

"Where are you from?" "Where are you going?" Zambians sure loved getting existential.

English was Zambia's official language and so when we responded that we were cycling from Cairo to Cape Town they gazed at us lunatically. They knew Egypt, they knew Cape Town and they knew all the kilometers between. "God Bless" was all they could whisper as they backed away slowly. One hundred and eighty two kilometers stretched ahead, another long day in Zambia which meant less time to stop and explore. Zambian winds prefer the least straightforward route playfully flirting this way and that without rhyme or reason. They toyed with our minds making every road feel uphill. The gang struggled for the first forty kilometers until we reached a beautiful small town with a bakery serving an unexpected treat: fresh long johns. Gustatory bliss! Straight across the street was a tea shop serving chai. Our lucky day! We cycled onward past manicured markets of fat luscious fruit and veggies lining the roads between rows of gourds, seemingly operating on the honor system. The people were equally manicured, healthy and athletic. On our final stretch we could no longer avoid the tropics, we could no longer stay dry. First, we made a quick stop for our first (of many) Windhoek beer, then we cycled straight into a powerful storm. As if God grabbed every cloud, turned each inside out and shook with all his might, droplets dangerously descended stinging our faces and drenching our bikes and bodies within seconds. The road vanished under the pelting water. Massive thunder clapped while lightning raced all around us. Every second slowed while our concentration narrowed to a pinhole, I went off the road a few times without knowing where I was until I was cycling on slick grass. Intensity gifts a pivotal moment where you choose to hold tight or let loose. Long lost was our security blanket, long gone our sense of control, so we let loose. We laughed maniacally out loud for God to hear our surrender. Then Sharita showed out of nowhere. She warned us to stay close together for safety. Our laughter stopped. The last thing we needed was for a lorry to hear our cry of surrender and come looking for us. We made it to camp soaked, released and gracious.

D-Day + 89
The one with 'Smoke that Thunders"

One hundred and fifty one kilometers separated us from a double rest day in Livingstone. Separated us from Victoria Falls — the world's largest waterfall. Separated us from a bicycle donation. Paramountly, separated us from a booze cruise on the Zambezi River. Unfortunately, and perhaps because of these facts, my alarm clock didn't sound. Since the beginning of tour, I had never possessed a material alarm clock. I, like many others, relied on the noisiness of others leisurely preparing for their day to awake me from my slumber. Today was different. Riders quietly and swiftly packed, ate and mounted, desperate for what was to come. Everyone who relied on the noisiest laughers, loudest eaters or champion flatulators slept in. Suddenly we alarmless riders awoke panicked, it was too quiet. We could not miss the booze cruise! We hurriedly threw our belongings into the truck, ate a PVM energy bar and grabbed our bicycles. Conversely, tardy racers were not panicked. There was no rush for riders who regularly travelled at thirty-five kilometers per hour.

The gang set off thankful for the underdevelopment of the ride into Livingstone. Not only was lorry-dodging not required but there were literally zero rest establishments to tempt us en route.

When the racing peloton rode by, Jenny commanded *"Attach on!"* and so we joined our second peloton of tour.

I pedalled and concentrated furiously as sixty minutes simultaneously dragged on and blinked by. My brain processed nothing in it's heightened fearful state. Suddenly I was thrust to the front of the peloton. I pushed with herculean force at the front and maintained a speed of thirty four kilometers per hour uphill. This was fear at its most effective. When I dropped to the back, Marita mentioned that she had to pee so the gang fell completely off the race. I was fully mentally and physically exhausted with over half the day remaining.

If there was one cure for mental and physical exhaustion it certainly wasn't eating insects. For lunch, Noah had prepared a rare delicacy of bugs. A few brave souls crunched away on Noah's terrifically ugly bite sized protein chips, but I bowed out. Having eaten crickets in my teens, I knew insects would do nothing for my already depleted morale. After lunch the gang battled a strong headwind for the remaining seventy six kilometers. Headwinds strong enough to make me miss the peloton. Zambia was having it's way with my mind. Then at twenty kilometers from camp something spectacular happened: we cycled through a cloud. Not a cloud of pollution, nor a cloud of humidity, but a proper cloud fallen from the sky. Our bodies were enlivened by the misting of our ears attuned to a humming roar. Like a lion warming his vocal chords, the noise got increasingly guttural and loud as we rode into camp. This was Mosi-oa-Tunya's greeting party. The smoke and thunder of the mighty Victoria Falls was upon us all, one of the seven natural wonders of the world.

Camp was Eden. Our tents nestled amidst beautiful shady trees, swimming pools and Lake Zambezi; home to crocodiles, hippos and elephants. Monkeys danced overhead to birdsong. We sat in the shaded awning of a restaurant, ate and observed a donation ceremony. Then the booze cruise boarded but I stayed behind. Having learned my lesson in Bahir Dar, I did not want to be hippo bait for a second time. I briefly considered the effects of mixing anti-nausea medicine with alcohol and settled on drinking at the perfectly good bar on dry land overlooking the Zambezi. Alaric, Holly, Dareo, Ton and I laughed as we recounted adventures reminding me that this odyssey was entirely perspective.

D-Day + 90, 91
The ones with breathlessness

Alaric had won tickets to go abseiling and zip lining over the Gorge. There was one small problem. Alaric was afraid of heights. Graciously he gifted me the tickets and came with to watch the spectacle from solid ground. I was surely the evolutionary anomaly as I lacked fear of heights entirely. Leaping from the edge on the Flying Fox zipline I felt nothing but freedom racing forward suspended from the line face down over the abyss. I took in the measure of the gorge. In a world where everything presents itself a few feet from your face, my eyes felt unusually liberated. They refracted wildly to soak in the extensiveness. Stiff rock cliffs sheenly defined the Gorge while monkeys cried out in excitement. The mist from the falls hung underneath and I felt on top of the clouds. Abseiling afforded more time to look around, while getting intimately acquainted with the cliffs. Then we hopped on our bicycles and rode to the main attraction.

Cycling towards Mosi-o-Tunya, Alaric and I encountered our first roadside giraffe. If you ever want to feel small and vulnerable, cycle to Victoria Falls. From the bicycle, the giraffe's presence felt immense. But this was only the beginning. Breathtaking was but a metaphor until I saw Victoria Falls. Sheer awe can override the autonomic nervous system; this I discovered in Livingstone. As I dismounted at Victoria Falls, disbelief at the grandeur took my breath, and left me gasping and gaping for the first time in my life. I grew up in St. Catharines, a neighbour city to Niagara Falls. More than once I boarded the Maid of the Mist and toured the mighty Niagara Falls. The beauty of the falls never normalized and I appreciated each visit equally. But I never lost my breath. This may have given me an arrogance as the bar was certainly set high for waterfalls. The moment I glimpsed Victoria Falls I stood transfixed. Was the scene even possible? Could that much water fall continuously? The immensity was not translatable to the human mind. Energy transformed at mind boggling speed and entered our bodies via the thunderous roar. It felt like witnessing the world's greatest magic trick. The illusion of enormity. But it was no illusion. Victoria Falls was the real deal. I reminded myself to breath if only to have a few more moments humbled at her entrance.

Measuring only one hundred and eight meters, Victoria Falls is not amongst the world's tallest waterfalls. Angel Falls in Venezuela holds the record measuring nine hundred and seventy nine meters. Neither is Victoria Falls the widest waterfall. The Chutes de Khone are over six times as wide as Victoria Falls. Nonetheless, Victoria Falls is often considered the largest and greatest waterfall in the world. It boasts the largest sheet of water cascading with enough ferocity to be felt over twenty kilometers away. The gods dump two hundred Olympic-sized swimming pools every minute over the edge of this magnificent host. Waves upon waves of rainlike mist float back up and spill all over the lookout, soaking onlookers and taking payment for witnessing arresting beauty. Victoria Falls is the act of falling into passionate love. Even the moon falls in love at Victoria Falls, as it is one of two places in the world to witness "Moonbows". Lunar rainbows can be seen as moonlight bounces off the wall of water. Love swirled inside and out alternating between a serenely calm flow at the crest and base and a tumultuous fall, bumping uglies with protruding rocks, rubbing off on each other and both leaving just a little changed. I felt magnified in force but infinitesimal in importance. The next day I rested and regrouped grateful to Zambia for drying out my dampened spirit and eager for our upcoming venture into Botswana.

Botswana

D-Day + 92
The one with four countries

Botswana, the only country in the world that had more elephants than people. Today we would cross into this mythical land. The gang had planned the perfect border crossing garb; Mardi Gras costumes! Surely elephants would appreciate carnivale attire — the response was immediately and glaringly obvious. As unimpressed as the elephants would soon be, nothing showed more disdain than Sharita. Our t-shirts had come in. We sported them proudly with "We impressed Sharita" boldly emblazoned across the front. Sharita was most certainly not impressed. She begrudgingly wore her gifted shirt for one quick photo then removed it quickly to reveal a black t-shirt bearing the superman logo. Nothing could be more fitting. Undeterred, we wore red, purple and gold masks and blew in party whistles. Faces were painted Carnivale-style and green streamers were attached to our helmets. We set off in celebration.

We had a new custom at customs. Just before entering, we would head to the nearest restaurant and blow all our remaining currency. Money changers were corrupt the world over and so we toasted many Smirnoff to them within feet of the Zambian border rather than supporting their scams. For the second time, Sharita sent someone to fetch us as the border was closing. We downed our drinks and then found two customary flat tires. To save un-impressing Sharita even further, we walked our bicycles the five hundred meters to the border. We passed through customs quickly with Zambian officials appearing relieved to get rid of such a festive bunch. Then we mounted a ferry boat on the Zambezi River en route to Botswana and started changing our flats. It was fitting that our border crossing should be by ferry boat. Rainwater was the ultimate blessing in Botswana, a country well accustomed to drought. Their devotion ran deep enough to name their currency the Pula, meaning rain in Setswana, their national language.

Competitive travellers love the Zambezi River. In a one hundred and fifty meter ferry ride you can visit four countries. Travel the Zambezi River a bit farther if you wish to add a total of six countries to your passport: Zambia, Angola, Namibia, Botswana, Zimbabwe and Mozambique. Hippos and crocs change citizenship daily in the Zambezi River. Every country needed a piece of this truly remarkable waterway. We entered Botswana's customs and received a warm welcome. Carnies were welcome in Botswana. Jenny handed her mask to one of the officials who sported it proudly while filling out our forms. Then her friend grabbed the mask and wore it while trying to help Sharita. We had done it. We had thoroughly unimpressed Sharita who scowled at the 'not-so-official' official the entire time. Ironically, superwoman had no time for dress-up. Within the first few kilometers of cycling we spotted our first warthog. That was thrilling enough until we peeked over the warthog's shoulder into the distance. There was an elephant traipsing along. He was quite far in the distance and paid relatively little attention to us once he saw how we were dressed. No self-respecting elephant gives the slightest mind to carnivale folk. From a safe distance the elephant seemed small. Soon enough we would recognize our folly, but in this moment we were thrilled. The gang cycled the remaining ten kilometers to camp and arrived just in time to sign up for the sunset cruise in Chobe National Park. Trucks were mounted and we were driven to a wide ferry boat on the bank of the Chobe River. Botswana welcomed in style.

People were an afterthought in Chobe National Park. Animals owned the land and tourists were only there for the animals' amusement. Nothing was contrived. Elephants lazily ate from trees while nearby crocodiles sunbathed. Eagles flew majestically and impala leapt across fields. I realized that I had been misled by every nature show since birth. Or perhaps I had simply put my own 'human' spin on things. Nature's penchant for survival was quintessential. But the manifestation was not nearly as acrimonious as I imagined. Nature lived harmoniously most of the time, elephants could eat close to lounging crocodiles, hippos and elephants could share swimming pools playfully together. It was all very paradisiacal — until it wasn't. We humans sensationalized everything with our every media focusing on fierce emotion-triggering moments. Nature was no exception. I had grown to believe nature was in a constant survival of the fittest warzone. Nothing was further from the truth. Nature was on guard, but also assured in balance. Violence was only parcelled through necessity. This was harmony, co-dependence and oneness. This was mutual respect. This was a better community than I had ever lived. I studied a male impala who was being trailed by a harem of twenty females. When a female peed, the male would scuff up the ground to avoid detection. Nearby elephants played happily in the water, dunking, swimming and splashing around in circles. Nearby a large hippopotamus opened his mouth one hundred and eighty degrees and yawned. The sunset providing the backdrop for this incredible scene was what mysteries were made of.

D-Day + 93
The one with the elephant

Elephants always had right of way on the Elephant Highway. Even if they hadn't, who would have stopped them? Not us, yet. We still had all enough marbles to know better. We were just beginning the second to last section of tour: the Elephant Highway. Famed as the section where many riders go nuts — days were long, roads were straight, fenced and unoccupied. Aside from the occasional elephant sighting, riders were left to their own minds' entertainment for up to ten hours per day. Endless kilometers of nothingness lay in our immediate future, so the gang devised a plan. We played brain teasers for the first forty kilometers. We created a murder mystery which passed another ten kilometers. Then we were out of ideas. Desperate to end the mind-numbing monotony, we happened upon our best idea yet: we would create a quiz night. This would occupy our minds for the remaining one hundred and thirty kilometers, AND take our minds off our symptoms of serious caffeine withdrawal. There were no rest stops along the Elephant Highway. No tea, chai, coffee or Coca Cola. When Sharita passed, we flagged her down and pleaded with her to allow us to stash caffeine filled items in her Hilux for our daily fix.

Sharita half smirked and rode off claiming she needed to "Go save lives."

Twenty kilometers later the gang saw a strange roadblock next to a sign that warned "slow down". Uneventful riding had put us in such a hypnotic state that we failed to heed the sign's wise advice and almost crashed into one another in a quick effort to preserve what lay strewn across the road. Sharita had left us COLD Coca Colas, lollipops and a jar of Marmite. This was better than an elephant sighting and we did not approach cautiously. Within seconds caffeine released the dull ache lounging between our eyes and the great marmite debate gave us plenty to discuss for the remaining kilometers. Delicious? Gross? Pairings? Wherever did Sharita find marmite?

A few kilometers down the road, Darryl was stopped at an elephant. Darryl was a local wildlife expert tasked with keeping us safe along the Elephant Highway. The founder of TDA Global Cycling had experienced a major run-in with an elephant and knew the heightened risks to cyclists in a country with over one hundred and sixty thousand elephants. The bull was majestically huge. I stood transfixed for long enough that most of the gang departed without me. Jenny, Natalie and I remained. Earlier at camp, Darryl had communicated the Elephant Encounter Rulebook prioritizing "do not panic", "do not approach" and "do not leave your bike". Darryl was a rule-breaker. Darryl told us to "leave your bikes, let's go" and brought us by foot through the bush to within twenty meters of the massive bull. I tried my best to obey the first rule and not panic when I saw how close we were. What a chilling thrill to see such a massive creature up close. We were exposed and vulnerable, but with Darryl by our side we felt some sense of security. Our next elephant encounter was at camp. An elephant decided to mosey along around our tents, unbothered by our presence. As thrilling as it was to see a wild elephant, I could not help wondering how I would sleep knowing a giant foot may decide to stomp my tent and crush all my bones. In my red tent, I felt doomed. Steve and Miguel assured me that if all my body parts remained inside my tent, I was extremely likely to wake up with them all still attached. Oddly, this was somewhat comforting.

D-Day + 94
The one with quiz night

The gang was extremely lethargic after a busy evening and morning preparing for quiz night. Before enjoying the fruit of our labour, we would need to complete one hundred and forty-eight boring kilometers in a headwind. Headwinds were gang-divisive. Jenny, Femke and Rachel raced ahead —

Rachel was a new sectional rider and Jenny's friend from England. Marita and Esther retreated to a slow methodical cadence. I cycled right in the middle of the two groups. Headwind-days nourished my introverted soul as I grooved along alone to music quite contentedly. Soon enough, the gang was reunited by elephants. Darryl was nowhere in sight and so I couldn't treat this encounter like a trip to the zoo. Step one was to shake my North American head and dump out that zoo mentality. Given that I still had an unsquashed head to shake, I knew enough to feel awestruck and apprehensive of what I was seeing. A parade of elephants ran across the road ahead of our bikes. These wild, unpredictable and temperamental mammals glanced our way and thankfully continued on their path. My reaction was exactly opposite from my last encounter. I did not dismount, nor approach, but kept a respectful distance while slightly panicked. Once they were no longer visible, we rode to camp and prepared for quiz night.

Nata Safari Lodge had a large outdoor patio bar which was perfect for hosting. Andrew agreed to be Master of Ceremony while the gang waitressed and tallied scores. Almost everyone took part in answering questions in our four categories: "Quotes and Bike Facts" featuring famous rider quotes on tour, "Who's Who" and "Staff Facts" guessing the secret past of tour members, and the ever popular "Whose Bums Are These" featuring a lineup of shammies. Andrew created the most magic, reuniting us all in over an hour of continuous laughter. The staff table won and Sharita bought the gang a celebratory beer. It would take moments like this to fill our heads for the long monotonous days ahead.

D-Day + 95
The one with the puff adder

Botswana by bicycle was an endless highway. One hundred and eighty seven highway kilometers to our next camp. For me, this would be a new record. We buzzed about the successful quiz night for about five kilometers. Then Esther, L.S, Ian and I spent fifty kilometers profiling over sixty characters for a Days of our Lives Theme Party. Esther cycled no-handed the entire fifty kilometers over pot-holed cement writing down all of our ideas.

Creativity was our mind's lifeline. We still had one hundred and thirty two kilometers to go. I tried to create mental poetry for Botswana's flora – rusty orange, mustard yellow, all shades of green and brown hung from trees. The illusion was not fiery like Canadian Autumn, but rustic, ancient and wise.

Finally we arrived at the lunch truck. It was parked directly beneath a giant mystically alluring baobab tree. The tree of life looked perfectly deformed, unfortunately I couldn't stop staring. Antoine de Saint-Exupéry alluded to the dangers of allowing the Baobab to grow in his famous book Le Petit Prince. The immature baobab strongly resembled a rosebush. If not seen for the weed that it was and plucked from the soil, it would grow to prove hideous, rather than beautiful. A metaphor for our deeper consciousness. Also a useful tidbit for today. Sharita concurred with Antoine when she tried to ban us from Planet Baobab, our next rest stop. Although Planet Baobab had the appearance of a rosebush, complete with a pool, fur chairs and a wrap around bar, it had the makings of a weed, taking over and eating up more than a few EFIs. Bored, we promptly ignored Sharita's sage advice and cycled madly the twenty kilometers to Planet Baobab. We guzzled a cold drink and went for the world's most refreshing dip in the pool. We had a photoshoot. We celebrated my Mom's birthday and Ian's Mom's birthday with shooters and cake. Most cyclists made this their final riding destination for the day. It was too good. Sharita showed up to collect drunkards and gave the gang a stern look. We heeded. Against all odds the gang cut their way through the metaphorical weeds and ended up back on the bicycle, slightly inebriated with slightly less than half the day to go.

Weaving around donkeys and cattle as a strong tailwind pushed us onward, we were grateful and grumpy. At the final refresh stand, Claire told us that camp was unexpectedly fifteen kilometers further. We would never make it before the setting sun. She laughed at our defeated faces and confided that Sharita had put her up to it, concerned that we were not taking the day seriously enough. Darryl showed us his hunting rifle and we ate watermelon until we were sick. The next time we saw Darryl was right after one of our frequent alcohol-ridding pee stops, he was hunched by the side of the road with his kill. Not far from where we peed, Darryl had caught and killed a Puff Adder – the deadliest snake in Africa. He showed us the Adder's venom and I committed to search for adult diapers in the next big city. The dangers were real, even when camouflaged. We arrived at camp just as the sun was setting and I felt physically, mentally and spiritually drained. We had done fierce battle in effort to uproot the baobab. It nearly got the better of us.

D-Day + 96
The one with the musical

"This tour is really difficult. Just when you finish the physically challenging days due to elevation and off-roading, you enter the mentally and emotionally exhausting days.' Alaric coined it well.

Crisis had entered camp. Cyclists rebelled wholly against the boredom of cycling Botswana. The desire to get on a bicycle every morning was waning as more and more riders piled their bikes on the tour truck and were driven to camp. The Ethiopian mountains had nothing on the mind-numbingly straight Elephant Highway. The gang was holding it together, by a thread. Today that thread was musical. For one hundred and thirty one kilometers we serenaded every rider who managed to haul their weary mind on a bicycle past us.

"Now I've, had, the time of my life, no I never felt like this before!"

We created new lyrics to Puddle of Mudd's "She F(@*#($* Hate Me" and serenaded Sharita proudly when she rode by in her Hilux. We named, watched and sang to a dung beetle. Leonard. Leonard the dung beetle. This was THE ONLY wildlife we saw the entire day thanks to fencing on either side of the highway. So we studied his movements for nearly thirty minutes. This was pure excitement. We were losing it.

D-Day + 97
The one without camouflage

The Sedia Hotel in Maun boldly offered an all-you-can-eat breakfast buffet. Cyclists on a rest day typically had time and hunger enough to eat such establishments out of business but the Sedia Hotel was different. It was calculated. It charged an exorbitant fee for breakfast knowing full well we would be gone within the hour. The Sedia Hotel was located in close proximity to the Okavango Delta; one of Africa's Seven Natural Wonders and the very last wonder needed to finish our bucket list. Okavango was the largest delta in the world formed by a tectonic trough. It held such wonder that I willingly broke a promise to myself made years earlier and boarded the tiny eight seater fixed wing named Fiona with Natalie, Alaric, Hermon and Femke. While boats made me want to throw up, small planes made me want to die. In small planes my stomach flipped and turned until it felt like I had drenched my brain in gastric acid. Yet, I willingly got on board with a few minor concessions. I sat up front with an open vomit bag on my lap. That was how spectacular I expected the Okavango Delta to be. It was spectacular. Well worth every gastric somersault.

The Okavango Delta was God's interactive art installation. It shifted and changed as animals came to drink from it's golden pond of life. The water resembled a liquid mood ring with a bronze tinge giving way to a brownish black surface. Bone white dead trees sprouted from the center of black lakes and gave the entire landscape eerie shadows. Admission to the Delta included coat-check; one after another animals surrendered their camouflage suits as they traipsed through the wet soggy ground crushing vegetation and veining obvious tracks with every step. No one entered the Okavango Delta unannounced. Pools of golden mineral-rich water snaked around for miles mesmerizingly while animals lounged at the ever expanding edges. Where elephants, giraffes and hippopotamus' were alarming up close, they were menacing from afar. Flying high overhead we felt omniscient viewing the entire jungle landscape. It looked as if miniature plastic animals had come to life, naked and exposed to predators. Predators stalked and tracked each other ominously through the water-filled trenches. Giraffes moved about in towers, resembling moving twigs. Buffalo, deer, cows and monkeys filled in all extra spaces. Unbelievably, we saw smoke coming from a swampy section of the Delta. Darren, our pilot, told us that vegetation in the Okavango Delta dried out under the fiery hot African sun. When completely dried, a single droplet of water could magnify and set the stalk on fire. Darren was unconcerned knowing the fire would quickly be quenched by the land's oversaturation.

Suddenly Darren swooped the plane and I felt like nausea was brimming out of my lungs. With the puke bag at the ready, I took my second gravol and focused on the horizon, it was no use. I felt my throat fill when suddenly Darren reached over and opened an air vent blasting me with cool air as he commenced his descent. It was just enough to get me safely to the ground, buffet breakfast unspoiled.

D-Day + 98
The one with the penis

Queasiness sat within heavily. My already angered stomach knotted over the anticipation of cycling past thousands of Delta-dwelling jungle animals in the upcoming one hundred and fifty-seven kilometers. I hoped their camouflage remained with a coat check so we would see them at a comfortable distance from the bicycle. The gang was fortunate, although we did see our share of roadside wildlife it was of the plump and happy variety. Darryl told us that the animals were currently at their best, having spent the rainy season fattening. They would trim down to nothing soon as the dry season rendered food scarce. We rode by snobbish donkeys who quite obviously preferred their own company. Goats and sheep communed with cattle. Then at fifty kilometers, two massive bull elephants ran full speed across the road fewer than one hundred feet ahead of our bicycles.

I stopped quickly, my mind slipping immediately into tourist mode when Jenny's yells "DON'T STOP! GO! GO! GO!" jolted me back to awareness.

The two massive bulls appeared to have four trunks. We were being challenged. Their massive penis' dangled low and seemed to look our way with their one menacing eye. Possibly, this was the elephant parade's reconnaissance element. Flashing back to a Kenyan safari in two thousand and ten, I remembered the Maasai women casually mentioning that before venturing into the jungle they always stripped a young boy and made him walk out front. This was not an unforgivable form of sacrifice but a true testament to the might of male virility in the animal kingdom. Animals didn't mess with the penis. They respected and kept their distance from the penis. We would be wise to heed this practice. Just thinking that these two massive bulls may be the smallest calves of the parade, we pedalled past furiously and onward to camp.

D-Day + 99
The one with 120 km/hr

Nearing the end of the Elephant Highway, cyclists were riding closer and closer to the edge of mental breakdown. Staff decided to break the monotony with a scavenger hunt. The race was suspended as riders grouped to accomplish all tasks on their list. The moment we were given the list, the gang got to work. Perusing the list quickly, we went on the offensive. Knowing full well our legs would never compete for quickest speed on an odometer, we put our hands to work. With one month of Ethiopian tutelage, we stole odometers from every bike left unattended. Unstealthily. We only managed to pilfer Peter's. All was not lost. We were tasked with finding items that began with the letters in Botswana and the odometer would serve nicely as the O.

One by one the gang, Rachel and Natalie (an Australian sectional rider) tackled all items on the list: longest thorn, items that begin with the letters in Botswana, roadside treasures. En route, we found a termite hill, bared our bums and pretended to have collectively pooped it out. Biggest turd. We inspired Doug to bare it all for a shot of a roadside treasure. Then we went in search of cyclists to exchange clothing for impersonation points. We happened upon Ming. His nose was significantly bent out of joint. Ming did not understand the concept of a scavenger hunt. To him, people had been acting excessively erratically and unjustly bossing him around all morning. We quickly explained the premise of a scavenger hunt. Always the photography opportunist, Ming's face radiated as he stripped shirtless and immediately embraced the fun. This was to be Ming's day.

A photograph with elephants would have been an easier accomplishment than the next item on our list: we needed a photograph with locals. Nobody travelled the Elephant Highway. When one lone truck rode by though we desperately stood in the road trying to flag down the vehicle. Against all odds, the truck stopped. Four ladies and one massive transistor radio piled out the truck. We posed in the cab of the truck together and then Natalie convinced the driver to pile her bike in the back and speed away to the lunch truck so she could photograph the truck's odometer at one hundred and twenty kilometers per hour.

In one morning, morale was lifted so high by the collective fun that riders didn't even grumble when our organized camp with hot showers suddenly became another bush camp in the middle of nowhere. Our designated camp had shut down without informing any tour staff. So we stayed in an open field, happily fueled by conversation. This was the power of community. Nobody internalized that this little detour to our surprise bush camp would make the next day the longest day ever recorded on any Tour d'Afrique.

Namibia

D-Day + 100
The one with the record

This day had loomed ominously for weeks. It was a day to set records. For all, the day would break the record for the longest road travelled in one riding day ever in the history of the tour. For some, the day would break personal records of longest distance travelled. For few, the day would break tour records for quickest travel time. We would travel two hundred and seven point seven kilometers along the Elephant Highway and into Namibia, in a fierce headwind. On a typical headwindless day, the gang liked to comfortably ride around twenty-five kilometers per hour. At this pace, the day would take over eight hours without a single dismount. We needed to get to the Namibian border before closing. Our hopes rested on the one thing we despised: the peloton.

Jenny and Femke had decided to go for gold. Together, they raced all day to the finish line in anticipation of winning quickest completion time. Raphael, an incredibly strong German racer who held the second place in the race standings, and Bryce were attempting the same. Esther, Marita, Jen, Natalie, Rachel and I had a quite different ambition; not die. We set out riding at a comfortable twenty-eight kilometers per hour. We picked up Ton and Ian along the way. The comfort in numbers was indescribable, we couldn't ALL fail, could we? We worked together in mutual support. After a quick twenty-five minute lunch we were back on our bikes, the day was beginning to feel like a broken record. We pushed and pedalled for hours on end, struggling to keep formation. It was all I could do. This revelation hit me like a brick wall. Since youth I always believed in exploring my physical limitations. Part of my confidence developed because I never truly believed I had physical limitations. Never had I considered an athletic skill beyond my ability to learn, beyond my will to perform. Until this day. For the first time in my life I felt limited. My iron will could not possibly push my legs harder, faster, or longer. I thought about Jenny and Femke and realized that I absolutely could not race as they did, for as long as they did. No amount of desire would change the fact that I had physical limitations. Records were not the only things breaking this day. Internalizing limitations broke a piece of my longstanding spirit. I arrived at the border defeated and emotionally unable to genuinely celebrate our accomplishment.

At the border, Esther, Marita and I took the time to dress up as Ninja Turtles to have a bit of fun with the border officials. The superhero attire lifted my spirits slightly. I could hardly keep it together when I noticed that Esther wrote "Ninja Turtle" under her occupation for Immigration. The officials kept their stony faces but permitted our entry. At camp we learned that Raphael and Bryce made it to camp in slightly over five hours. This new tour record was unexpected as they battled headwinds and a longer route. They were the true superheros! Femke and Jenny missed the best female time by about twenty minutes, a strong showing under less desirable conditions. I was humbled. From this day forward, my newly limited body no longer recovered at night. Day after day my body progressively broke down. I was permanently in survival mode, hoping what I had left would last the eighteen days to the finish line.

D-Day + 101
The one with impersonation

I woke up with a leg cramp. The soaring pain dulled to the previous night's familiar ache. Sleep was no longer muscularly restorative. I had traumatized my muscles enough that they burnt out and Cape Town was still eighteen days away. Mercifully, Namibia greeted us with the strongest tailwind of the tour. I was grateful as we had one hundred and sixty-two kilometers ahead. With minimal exertion, the gang soared at thirty kilometers per hour. We cruised effortlessly to lunch, and then coasted just beyond to second lunch at our first Wimpy's Burger. Alaric's charity met us at Wimpy's Burger donating energy drinks and chocolate bars. We were formally greeted by the Deputy Elizabeth Amutenya and the Chief Executive Officer of the Town Council Efraim Dawids. Alaric was finally home and Namibia was celebrating his arrival. Alaric was the pride of Namibia. A local reporter interviewed me and when the article was printed I was mistakenly given the appointment of

Tour Leader. I cringed wondering what Sharita would think. Luckily, she never saw the article. Unluckily, this was due to the fact that she was extremely unwell.

After second lunch we cycled five hundred meters to our first German bakery for third lunch. We stayed for hours, overly confident in our understanding of Namibian weather patterns. Then we turned straight into a violent headwind. Discouragement seeped it's melancholy thoughts through my head. Suddenly I felt too sore, too grumpy and too tired to continue. We pushed onward but Marita who had just downed a double thick strawberry milkshake pushed back. Jenny recommended that we try a loose peloton formation to cut the crosswind, Marita opted for some quality alone time in a ditch. One kilometer down the road, the gang decided to wait for Marita under a tree. Twenty minutes later Marita woke us up. Exhausted to the point of failure, we had all fallen asleep in a thorn bush. We pressed on together. At fifty meters to camp we stopped for a beer. Sila Bezuidenhoudt, the mayor of Gobabis, stopped by the bar to greet Alaric. She was a powerful woman in appearance and personality. She had vibrant hair colours and a great set of grills. Mrs. Bezuidenhoudt welcomed us warmly, questioned riders on the need for speed as we sprinted to the finish line, then burned rubber leaving the establishment. Her power was matched only by her approachability. It was thrilling to be in a country that celebrated strong women.

D-Day + 102
The one with Fristmas

Windhoek translated as Wild Corner. Never had a place matched so closely it's description. Windhoek winds cut into each other angularly, often pushing different parts of our bike left and right simultaneously, impossible to escape. Windhoek was secluded and remote, yet controlling and dominating. Even at one hundred and sixty kilometers away, we felt the effects of this Wild Corner. Trying to make sense of the crosswinds, the gang began the day in our vertical draft formation. The peloton passed as we belted out Christmas carols, it was the 25th of April, Fristmas. Doug was setting a frenetic pace at the front of the peloton and they had lost Peter and Alaric. When the two raced by trying to catch the peloton, Peter decided to stop rushing and meander with us. Peter taught us German Christmas carols. We plotted the twelve rest stops of Fristmas. Soon enough, we found our first stop: a German bakery. As we entered the establishment we delighted in the fact that the matron bore a tremendous resemblance to Kris Kringle himself. We convinced him to sit with us for a photograph and then we feasted on coffee, tea, beer, pie, bread with cheese, salami, and tomatoes. L.S and Holly joined us as we stayed for a really long time. Annelot, the staff sweep passed us by without stopping. This was ominous.

We mounted our bicycles begrudgingly, and took off, leaving Holly and L.S to enjoy their meal. Twenty kilometers down the road a lorry flagged us down. It informed us that two cyclists had been hit. Devastation. Knowing that Annelot was far ahead, we tried to contact Sharita to no avail. So we mobilized. Esther, Rachel and Marita carried on to lunch to tell staff what had happened. Jenny and Peter flagged down a car and went back to the site of the accident. I stayed with the bicycles. For two hours, I baked in the hot sun wondering what was happening and praying that L.S and Holly were okay. Every so often a nice local would stop to ask me if everything was okay and I could usually get tidbits of information out of them. I learned that a lorry came very close to L.S and Holly knocking them off their bicycles and into a ditch. L.S was talking a blue streak about dangerous drivers and clutching her wrist while Holly was screaming about African Black Magic and how it was out to get her. Holly had a sore back and a cut knee and she was fearfully threatening anyone who came near her injuries. Holly allowed Jenny to conduct a primary search to determine that although injured, she was not in immediate danger. We later learned that she had broken her pelvis and spine. L.S's wrist was swollen and also turned out to be broken. Finally Annelot had arrived with Sharita in tow and they took over the scene.

Jenny and Peter raced back and we sprinted to lunch with literally no time to waste. We were only eighty kilometers into our day, it was already the afternoon and we had eighty kilometers left. In steep hills, and violent headwinds. Sharita called Chad, who was our newly appointed staff sweep to pass along a dire message: hurry up or lose EFI. After a quick twenty minute lunch we got back on our bikes and cycled wildly. Panic ensued as everyone tried to calm each other down but the repetitive communication around losing EFI did nothing for our nerves. We assumed a peloton formation with Chad at the helm. We drafted behind Chad and Peter for most of the afternoon. It was still very hard work with failing muscles but my slow leak of adrenaline kept me racing the clock. At long last, we found ourselves coasting downhill into the bowl that is Windhoek. The city was surrounded with steep hills and hardly looked like the most hospitable land in which to settle such a modern city. I immediately noticed that the houses were unique, expensive and gated. They seemed to be built in the middle of mountainous land. With great relief, we got to camp after an exceptionally long day in the saddle. We had thirty minutes to prepare for a BBQ banquet hosted by Alaric's family. The banquet was beautifully situated beside an Olympic pool. We feasted, we drank and we danced the mountainous stress away. Windhoek had warned us, it certainly was a Wild Corner of the World.

D-Day + 103
The one with the new goal

Our lodgings in Windhoek were superb and I awoke the next morning in a room with four walls lying on a long forgotten luxury: a mattress. I made myself some tea. How civilized. While digesting the previous day, I suddenly realized that I had changed. I began this tour with only one ultimate goal, and EFI defined my tour. Although still willing to doggedly defend my EFI, tour had slowly become much larger than this small singular goal. Finally, with two riding weeks left, I knew that EFI mattered far less than the spirit of what we were accomplishing together. I vowed that one day I would try to capture the very spirit of our collective adventure. I would write a travel memoir.

D-Day + 104
The one with probable death

Esther coined it best "I used to have a few grace days before my body started to break down, now I'm beginning to break straight after a rest day."

My muscles no longer knew how to relax nor recover. They were sore from first pedal to last every single day. And we had eight consecutive days of offroading ahead. Everyone was feeling similarly worn and this made us feel more vulnerable to accidents. Knowing that we needed to climb out of the Windhoek bowl we looked at the steep cliffs with dreading minds and depleted bodies. Winds cut from all directions in front of our bicycles. Winds flooded our ears and blocked out all hope for conversation. We were to be prisoners of our own minds for one hundred and fourteen kilometers of dirt roads. Deciding self-pity was futile, I looked up and around for the first time. I was immediately transported into a pastel painting of indescribable beauty. Three soft shades of pastel green covered every visible surface for miles. The chartreuse grass danced a ditty while dark seaweed green trees highlighted the backdrop. Tamarisk trees heralded the need for shade under the fiery sun. Longer grass shimmered like translucent silvery blue tinsel in the surging wind resembling snow. Springboks grazed lazily. Lost in the scenery, I suddenly heard tires squealing and looked rearward to see the expression of shock on a teenaged driver's face. *This was it*, I thought to myself fleetingly. *This was how I died*. He was a few feet away from hitting me, time slowed. In mere seconds that felt like an eternity I considered zigzagging left or right, but I was unable to make up my mind. Inches from my back wheel the young boy swerved sharply off the road and into the ditch. We were both in shock. Instead of a coroner, he would need a tow truck. The great game was one of chance.

D-Day + 105
The one with vultures

With a headwind and a new lease on life I set off determined to enjoy the beautiful scenery. Mountains fenced roads of loose dirt, fields filled with wondrous white shimmering grass provided endless scope for the imagination. It required an imagination to even believe such a place existed. Namibia was utopic. Namibian nature was modelled by a fairy tale fanatic. Wind energy was the fairy tale creature blowing through the landscape, magically making the divine even more beautiful. Marita, Esther and I stopped to soak in the aesthetics. Then we got brave. With seemingly decaying musculature we decided to climb an acacia tree and rest in a vulture's nest. Acacia trees are a climber's paradise with a short, branchy stature. As we rested near the soft nest we noticed small kamikaze birds entering the vulture's lair. Hundreds of them.

We had it all wrong. The vultures we had seen perched atop these platforms were visitors. Welcome to aves masterpiece theatre. The hosts: sociable weavers. Sociable weavers were mighty sparrow-sized birds. Sociable weavers did not build nests, they build masterpieces. Living in muti-generational communes, sociable weavers created the largest manors of any bird worldwide. The manor was carefully designed to be multi-purpose. Each weaver family had an inner and outer chamber to their dwelling. The inner chamber was warm and used for roosting, while the outer chamber provided daytime shade. They rented their manor as a love motel for paradise finches and rosy-faced lovebirds, and often had sleepover parties with ashy tits and familiar chats. Owls, falcons and vultures used their platform commensally while snakes, cobras and pygmy falcons looted eggs. As such, sociable weavers were a staple to the fabric of African wildlife.

At five kilometers to camp, we stopped. We had to stop as something momentous occurred. Ten thousand kilometers. We had cycled ten thousand kilometers and deserved a beer. We stopped for a Windhoek beer at an eclectic establishment housing a variety of taxidermied animals, antique lawn mowers and wheelbarrows. Two rhodesian ridgebacks came and lapped salt off our faces. I made myself another kept promise: one day I would own a rhodesian ridgeback. The remaining five kilometers to camp were unexpectedly challenging, as we descended into a huge steep crater. The descent was terrifying as we jiggled so much that our feet repetitively dislodged from our pedals and the only thing keeping us on our bicycles was our tenderized and shrinking derrière.

D-Day + 106
The one with naked drinks

Before exiting my tent, I sunscreened my nipples. This was a first. Naked, I resembled a panda. Darkened by constant exposure to radiation, my extremities contrasted strongly to my pallid torso and face. I wondered what predators a Panda has in Namibia as I was about to ride naked. We all were. The Naked Mile was a tour tradition, making clothing optional for one mile between the towns of Solitaire and Sesriem. Naked riding achieved a new level of fame in two thousand and four with Canadian Conrad Schmidt's conception of a World Naked Bike Ride event to promote sustainability, peace and body positivity. I was failing Mr. Schmidt. Relating my body to that of a panda was not the height of body positivity. Even after one hundred and six days on tour, my body's greatest manifestation of ability, endurance and power, I sat critical of its appearance. Indoctrination to body negativity is sewn into the fabric of North American society that held our weight accountable since birth. Body positivity was rejected in favour of selling diet plans, prescription drugs, and magazines. Media defined beauty within unattainable parameters. We evaluated our bodies by form, not function. The fact that this was a new phenomenon became evident the moment we went to bare all. Women spanning five decades stripped down together and steadied their vaginas for a rather unusual voyage. Those women in their twenties and thirties, undressed uneasily or remained partially clothed.

Those in their sixties threw their clothes to the ground confidently and ceremoniously, Gennesse exclaiming "I have been working for months to look this good!"

Being naked in the birth canal of civilization felt deeply au naturel. Vitamin D shocked cells while air travelled to my most shuddered places. I was so lost in elemental communion that didn't notice that we had visitors. The desolate road was suddenly populated with drivers who just happened to be videotaping the local "scenery". Their vista must have been spectacular as they made multiple passes. Shyness melted away as we laughed and waved. Suddenly Gennesse veered left. We followed. Gennesse. It turned out that our naked matriarch was parched, she desired a Coca Cola so she stopped at the only local establishment we had seen all morning. Though Gennesse's clothes were available, she was unabashed. Naked, she marched right into the front lobby and asked the matron Nadine if she would serve eleven naked women Coca Cola. Nadine didn't miss a beat and so we all marched in. I stood nakedly envious of Gennesse's body positivity while sipping cold Coca Cola and shooing away Nadine's two overly friendly dogs.

Nadine was understandably inquisitive, and oddly took detailed notes of our answers. She told us that she had a background in journalism, which explained this oddity. Nadine offered us shots of sambuca and took a group photograph on her balcony. Then she offered her pool, which was beautifully situated down a precisely zigzagging rock path surrounded by manicured lawns. Sunbathing naked and diving in freely, we soaked in the moment of sisterhood. It felt as close to freedom as I had ever experienced. We would have liked to stay all day but cognizant of time, we bid Nadine adieu and cycled to lunch.

Most riders were happy to robe at lunch. We were apprehensive of getting sunburns in sensitive areas. Not L.S, she was on a mission. L.S. would ride the entire eighty-three kilometers in the buff setting a new tour record. It was not easy for her as the roads became increasingly difficult after lunch. Loose gravel spun our wheels while the hot sun of the Namib Desert beat our bodies with temperatures we had not experienced since Sudan. Additionally, I had a bum-burn. The sun had rendered my lily white bottom angry scarlet. I needed a break. I was only four kilometers to camp, but I was DONE! I rested under an awning and seriously considered quitting for the day. Esther, Marita and Mark caught up with me and eventually got me moving again. Good thing. Ten minutes more of self-pity and I would have missed one of the most memorable sights of my life.

Arriving at camp, we had just enough time to change our clothes before boarding an open-side safari vehicle en route for the live desert. Living desert seemed an oxymoron. Deserts deal in death. One wrong move and your life is jeopardized. Contrarily, the Namib Desert was a coastal oasis. Earthy red dunes lush with soft green vegetation flanked the road we travelled, the contrast of these two opposite colours was stunning. A colourful palette signifying the constant tug-of-war between life and death. Layers of sharp peaks and curved edges mesmerized the brain, interspersed with the occasional animal. Even in the extreme heat and drought, animals flourished. The Namib Desert was home to antelopes, springbok, ostriches and desert elephants all boasting evolutionary adaptations to their dry home. Salt lakes hosted beautifully haunting white trees which sprouted from their centre. This was diamond country. We frolicked up dunes and played in the sand. From atop a dune, we watched the sunset and I introspectively considered my concluding journey. I knew that a new journey would rise as I was listening strongly to my heart's voice.

D-Day + 107
The one with truth

For hours, I watched the quiet movement of nature restfully in Sesriem. Feeling serenely peaceful I knew that a transformation was complete. Real change had settled deeply into my soul. I was fully present. I felt no pressure to accomplish tasks. I was closer to quiet. I knew that this transformation would stay, it felt permanent. I would no longer define my worth by how occupied I was, how competitively I lived, nor how acceptable my actions were to others. I would keep this quiet and live as life unravelled. Being was enough.

D-Day + 108
The one with sirens

The road ahead was unpredictable. I no longer assumed days would be easy or simply because they weren't listed as hard at rider meetings. In this way, cycling was a lot like rock climbing. In my late twenties I started rock climbing at Coyote Rock Climbing gym in Ottawa, Ontario. I immediately fell in love with the sport and into a fantastic community of climbers. It looked so simple, grab hold and climb up. It was anything but. Every route needed a precise measure of strength and finesse. Some of the routes that appeared easiest, would be most technical requiring hours of planning, trial and error. Climbers called the sharing of technical information "beta". Beta was freely shared as climbers competed only with themselves. Everyone encouraged each other towards success. No matter how much you planned or anticipated, it was often beta that got your through the climb. Even with the best beta, routes were unpredictable. Holds would suddenly break off, sweat would slicken rocks, muscles would fail. Cycling routes were as unpredictable as climbing routes. A strong wind, rain, or a moment of distraction could transform days. We had beta on the route to Betta, Namibia. The ride was touted as the most picturesque day on tour with no sharp climbs nor steep drops. Esther, Marita and I anticipated a gloriously easy riding day knowing full well this could change in an instant. It did. Truly the road was picturesque, we were travelling through a living painting. Soft pastel colours welcomed our eyes invitingly. Light green vegetation eased into the burnt reddish orange road. Overlooking, birds coasting in a baby blue sky sang gracefully to steep taupe mountain tops. Grass shimmered silver in the strong wind. The strong headwind. Strike one to our perfect day. Wind sirened past heralding nearby beauty, luring our eyes from the road. At great peril. Strike two: the road. The rocky road was heavily corrugated with patches of sand waiting to steal our bikes from under us. We could not look up and it was torturous. An oryx crossed our path but we glanced fleetingly before returning our gaze downward to safety. Our maximum speed was only sixteen kilometers per hour. With one hundred and thirty nine kilometers to camp, we calculated almost nine riding hours to camp. On sunburned tushies. Strike three. Every so often we would stop and take a moment to marvel at the most beautiful place on earth. It was challenging to believe such a utopia even existed.

At camp, the day went from bad to worse. Gennesse had fallen on a dodgy downhill and had been knocked unconscious. Her collarbone, ribs and pelvis were broken. I remembered just the day before when she was outlining her grand cycling plans for the year. She had planned on cycling the Tour du Canada and then journey on a self-supported cycle through the United States. Unpredictably, mere seconds changed the course of Gennesse's life. Predictably, her spirit was unbreakable. Gennesse sent us photographs from her hospital recovery room wearing her cycling helmet and giving us the thumbs up. Once healed, Gennesse continued her cycling odyssey. In a world of unpredictability, the only reliance was an unbreakable spirit.

D-Day + 109
The one with brakeless riding

Within minutes of setting out, the gang encountered our first roadblock: a wild horse. His massive frame was in the middle of our sandy road and was moving for nobody. We tried to wait him out, in vain. Finally, with one hundred and fifty three kilometers of off-road looming ahead Jenny decided to go for it. She rode by the horse and he didn't charge. We followed her lead. The horse stared at us but didn't budge. We were in his territory and he wanted us to know it. My second hurdle was three flat tires. The gang stayed for the first two but I shooed them away at my third. I could tell that they had itchy feet with such a long day ahead. Minutes later I realized that I did not have a single functioning bike tube left in my spares. Would EFI be lost with ten days left on tour? Perhaps this was it for me. Perhaps not. Deeply cognizant of the unpredictability of each day I felt suspended in midair, awaiting what would come. Katarina came. She was staff sweep. I asked Katarina if I could use the satellite phone to call for a tube drop off. She told me that the phone hadn't worked since entering the Namib Desert. My emotions teeter-tottered down. Then I glanced at her wheels and was whisked back up. Twenty-six inch rims...same as mine. Africa wasn't done with me yet. Katarina gave me a spare tube and I quickly fixed my flat tire but when I went to re-engage my front brake the wire seemed to be drawn too tightly to engage. Neither Katarina nor I could engage my brakes. Perhaps Africa was done with me. I did what any panicked cyclist facing a century of offroading would do. I rode brakeless.

I raced for thirty kilometers keenly anticipating injury, but unwilling to surrender my EFI without a fight. My heartbeat pounded through every cell as I gunned downhill over rocky corrugated dirt roads, wishing beyond measure that I had a spare sandal to slow my bike African-style. In moments of extreme panic, I forgot and pressed the brake lever. Adrenaline shot through my body as the level offered no resistance and jolted me off balance. Somehow, I caught up with Marita and Esther. What a relief! At fifty three kilometers, I needed a break. With only one third of our day done, the stress of riding brakeless was wearing my already worn body. We collapsed in shade and devoured PVM bars until Sharita swooped in to save the day. She grabbed my multitool and fixed my brakes within seconds. Perhaps Africa wasn't done with me. Within a few kilometers of setting off again, I got my fourth flat. Luckily Katarina had given me an extra tube so I fixed my flat yet again and we set off together. We were not alone in the Eden that is Namibia. The moon was already rising on the left, while the sun shone brightly on the right. With mountains and valleys sandwiched everywhere in between. Namibia smelled like my grandfather's well loved basement armchair. Comforting and earthy. The remainder of the day was completely physically and emotionally exhausting. Would Africa work us doggedly right to Cape Town? I wasn't sure I would make it to find out.

D-Day + 110
The one with patience

The German pancake house, an alluring staple of Namibian society. So enticing that racers stopped in the morning mid-race to devour chocolate cake, waffles and ice cream. So rich that long after everyone left, the gang spent one hour digesting, while restfully slumped on the patio. One blissful hour, for us.

One terrible hour for Ming. "One hour!"

Ming yelled at us when we caught up with him later that afternoon. "One hour! With only one apple, one PVM bar and one water bottle."

Ming had been waiting at the top of a large hill. He couldn't help himself. Ming, the photography addict had found his drug of choice - the perfect panorama. The light played perfectly off our faces, casting no silhouette as we struggled uphill. The texture of the dirt road contrasted with the smooth flanking greenery. The only consideration was proportion. In order to achieve photographic nirvana Ming cycled downhill and snapped the shot from a perfect position to capture the struggle on our faces yet equally represent the magnitude of the climb. Ming cycled uphill and downhill all afternoon capturing every rider. All afternoon with only one apple, one PVM bar and one bottle of water. This was devotion.

D-Day + 111
The one with the birthday suit

It was my thirty-second birthday and my wish was granted: a flat ninety-four kilometer day. I would receive three gifts. My first gift was thoughtful, a Namibian mug. After three months I would no longer drink watered down caffeine from a soup bowl. Small luxuries were life changing. The second gift was impressive, "The Golden Rack". The gang affixed two balloons to my chest, double E knockers to replace my dwindling mammary. Instantly crowned gang matriarch for the day, they let me talk to my heart's content about previously banned topics: my elbow bursitis and strange fingernail bed pattern, they even feigned interest. I was touched. This was true friendship. About ten kilometers down the road I received my third gift. Sharita had left a head of broccoli, bread, chips and powerbars, all wrapped in flagging tape on train tracks. Beside the African gift bag was a note: Happy Birthday Jana! This was thoughtful and fortuitous as we anticipated missing the lunch truck after our late departure.

A few kilometers later we happened upon a construction site. Parched from the raw broccoli and bread, Marita asked the gentlemen working if we could stop for a coffee.

"I know you! I just read about you in the newspaper."

Thinking he must have meant the feature on Alaric, Marita nonchalantly replied "Oh, what about?"

Reaching for the newspaper the construction worker exclaimed "You are the ladies travelling from Cairo to Cape Town and you get naked!"

Racing from our bicycles we snatched the newspaper from his hand. There we were, all eleven ladies, naked on the front page of the Republikein. I was in my birthday suit on the front page of an Afrikaans newspaper with a subscription of eighteen thousand. Nadine, the matron at our naked rest stop, hadn't told the entire story. She was a popular newspaper reporter. Unbeknownst to us, scribbled on her notepad and in her camera's memory, was our interview. Misquoted in the text, Nadine wrote that we rode naked for one mile each day on tour. Instant fame. For the remaining two cycling days in Namibia, cars and vans slowed and followed in hopes of catching that one naked mile. Predictably, the construction workers welcomed us for coffee and we shared a good laugh.

We thanked the construction crew for their warm welcome and hurried to our campsite at Roadhouse Canyon. We arrived in time to mount a bus to Fish River Canyon, the largest canyon in Africa. It felt paralytic looking so far off in the distance. I stood transfixed by the vastness of the canyon, it's edges felt world's apart. I looked down and my knees wobbled. My knees never wobbled. In many years of rock climbing, I had never reacted to height. I would stand at the edge of a gorge or a sheer rock face and contemplate whether my comfort was evolutionarily sound. Surely, humans survived by having some fear of heights. Here was that fear. If my brain wasn't evolved enough to feel it my body certainly was. *SIT DOWN* screamed my body, so I did. Fish River Canyon was THAT large. I soaked in the depth of scenery until

I felt saturated. The setting sun played off the rocks, stripping the cold greys of their harshness and replacing them with warm ambers before enveloping the entire canyon in darkness. It was time to retreat to camp. My first day at thirty-two had certainly been memorable. As I reflected on the day a new feeling washed over my body, homesickness.

D-Day + 112
The one with homesickness

Nomads defined home differently. In the absence of walls saturated with history, nomads defined home similarly to that of Scandinavian hygge: a cozy intimate feeling of comfort and belonging. We tried our best to create 'home' on tour but I felt homesick. Within two weeks, the home we built on tour would be broken as we scattered in all directions trying to fit into past lives as changed people. I craved the comforting arms of my parents and sister, who were the one consistent home in my life. I knew I would not see them for months and a great sadness enveloped me. So I decided to cycle alone, for one hundred and seventy-two kilometers.

Namibia was a beautiful place to be in a foul mood. Two bushbucks leapt nearby and their movement was a perfect projectile. They floated across the landscape with every part precisely tucked in. A kudu ran across the road ahead of me quickly camouflaging in the surrounding mountains. The kudu was as large as a moose and had massive spiral horns pointing back and out. Pink mountains ended in pastel pastures, deep blue skies hung over red roads. The beauty was so serene that I almost forgot that I was struggling physically and mentally. Almost. Headwinds beat my already vulnerable mind, while my body struggled to pedal for eight hours straight over corrugated rocky roads. I was tired, stressed and mentally ill.

At camp, Bob stated "I had no desire to go to Mars but after today I'm thinking about it."

Namibia was otherworldly. It's beauty and exoticness was hard to fathom. Namibia was divinity's art museum and we stood in awe.

D-Day + 113
The one with eating

Our final rest day on tour. The campsite at Felix Unite had a buffet breakfast. Eating was my only accomplishment. I ate away my homesickness.

South Africa

D-Day + 114
The one with terrorists

Brazen from our previous border crossings, the gang decided to push the envelope and dress as terrorists. Fake guns, a knife and a bow and arrow in hand, we rode towards immigration. Listing our occupation as casual terrorists, and threatening immigration officials with our fake weaponry they still granted us entry. We rolled across the Orange River, the longest river in South Africa and entered our final country on tour. South Africa was a rock climber's paradise. The Great Escarpment extended endlessly calling all mountaineers to explore her rocky cliffs and outcrops. The boulders lining the escarpment entrance called to me and for a moment I considered trading my cleats for climbing shoes. Then I remembered that I was operating at failure and would need whatever reserves I had for the following few days. Resigned, I forced myself not to look at the tempting boulders, but focused instead on the changed faces of the locals. In the mining town of Springbok, the locals had high cheekbones, long straight hair, sturdy builds and beautiful dark olive skin. They possessed a look I associated with Indigenous cultures. I later discovered that genetic testing suggested that the people of Springbok had one of the most mixed ancestries in the world. Descendents from at least seven cultures, the people of Springbok had a rich family tree. History lined their faces which stood in my mind as remarkable.

D-Day + 115
The one with a terrible boss

This morning, my body handed in its letter of resignation. Unhappy with the long working hours and strenuous conditions, it quit. I was an unfair boss. I didn't allow for work life balance. While most riders pushed through the kilometers in the morning, arrived at camp in time for a midday nap, then relaxed in the afternoon and went to bed at seven, the gang did things differently. We pushed for experiences en route, the entire day. More often than not, we would show up moments before supper, eat, hastily set up camp and hop in bed at nine without a moment's recovery. I seem to be more tired than Esther, Jenny and Marita, which I excused as my prerogative as the eldest, but really I was simply less in shape. Still. As a boss, I sternly reminded my body that it needed to give at least one week's notice and prayed that it would show up the next day for one hundred and sixty-four gruelling kilometers. The gang set off on our one hundred and seventeen kilometer day. We spotted sheep grazing in meadows at the base of pink-tinged mountains. Having very little left to chat about and feeling sombre as we contemplated the finality of the week we rode in silence. Suddenly we heard a soft crying noise approach from behind. L.S caught up to us, she was shaken. Still shaken from her accident near Windhoek, L.S swerved off the road every time a vehicle approached from behind. We sandwiched her in and rode protectively beside her. Later that afternoon we stopped for Coca Cola at a country shop filled to the brim with trinkets. Ton found the gang the perfect adornment for our final voyage together: fascinators. We also bought pipes, superhero underwear and plastic gloves. The end was near and we needed to be ready.

D-Day + 116
The one with a stage

Our last exceptionally challenging day was upon us. I didn't know if my body had shown up to work, so I set off early and alone, worried about keeping pace with the gang for one hundred and sixty-four kilometers of hills. My legs felt uncustomarily strong, pushed by adrenaline. As I passed cyclists, I gained confidence. My body had shown up ready to fight.

Suddenly Alaric passed and uttered three words that irrevocably altered my day "Hop on lazy!"

Typically I would smile and wave him off, content to meander at my own pace. Not this day. Nobody called me lazy after a gruellingly long expedition completed in my thirties without any training. This was my last day to show Alaric, what he thought impossible since our strange meeting in Cairo. I could keep pace. So I hopped on his back wheel and pedaled like mad to keep up with him.

Finally, at the top of a hill he said "Right, I'm off!" and took off racing downhill.

Buck was a heavy beast compared with Alaric's racing bike and so I had no trouble keeping up on the downhill. He looked back, noticed I was still there and recognition dawned on both our faces simultaneously. This would be the day he supported me in a stage win. A stage win was awarded to the quickest male and female to complete the day. Alaric had already won. I had never come close. This was my last day to go for it.   Everything aligned. I stuck to Alaric's back wheel as he pulled me all day yelling motivational gems like "Suck it up!" and "Get up here soldier!" the entire day.

Alaric set victims cycling ahead of us to catch (we always did) and talked me through the pain of cycling uphill. At lunch, he coached me to forgo my quadruple decker sandwich in favour of five orange slices, one banana, a quick pee and back on the bike. The life of a racer was foreign and filled with adrenaline. After lunch the offroad turned to tarmac and was overcome with mist from the Atlantic Ocean. It whipped us fiercely, drenching our clothing and reducing visibility to a few feet ahead. The headwinds and water droplets stung our faces but Alaric kept pushing, determined for me to win.

We saw Bryce up ahead. My legs were aching and every muscle screamed to stop but Alaric commanded "Let's catch Bryce!" I knew it would mean the world to him and he had sacrificed all day for my stage win so I sturdied my mind and said "Let's go!" We pushed when I had nothing left. I forced my legs to exert muscles that were far beyond the point of fatigue. The next thing I knew we were alongside Bryce and he nearly fell off his bike astonished when he caught a glimpse of me. I saw the finish line flag and sprinted alongside the boys. Alaric crossed the finish line first and he was ecstatic. We had done it together.

Camp was set alongside the Atlantic Ocean. For the second time on tour, I was cold. The mist enveloped us as we huddled around soup. At the rider meeting I was presented with a stage plate, which surprised most. Although I felt proud, I was more thankful for the tremendous gift Alaric had bestowed upon me. Since the two hundred and seven kilometer day I had been doubting my body. I had been defining new limitations and believing that they were insurmountable. A piece of my spirit had been broken as I considered levels of athletic skill beyond my ability to learn. This was all untrue. I could do more, be more, achieve more. My mind had defined limits, but on this day my body had pushed through and conquered all perceived limitations. My body image shifted as I stood in awe of all I could accomplish. Alaric had helped me believe in myself again.

D-Day + 117
The one with vacationing

This was our last full day of cycling without any obligations or timings. It was also Jenny's birthday and a short seventy-seven kilometer day. Perfection. We decided to take a mini-vacation together. In celebration of Jenny, we detoured half a kilometer from camp for champagne breakfast overlooking the Atlantic. The Atlantic Ocean put on a mighty display, crashing and churning against the shores as we casually sipped our champagne in tune to soft classical music. It felt strangely civilised to watch forces of nature from behind a window pane. We were used to being in the trenches, drenched and fighting alongside nature. Now we were spectators. Herein lies the root of a cyclist's passion, cyclists seek oneness with nature. Cyclists want to feel in communion with the world. The same feeling can never be achieved in a vehicle. The transparent window pane is as great a barrier as any concrete wall. Civilization is the antithesis to nature. We cycled five kilometers and spotted a lighthouse surrounded by a fence with barbed wire. Someone had forgotten to lock the gate. So we entered and climbed to the lighthouse lookout shocking a soldier out of his slumber.

"You are not supposed to be here! This is a military establishment." the man exclaimed.

Seeing so many women in tight cycling shorts, the soldier relented, "Since you are already here, you might as well look around."

As we enjoyed the view, he did the same. The Atlantic raged as we listened, watched and felt her might. For a moment, it felt like she was cheering us on.

A few kilometers into town we saw a dangerous sign "Wine Tasting Offered". Like a moth to a flame, we were drawn. The sign was written on a dilapidated building that had been modernized. Alberta, our sommelier spent two and a half hours teaching us about South African wine. We tasted seven wines, selected a bottle to toast Jenny's birthday and accompanied it with a cheese platter. My legs faltered as I staggered back to Buck. He eyed me reproachfully as I plunked on his seat. We had fifty kilometers to go. The gang had missed lunch. Feeling lethargic as the wine dissipated and cheese settled deeply, we needed a boost. The gang found a beach hut, stripped down and took a quick dip in the Atlantic. The frigid water shocked our cells enough to make it to camp for the evening. Complete with champagne breakfast, sightseeing, wine tastings and swimming, cycling had been an afterthought.

D-Day + 118
The one with gatvol

The end of a journey is met with mixed feelings. Excitement for a new journey is tapered by the sadness of conclusion. My feelings were jumbled. I felt excitement for the tour's conclusion and sadness for what lay ahead: life off tour. I craved the finish line but nothing that came after crossing it. Moreover, I felt like a failure while accomplishing a lifelong goal. I knew that a journey's end was a time for reflection, mindfulness and savouring. I couldn't. Doug coined it best with his South African slang "We are all gatvol." I was gatvol. I was completely fed up. The present felt bleek while the future appeared bleeker. This was not how I envisioned the end of tour feeling.

The gang dressed up for our final full day together. Ninja turtle tights were worn under superhero undies, mad hatter neckties peeked from under transistor radios, our Scuba Steve lifepreservers draped over our shoulders. Nonetheless, the day did not go swimmingly. Every road felt like an uphill battle as I shook away my hangover on gravel, dirt, then pavement. In moments of extreme gatvol, I wanted to throw Buck off a cliff. I'm positive the feeling was mutual as Buck and I were barely tolerating each other. Just pedal I coaxed myself. One more day. EFI. I mentally repeated these words for hours. Mercifully, the day could not drag on endlessly. We had a timing. Staff had prepared an awards ceremony and dinner for riders and it commenced at four thirty sharp. Staff had selected special gifts for every rider and had cooked a delicious meal. The gang received pom poms for cheering the way. I had lost my cheer.

D-Day + 119
The one with the finish line

Normalcy had become awaking on the hard African soil under a canvas canopy. Normalcy had become journeying, hardships and communal living. In fewer than twenty-four hours normalcy would be obliterated. As much as I tried to imagine myself waking up surrounded by walls, and leisurely making myself a solitary tea while contemplating how to occupy my day, I couldn't. I didn't want to. Four months communing with nature had brought more quiet to my soul than any civilized contemplative tea. Experiencing life through the core lens of survival had enlivened me more than a good night's rest. Civilization was veiled apathy and I was afraid to lose myself once again in it's trance. I briefly considered turning my bike around and cycling home to Cairo, but my muscles sharply reminded me of the contract they signed for four months ONLY. They would begrudgingly hold up their end of the bargain, and not one kilometer more.

So fascinators were fixed securely to our hair, and pipes dangled from our mouths, the gang was almost ready for our final voyage together. We only needed capes. Luckily one kilometer from camp we found a used clothing store. It was made for us. Perusing the aisles, we selected our best journey's end outfit, hot pants and pink capes, and set off towards Cape Town. It felt bittersweet to reminisce highlights and challenges from our journey together as we closed in on Table Mountain. Staff had organized a fancy lunch on the ocean's coast. Table Mountain provided the perfect backdrop for our final group photos. As I raised my bike high in victory, I was perturbed by the fact that I didn't feel victorious. As we gathered for EFI photos, I felt no pride in accomplishment. It all meant nothing. Quickly I was swept back into the fanfare as interviewers approached. The gang had planned for this moment, deciding to have one lask lark. Knowing that the press would be there to interview cyclists, we had decided during the morning cycle on four sentences we wished to insert into any questions asked:

"When in doubt, pull out!"

"But otherwise you are well."

"Tomorrow is a brand new day."

That would be an ecumenical problem."

One last laugh. One last moment of a truth learned on tour: a sense of humour is quintessential to survival. The interviewer looked slightly perplexed at moments but we managed them without straying too far from the question. One last gang victory. Finally, we convoyed to the finish line near the base of Table Mountain. I saw the orange flag only from a few meters away and the gang passed through the landmark together, hooting and hollering. Still, I did not feel victorious. I faked elation and wondered what was wrong with me. Then it hit me. This particular moment was unimportant and staged. The only meaningful bits had already passed, they had already been internalized. I had learned that the best bits of life were unstaged, unpredictable and truly captivating. They happened frequently to a receptive host, and to be receptive you needed quiet, not fanfare. Fanfare glaringly marked moments in a hurried life, but I no longer led a hurried life. The moments I marked and internalized were moments of reliance, of oneness. I marked the moment Peter helped Esther to the finish line when she was ill. I marked the moment the Ethiopian child threw Marita's camera back at her. I marked the moment I met Salamo. I marked the moment we danced on the streets of Tanzania. I marked the moment the kind stranger told us that "tomorrow is a new day". These would be the lessons I carried forward. I would think about the millions of people it took to keep us safe throughout our voyage. I would consider my own misconceptions, prejudices and human nature. This memoir is what I marked. The end was unimportant, the journey held all.

Acknowledgements

A teaching assistant at Brock University once wrote the following feedback on my assignment: "Largely crap with moments of sheer brilliance." If this memoir contains more brilliance than crap, it is due to the editing talents of Min, Mom, Steve, Jane and Mary-Lyn. To Rebecca, Kareena and Jodie, thank you for paying for this book a decade ago and for your patience. To the family. Bryan for being the guardian of my solitude. Emmett for being a champion napper allowing me the time to write. Elson for kicking me from the inside into action towards publishing before all hell breaks loose. To my late grandfather, whose short memoir sparked the embers caught in a long slow burn.

Disclaimer

Made in the USA
Monee, IL
14 May 2021